FROM DUBLIN
TO JAILBREAK

1969-76

MARTIN POPOFF

FROM DUBLIN
TO JAILBREAK

1969-76

MARTIN POPOFF

WYMER
PUBLISHING
Bedford, England

First published in Canada in 2011
This edition published 2016 by Wymer Publishing
Bedford, England
www.wymerpublishing.co.uk
Tel: 01234 326691
Wymer Publishing is a trading name of Wymer (UK) Ltd

ISBN 978-1-908724-39-7

Edited by Jerry Bloom.

Every effort has been made to trace the copyright holders of the
photographs in this book but some were unreachable. We would
be grateful if the photographers concerned would contact us.

Front and back cover images © Steve Emberton.

Printed and bound by
Clays, Suffolk, England

A catalogue record for this book is available from the British Library.

Cover design by Andy Francis.

CONTENTS

PROLOGUE

I've been asked repeatedly over the years by many of you for a Thin Lizzy book. But even if they are one of my top fave handful of bands ever (and even more so on how much I've played the albums over and over again through the years), I never thought it possible because I didn't have enough new personal chats as to make a contribution to the fine body of work already on the band.

That's changed to a fair extent, given that most of the principles I've now talked to a bunch of times, as well as some of the lesser players. A fair bit of this contribution was prompted and cajoled by Peter Nielsen, who was absolutely the defining personality in finally getting me to embark upon this birch bark.

For not only did Peter – keeper of the Lizzy archive, pretty much above all others, at thinnlizzyguide.com – help me with interview contacts, he also threw open the doors to his vault of images, a mountain of goodies that put this project over the top, in terms of offering something that hasn't been in print before, in terms of speaking right to my heart.

What follows is more a biography of the records than the people. And that is actually more deliberate this time than ever. Being in a zone where there are already other fine Thin Lizzy books out there.

Nonetheless, I still find myself scratching my head at how fast the albums are dispensed with in these specific rock bios and rock bios in general. As a result, I felt I'd further pick my spots and try and offer more in this area (and like I say, it's my way anyway), even if some of this information might be seen as geeky, or not as dramatic and instantly entertaining as the personal stuff. As usual, I want you running back to the records and playing the songs again, seeing if I got it right, seeing if what the guys making them said rings true to your experience.

Enough said, besides thank you for reading this book – we're definitely of a small funky nomadic tribe.

Martin Popoff
martinp@inforamp.net
www.martinpopoff.com

1

DUBLIN DAYS

"Like a duck to water"

T he good bands seem to have complicated histories, or rather, histories that contain within them a goodly chunk of learning and leaning this way and that, some thought, some elbow grease, good values and their effect on work ethic.

Thin Lizzy's got all that and more. The more embodied in a tall, skinny black man, further uncommon for being Irish, but I separated that out, 'cos the Irish component applies to the whole band, and that in itself is indeed uncommon and exotic, given that so few acts have ever broke out of the Emerald Isle.

Those who've read my biogs know that I tend not to dwell or elaborate too long on pre-histories, yearning to get right into the records - indeed the main topicality of these books I do, the reason I do them. That promise I'll make again, and yet, there are definitely a number of salient details in the pre-history of Lizzy that need telling, as they affect what the band would become, forming echoes and under-currents that help the listener understand the material right through to the tragic end.

Philip Parris Lynott was born in Hallam Hospital, West Bromwich, Staffordshire, England, August 20, 1949. His mother Philomena, keeper of Phil's flame and fire for decades after his death, was born in Dublin but had been setting up a young working life for herself in Birmingham, where at the age of 18, she found herself pregnant by a black man of South African descent, one Cecil Parris. Once the scandalous pregnancy was discovered, Philomena was tossed out of nursing school, taking a job at Austin Motors, upon which she disguised her pregnancy as long as she could.

Philip now born, returning to Dublin, she brought a baby of coffee complexion and a rock star in the making. Although Philomena and

Phil's father stayed in touch for four years and marriage was discussed, it was not to be. Mother and son were bounced around between homes for unwed mothers until Phil found himself back in Dublin being raised by his grandparents Frank and Sarah (Frank would pass away when Philip was 14), with necessity causing Philomena, popularly known as Phyllis, returning to England to work and send home money. The year was 1953, with Philomena now in Manchester holding down three part-time jobs and returning regularly to Dublin to visit with her family.

Much of the racism one might expect toward the situation seemed to fade as Phil came into his own, and one would have to attribute this to the charm of Phil Lynott, not to mention his talents, which both were manifest as early as school days. Said Phil to the *Los Angeles Times*, "Me mother is Irish and me father is from Rio. I haven't seen him since I was four. He's a real lover. He loved them and left them. I think that's the only thing I learned from him. Being a black in Dublin wasn't a problem. The Irish never showed me any prejudice. Besides, I'm a big lad and I'd deck anybody who said anything nasty to me."

Phil had a couple of uncles, Peter and Timothy, who became somewhat surrogate brothers, with the latter lighting the spark in Phil, his music hobby, namely the study and assimilation of a wide variety of pop and rock records. Peter on the other hand found himself addressing rock 'n' roll more directly, playing guitar and singing for The Sundowners, which 'round about led to young Philip having a go himself, winding up in his first band, The Black Eagles.

As local gigs piled up, The Black Eagles found themselves supported by a band called The Mod Con Cave Dwellers. Drummer in that band was Brian Downey, born January 27, 1952, right there in Dublin. A minor bit of miscommunication took place when the Black Eagles lost their drummer to the army. Phil had apparently promised the job to Downey, a school chum, if it ever came up, but placed an ad for a replacement instead. Downey answered the ad and called Phil on it, with the two patching it up over Downey's convincing blast through The Kinks' 'You Really Got Me'.

Phil experienced further the possibility of a show business life on regular visits to Manchester, where his mother and her new beau Dennis now owned and operated the Clifton Grange Hotel, which specialized in entertainers. It was a crazy place which further indoctrinated Phil into the surreal life, additionally, with a significant degree of music mentoring going on courtesy of a Canadian named Percy Gibbons, touring as part of The Other Brothers. Up into early 1969, Philip would arrange for his friend and leader of Skid Row, Brendan "Brush" Shiels, to have his honeymoon at the hotel (Phil was Brush's best man at the wedding), the place now colloquially known as The Biz.

"That was just for... what would you call them, old cabaret artists," chuckles Brush, recalling the ramshackle place. "In America, you'd probably call it vaudeville, for strippers and fucking impersonators. There'd be no stars there and the hotel would't have any stars either (laughs). It wouldn't be two star or three-star or four-star, it would be no stars with no stars in it (laughs). It was called a hotel anyway, and people were glad to stay in it. You can come in any time of the day or night and it wouldn't cost you too much money, and you'd get your beans and toast in the morning."

Back in Dublin, soon enough rock was becoming a force, Brian Downey recalling moving from the influence of his dad's pipe band music through The Shadows to the Beatles, Stones, Kinks and Yardbirds. Downey's first set of drums had everything except toms, but the enthusiastic learner soon found himself playing in his first band The Liffey Beats, followed by the aforementioned Mod Con Cave Dwellers and then The Black Eagles, this all taking place in rapid succession 'round about '64 through '65.

"I was always well into rock," explained Downey on the subject of his formative years, in conversation with *Sounds* magazine. "My cousin used to buy a lot of Jerry Lee and Shadows records. Little B was my favourite drum solo for a long time. After the pipe band, I was in a group with Phil called the Black Eagles. We did a lot of Beatles and Byrds numbers, playing in clubs and hotels. When the club scene really started happening, we began to write our own stuff interspersed with Zappa numbers. I began to get into heavier things when I played with a group called Sugar Shack. We had a hit in Ireland with a version of 'Morning Dew'. My main influences then were drummers like Ginger Baker and Mitch Mitchell. I also listened to a lot of jazz around that period and got into more intricate rhythms. When Thin Lizzy formed, I used to like listening to Noel Bridgman who was the drummer with Skid Row. He taught me a lot."

As part of The Black Eagles, Downey quickly learned about 30 numbers, and the band found themselves with lots of work, a seminal gig taking place at The Bastille Club where the booker of it was none other than Ted Carroll, who would go on to manage Skid Row and co-manage Thin Lizzy. But The Black Eagles, eventually a full-on raving Mod band and later briefly changing their name to Jigsaw, had dissolved by '67, with Brian drifting first, for two or three months, to a country and western act called Burma Boys Showband and then to Sugar Shack, taking us through '69.

Meanwhile, over in Belfast, Northern Ireland, one Gary Moore (born April 4, 1952) worked his way through The Beat Boys and The Method, arriving in what was to be the first significant rock band from Ireland,

Skid Row, who eventually wound up with a record deal with CBS. In '70, both Moore and Shiels also guested on the *Heavy Petting* album by Dr. Strangely Strange, a briefly fired hippie band that had ties to the pre-Thin Lizzy Orphanage arrangement as well.

Also in Belfast, guitarist Eric Bell (born September 3, 1947) gained experience with a number of acts, including The Deltones, Them Featuring Van Morrison, Shades Of Blue and John Farrell And The Dreams. Phil Lynott persevered through this period as well, singing with his old Black Eagles guitarist in soul band Kama Sutra and then performing lead vocal chores again in My Father's Moustache, which included aforementioned hotshot Brush Shiels on bass.

The outspoken and cocksure Shiels quickly became a mentor to Phil as the band ditched the whimsical name and became Skid Row, the two working together October '67 through the summer of '69. By this point, Phil had walked away from the metal foundry apprenticeship that had been draining his life force. He was sure rock 'n' roll would be his calling – it even paid better.

Skid Row was really a turning point for the Dublin rock scene. Before that band's manic, hard rock fireworks, rock of any sort had barely made a dent – Granny's Intentions had been the big band before Skid Row – with Ireland still being very much the domain of show bands and folk music.

"Before us, there was only really, as far as I can remember, Van Morrison, and then Rory Gallagher and ourselves around the same time," recalls Shiels. "But yeah, one of our missions was to be the fastest and the loudest band in the world (laughs). It was very fast and it was very loud; we came out of listening to The Cream and Jimi Hendrix, and we thought, we're going to take it up a notch. That's basically what we were going to do. And we were also influenced by jazz - Dave Brubeck, a little bit of Charlie Parker, the bebop. And for some reason, we were born showman. At the time you had The Who and Jimi Hendrix burning guitars and all that, and if you're going to go to America, you want to have a show. So we would've went on stage, at the Fillmore West, with Frank Zappa. We never used monitors; we didn't want to blow him off. We were touring America with the Allman Brothers, and we played at the Whisky A Go-Go, and Led Zeppelin turned up to hear the band, and John Bonham and Robert Plant got up to play."

"God, we were listening to stuff like Cream, again being a three-piece band," recalls Gary Moore on those Skid Row days. "But I don't have great memories of that band. When I listen to it now I think, oh shit, what was I doing? And I'm sure people who played music for a long time feel that way about stuff they've done earlier on. But particularly that band for me, the rhythm section was so busy. It was just like everyone was showing off. And the bass player, Brush Shiels, I think he saw me as this kind of little prodigy – because I was 16 when I joined the band – someone to show off to people. And he was encouraging me to play faster and faster, just so much emphasis on speed, showing off chops and all the shit that meant nothing, really. But I was so young at the time, I didn't really know what was going on so I went along with it. But I'm not really too keen on all that music. I just think it was very messy and frantic."

Frantic, yes, Cream-like, yes, but Skid Row were so far beyond the likes of, say, Them, that it entered the realm of prog. "Yes, there's a bit of a King Crimson vibe as well," agrees Moore, "all that unison, the fast breaks and stuff. But King Crimson was ten times better at it than anyone else so there wasn't much point getting into that. To be honest, when I joined that band, all I wanted to play was blues, but that's not what they were into. I came out of the blues into that band and I was asked to join and I wanted to get away from home at the time, because I was having a lot of problems at home in Belfast, and it was a great opportunity to get into a band. And Phil was in the band and it was him really that attracted me to the band and we became friends through that. Music sometimes is very strange."

Early days as it was however, there wasn't actually much competition one could hang Skid Row's sound upon, as a comparative. "There was Led Zeppelin, but I wasn't a great Led Zeppelin fan," says Moore. "Anything that rubbed off was probably accidental. I think the other guys might have been more into Zeppelin. There weren't that many heavy bands around those days. Zeppelin were the first band who acknowledged the riffs, although Jeff Beck had been doing that sort of thing with Rod Stewart. A lot of the Zeppelin kind of thing, the concept, the riff ideas, came from the first Jeff Beck album with Rod Stewart. I think some of our jamming onstage was like Cream, but again, it was a lot more frantic. Cream was a lot smoother, more fluid. When playing with Jack and Ginger you can be very fluid and the guitar kind of floats over the top. And I can see why Eric was playing those long fluid lines because there was a lot going on, a bit of a volcano going on behind him (laughs). It was almost like Eric had to hold it together at times, but it became a really beautiful sort of guitar playing, almost by necessity. But I enjoyed Eric's playing in Cream; it's just great."

As alluded to, the blues was very much part of Gary's DNA, as it was for Eric Bell, so much so in both cases that eventually, neither could do Lizzy for long.

"It's one of those things," muses Gary. "I feel it's where I come from in many ways. From the age of sort of 12, 13, I was just so into blues. I first heard the British blues stuff and then Eric Clapton, John Mayall, and then Peter Green came along. It was just a great time to be growing up with all these great guitar players just coming out of the woodwork one after another. Mick Taylor… and you had Jeff obviously and then Jimi arrived on the scene and he still had huge blues influence. Obviously he wasn't making blues records per se, well, apart from tracks like 'Red House', but it was inherent in his playing. But I was totally swamped with blues and then I started listening to stuff like Albert King and drawn to it. You must remember, the guitar at that point was more in the background; it didn't have a really powerful voice until Clapton made the Blues Breakers album, from my standpoint anyway, for my generation. It didn't have a strong voice. And that's when the guitar first really jumped out and spoke to people."

"Once I heard 'All Your Love' on the Blues Breakers album, I'll never forget that moment, you know what I mean? It's one of those thing; when you're a kid, you'll never forget it. It was a pivotal moment for me; it was like, there was no going back. I saw how the guitar playing, in A minor, just playing simply but with a lot of passion, could be so devastating, so passionate, so amazing really. And then I saw Peter Green play and that was another moment for me, when he walked into a club in Belfast. I had never heard anyone play a Les Paul live before. I remember the walls kind of resonating and the floors shaking. That's how I remember it. And he was just using a rented amplifier. It was an incredible moment for me. Same song actually, funnily enough: 'All Your Love'. He was playing Eric's lines. A hard act to follow, obviously. Only 20 years old; it was amazing, just walked onstage and fucking blew everyone away with his tone and everything. And when I heard all that, it was just so pure and so full of emotion and passionate, I really didn't want to play anything else. And it was some time before I started playing other music, actually, another three years after that."

"And Brian's got a really big knowledge of the blues," says Moore, with respect to Downey, a drummer Moore would not play with until his first brief stay with Lizzy five years later. "He grew up on the same music that I did. We started with the blues boom and got into the older blues after that. But I met the guy when he was 14. I was opening up for his band. He had come up from Dublin and I was from Belfast. He was in a band called Sugar Shack, which was probably the only blues band from Dublin at that time. There was a much bigger blues scene where I came from in Belfast, and we just hit it off. And he grew up liking the same drummers that I liked, like Aynsley Dunbar and Mick Fleetwood and people like that. So that, coupled with his kind of Irish feel, the Celtic thing – it's quite a unique style actually."

Ah yes, the Celtic thing, an element that would inform Lizzy's song craft nearly as much as the blues, if not more so in the literary realm.

Still, Ireland's rich folk heritage translates into a rich musical heritage, with the island country's rich musical heritage logically aiding and abetting so many lives forged in rock.

"On our nights off we used to go to the folk clubs and play acoustic guitar with the folk musicians," notes Gary, referring to himself and Phil. "It was something we were very aware of. And all our friends were from that traditional thing. And we also liked the blues thing very much. I mean, Phil was a huge fan of the blues. He liked different guitar players, he liked Mike Bloomfield very much, and he liked Peter Green obviously; we both liked him. And he liked a lot of BB King stuff so we had some common ground there as well."

However, before Gary and Skid Row managed to get their first album out, Phil Lynott was asked to leave the band. He had been singing off-key and getting progressively worse, the situation coming to a head during the band's version of 'Strawberry Fields Forever', as it was being filmed for local TV. As it turns out, he had gravely swollen tonsils, which he quickly had removed, on a trip to mum's home base of Manchester in the summer of '69. When he returned to Dublin and the band, a light bulb had been turned on in Skid Row, illuminating the idea that the band, a trio without Phil, were now very much in the mould of Cream, very much a band for the boys and not one that needed the looks and charm of Lynott to fulfil their newly academic mandate.

"Well, the reason he had to get fired," laughs Brush, "was we'd done this television show, and he wasn't pitching great, vocally. That was just an excuse. So basically, what he had, was bad tonsils. Tonsillitis. So when he went to England to get his tonsils removed, we were there like, it was just the three of us, Gary, Noel and myself, and we reckoned we could take on The Cream or Jimi Hendrix; we reckoned we could do it, no problem. But with Phil out in the front, the band had a different... Phil wasn't playing anything, so he's just standing there in front, so it wasn't going to work that way. And when he went to get his tonsils done, he wasn't pitching great, and so we basically stabbed him in the back when he was away (laughs). So when he came back, we told him he was gone. And then I taught him how to play the bass, and you know, in one way it was the best thing that ever happened, and in another way, who knows, but that's the way it was."

Still, Phil had been around long enough in Skid Row to strike out on his first officially issued recording, a single pairing 'New Faces Old Places' with 'Misdemeanour Dreams Felicity', issued in May of '69 on Ireland's Song label (SO 0002). Phil sings (very capably) on the Shiels-credited a-side, an acoustic ballad with tin whistle, its style closer to polite psych than Irish folk.

Now untethered, Phil subsequently hooked up with his also currently unemployed mate Brian Downey (indeed at one point Skid Row tried to poach Downey), forming Orphanage, in operation for eight to ten months, says Brian, and built around the idea of having a flexible, near spontaneous line-up. Hence the ten or so folks who have been cited as members through the band's short life.

"Not much use, "laughs Brush Shiels. "They were really just getting going, you know, great lads, Joe Staunton and Pat Quigley, and Brian; they were only getting the hang of it, you know? They were just learning what to do next. For Phil, it was just a means to an end, just a first stop on the way to where he was going. He learned there and went on to do what he did next. But Phil was always pretty showy, although it took him awhile to get comfortable playing the bass and being a showman at the same time. But before he played the bass, he was a real showman. But the bass kind of curtailed him for awhile."

Orphanage had been named for Dublin's premiere hippie house, a place where Phil's mind had been opened to the wider possibilities of music and art and literature, well beyond the strict guidance Brush had kept him under as part of the almost show band-like early incarnation of Skid Row. It was here that Phil discovered both fashion and soft drugs, along with a world of music from folk to world and beyond, played on record and by the crash pads-drifting troubadours. Orphanage soon gave way to the first Thin Lizzy line-up, namely Brian, Eric Bell, a keyboardist named Eric Wrixon (ex-Trixons), and Phil, now on vocals plus bass. The instrument he had learned from Brush Shiels who had felt bad for sacking Phil from Skid Row. Both Erics were from Belfast, and they essentially had hooked up first, separate from Phil and Brian, both frustrated with the show band scene and looking to do something more creative.

"I was singing in an Irish band called Skid Row when Eric asked me to join a band he was forming," said Phil in 1973, offering his abridged story of the founding of the band. "I said I would, providing I can play bass. Brian joined us shortly afterwards. I'd known him since my Skid Row days, when he was playing in an Irish show band."

"The funny thing is, Phil didn't have much experience in Thin Lizzy, playing bass," recalls Downey, thinking back to the origins of the band. "In fact, when the band formed, with Eric Bell, Phil was a singer; he wasn't playing bass when the band initially formed. It took him maybe a few months, taking lessons from his friend Brush Shiels, who he played with in Skid Row; it took him maybe four or five months to become really proficient on the bass. And then when Thin Lizzy formed, we wanted to play as many live gigs as possible, to make Phil comfortable playing the bass. He just didn't have any experience playing live, and he just took to it like a duck to water; he was just fantastic. It seemed to me, this was just waiting to happen, and Phil just jumped at the chance. He realized that he wanted to be a bass player all his life, it seemed to me. And it was much, much easier. Because when you have somebody who has no preconditions... I have my own style of drumming, honestly, from previous bands, but he had no preconditions at all on the bass, and so I don't think he knew what kind of style he wanted to play. He became a very, very steady, stable bass player. These kinds of bass players are very hard to find these days, because they seem to take off on all kinds of solos. Phil had a really good ear for the bass. He laid it down when it needed to be laid down, and he took one or two little breaks here and there when it needed to happen, and it's just fantastic to play with the guy. He's just so solid, you know? And he never made a mistake! He was phenomenal. And he was singing as well as playing the bass. And I think that was kind of a hard thing to do, to actually sing and to keep the bass line going. Without thinking about it, it's nigh impossible, and he did it – it was just fantastic."

"It didn't take any time at all," says Brush, on teaching Phil bass. "Like the reason I taught him how to play the bass... we were in a friendly way, he came on my honeymoon with me, and then I fired him (laughs). I told him I wouldn't let him down, like, I'd teach him how to play the bass. But when I say teach him how to play the bass, I don't mean 'do re mi fa so la ti do.' When I taught him how to play the bass, it was like, if he'd done what I asked him, I reckoned in three months he would have it together. Because that meant that we had to get together, you know, for five days a week for a couple hours a day and then he would have to work and practice for another four hours somewhere else. I started off teaching him stuff that was pretty complicated, and the first thing I ever taught him was the intro to 'Chinatown'. It wasn't the only lick he used (laughs). I'll leave it at that. But that was the first thing I taught him. And he eventually used it on 'Chinatown'. Because we used the same lick on a thing called 'For Those Who Do' by Skid Row, but we played it faster."

So Thin Lizzy was born, instigated by Eric Bell, who had brought up the idea with Phil and Brian after an Orphanage gig that both he and Eric Wrixon had just witnessed. Phil knew something of Bell's reputation from Gary Moore, a fan of Eric's playing, and decided to give it a whirl, but only if Bell agreed to take a few of Phil's original compositions into the fold.

"Eric was from Belfast, but Dublin was where it was happening," noted Phil, in a chat with *Trouser Press*. "So he came down there. He'd been playing in show bands. You see, the show band trip was, like, you got a lot of money but no satisfaction, because you're just playing the Top Ten hits. They're caught in a paradox, show band musicians; they either starve and play the blues or they join a show band and have money but no sort of musical integrity. Me and Brian had always been in groups, and we'd always done well. We met up with Eric Bell, and that was it."

"After I'd left the show band," explains Bell, "I'd saved up some money to live on, and I just went around the whole of Dublin looking for musicians, and nobody was interested in forming a band with me. I asked everyone. They just made excuses. Probably, it was because of my show band haircut (laughs), and my suit. You know, I had this mohair suit, and I had no other clothes at that time, because I'd just left the show band. So I was walking around Dublin with a mohair suit on and short hair, trying to form a group. I met Eric Wrixon one night in this pub in Dublin, and you know, we sort of hung out together for a while, and that night, that actual night I saw Philip Lynott and Brian Downey for the first time in my life. I went to this club with Eric Wrixon, and I approached Philip and Brian myself, went into the changing room, and after about 20 minutes talking to them, we decided that we would form a band."

Wrixon, like Bell, had played with Them, and as alluded to, both had been rebelling in their respective show band environs, on show band nights off, Mondays, sampling local bars like The Bailey and The TV Club for wild inspiration. They had tried to get a rock band together on the side, chatting up a third Eric, Eric Kitteringham, bassist for Rory Gallagher, but to no avail, leading up to the meeting with Phil and Brian at Ollie Byrne's Countdown Club.

The nascent sound, however, of this emergent "supergroup" soon to be called Thin Lizzy would not rock as hard as, for example, Skid Row did. Sure, there would be blues elements and stabs of electricity, even persistent flash, but rising surprisingly to the fore would be an emphasis on acoustic guitar applied to tender balladry, then laced with poetry.

"From an acoustic standpoint, we were listening to all sorts of music in Dublin," explains Brian. "The whole Dublin ballad scene was happening around that time – don't forget, late '60s. From '66 until '75, I think, this whole ballad thing was happening in Dublin. And we were very influenced by that whole scene, because of the fact that we were steeped in it, because we had friends and relations that played in different ballad bands and folk groups. So we had a good knowledge of what was happening in Dublin at that time. And don't forget also, Phil and Eric used to go out to the ballad clubs and stand in on certain sessions with guys. I know Eric and Phil became really good friends with some of the guys in The Dubliners, who are one of the biggest folk groups here in Ireland, and became very friendly with Barney McKenna, and Luke Kelly was a big influence on our band as well, because Luke was just a fantastic singer and songwriter. He was just an amazing guy to go and listen to. So if we were playing the weekend here in Dublin, we would end up at some of these folk sessions in some of the bars and clubs and whatever, and Phil might bring along a guitar and he would get up and sing a few songs as well, try to make it as folk is possible. Most of these songs he'd written were in a rock vein. And also he had a very soft side to him, as you know. So Phil and Eric, and I would tag along, maybe, set of bongos, sometimes I would get up, sometimes I wouldn't. But that whole period was very influential on the band, with the folk boom that was happening here and in the UK as well, actually not so much in the UK as here. So all that was a huge influence, yeah. It was just great to listen to all that stuff, because The Dubliners got into the charts with 'Seven Drunken Nights' in the UK, and that was one of the first Irish folk tunes to get into the charts, as I remember. So that was kind of nice to see."

After Phil had proudly presented to Eric Bell some of his earliest compositions, such as 'Chatting Today' and 'Saga Of The Ageing Orphan', all the while promising to him that his bass playing was really taking shape, the band got together for their first jam, oddly at the house of one of the Orphanage members that was about to be told the band was finished, namely Pat Quigley.

"I was really knocked out," recalls Eric, upon first hearing Phil's nascent compositions, spooled up one night on a borrowed reel-to-reel deck. "As I say, that night, the very first night we met in that club, he said that him and Brian would form a band with me, but on two conditions. The two conditions were that Philip would play the bass, because he was only singing at that time. And the other condition was that, would I be interested in doing a few of his songs? His original songs. So I said, 'Well, can I hear them?' He came up to my flat about a week later, with this reel with three of his songs on it, and it was just him singing with an acoustic guitar, and they were really good. And I said to myself, well, this guy, he's definitely got something here."

The band was yet un-named however, until one day Eric Bell had been flipping through a comic book at rehearsal and noticed a robot named Tin Lizzie. Slight in-joke about dialect later, and the newly minted Thin Lizzy (debut gig: Feb. 16, 1970, at Swords) were off and making a minor splash. The press expressing a spot of intrigue about the merger between two well-known musicians-about-town, namely Eric Bell and Phil Lynott. Lynott had indeed been voted as one of the Top 20 Irish rock performers, in New Spotlight as far back as March 1968.

"The name of the band… that's because I was from Belfast, living in Dublin," explains Eric. "And there's just a different accent completely. They don't pronounce their 'h's, so they say tick and tin and tree, instead of thick, thin and three. And so one day, it was about our fourth rehearsal ever, and we still hadn't got a name for the band. So Philip, as we were packing up our equipment, said, 'Hey Eric, I think we should start thinking of a name, you know, because once we start playing, we're going to have to be called something.' So as we were packing up the equipment – Eric Wrixon was still about at this point – we were all thinking about different names, so you think of book titles and film titles, all those types of things, Gulliver's Travels, and then we got onto comics. And I just had this idea in my head: Tin Lizzie, and they all look at me, 'What?!' 'What about Thin Lizzy?' 'No, you've gotta be kidding.' And I sort of stayed with it, and I said, 'Yeah, but, what we do is we put an "h" in it, and it's called Thin Lizzy. But people in Dublin will still pronounce it Tin.' And I sort of would say, 'No, it's not Tin, it's Thin Lizzy,' so they would have to make an effort to say the name, so the name would stick in their head more. That's the whole idea behind that. I don't know why they went for it. I really don't know why they went for it, Thin Lizzy. Because I remember seeing interviews with Philip later on, when I had left the band, and they were asking him about the name, and he said, 'Oh, that was Eric Bell's idea.' And they said, 'Well, what do you think of the name?' And he said, 'I think it's dreadful.' But he still kept it."

Next up for the band was a clutch of well-regarded gigs, culminating in a showcase on July 14, 1970 at Dublin's St. Aidan's Hall along with other Irish hopefuls such as Granny's Intentions, The Few, The Urge and Blueshouse. Management for the band at this point was a teenaged Terry O'Neill, who had fulfilled a loose collection of duties for the boys from the start for pretty much exactly a one-year period.

Explains O'Neill, on the subject of first hooking up with the guys, "I was a roadie with Skid Row (laughs). I was the West Coast or East Coast promo man, Brush used to call me, and I used to kind of put on events for them. I would be booking dates for their manager, Ollie Byrne, who is now dead. So when Thin Lizzy started forming, they really came to see Ollie, and every time they came to see Ollie, he would say, 'Talk to Terry.' So they talked to me and I started kind of going out with them at night, and it was like, 'What are you fucking doing? You're doing everything,' you know what I mean? And they said, 'Leave Ollie and manage us.' Which was a big step for me to do, even though I was only a kid. I was only 17 then, in fact, right? (laughs)."

"Ollie was a real character," adds Brush. "He really was a great character. But the only thing he loved more than music was soccer. He was running a semi-professional soccer team in Ireland called Shelbourne and he was finding it hard to pay the player's wages, and things went pretty bad in the downturn. And most people honestly believe that… Ollie got a brain tumour, and most people honestly believe that that was brought on by the frustration of trying to run a football team. It was really his first love – music wasn't. But you can honestly say he gave his life for this football team, Shelbourne. That's what cut him down. The strangest things happened. Like there was this terrible flood, and then the football pitch, the arena, got flooded; you know, and so everything went wrong, and then he found it very hard to pay the players. But he loved soccer even more than music."

Under the auspices of O'Neill, Thin Lizzy entered the nascent Trend Studios and cut five demos plus a debut single for EMI Ireland, pairing a Lynott original called 'The Farmer' with 'I Need You', a song written by studio owner John D'Ardis who, popular conception has it, offered free studio time in exchange for Lizzy covering his track. Curiously, both Eric Bell and Terry O'Neill, as we shall see, confirm this reading, but D'Ardis himself puts a different spin to the tale.

"Basically, I started the studio in '68, in a place called Lad's Lane, having previously worked in another studio here in Dublin," begins D'Ardis, referring here to Eamonn Andrews' studio, locally famous for its work with show bands. "I was really young, maybe around 19 or 20, and it was a pretty rough 'n' ready studio, as you can imagine. But we'd eventually put in an eight-track machine, which at that time was really leading edge. So although the setting, Trend Studios, was primitive, the equipment itself was the best equipment in Ireland at the time. That's why when we did the acoustic sessions and when we remastered them, they came out pretty well. But yes, because of that, a lot of groups and that who were more interested in recording better quality stuff, started to come into the studio. So one of those bands was Skid Row, and I think Phil was in Skid Row at that time, as a singer. At that time, prior to Philip starting up Thin Lizzy, Skid Row would've been more well-known, because they had a very colourful front man in Brush Shiels. He's what you would call a real character. I think he brought Philip in because, first of all, Brush wasn't a very good singer and so on. I understand there was a bit of friction between the guys, and I heard that maybe Philip was outshining him a little bit, which mustn't have gone down very well."

"So then after Phil was out of Skid Row, Philip started to come in with his own band, and himself, and to do demos and so on, of his songs, and it was very gentle stuff. So we recorded some of those tracks, and then, sort of a piece of trivia, I was writing songs myself at the time, so I asked Philip to indeed sing on one of my songs, which he did. So then that than just got filed away. And so after he had done the acoustic stuff, he then decided that he would do a single call 'The Farmer', which he did, which was much more of a rocky sort of thing, not too dissimilar from what he became famous for, actually, but it's sort of out there. It's very rare to see it; it's a very rare item now, and is worth about £1000. There were only 500 pressed; they were pressed in a pressing plant EMI owned in Waterford, which is a small city here in Ireland."

D'Ardis marvels at Lizzy winding up with a deal, as tiny as it was, with EMI Ireland, but if anyone could make it happen, he's not surprised that it would have been Terry O'Neill. "Terry was a very important figure and an interesting character, 'related D'Ardis. "He basically was a kind of publicist, I suppose you would say. Very much involved with the groups on a personal level, Skid Row, and with Phil personally. And probably Terry was the instigator of the recording session as well. He did a bit of marketing for me, publicity and that sort of thing, and I can well imagine that he might have persuaded me to put up some free studio time for something like this."

"See, in those days in Ireland, really, the scene was dominated by show bands, which were kind of cabaret acts with brass and so on, and they did records just entirely as promotion. So they would actually pay for the recording themselves and then they would bring it to a record company who would release it. And they'd basically sell records to the band who would then sell them at gigs. That's how it operated. So somebody like Philip who didn't have gigs and didn't have much of a following, he's very, very unattractive to record companies. So there would be no way to make any money. So for him to get a deal, which he did with EMI, was absolutely astonishing."

"But yeah, the groups, would be so small, and insignificant, that the show bands wouldn't even have considered them adversaries," continues John, underscoring the sequined state of disgrace Lizzy were up against. "The demand, really, from the dance halls, was where the money was. They wanted to have a show band line-up, and it would basically be that there was brass in the line-up. There would be like seven people in a show band, where a group would be the traditional four. And so they weren't competing for gigs or anything like that. The groups were generally playing in very small beat clubs, for derisory money, really. And very few of them were making any kind income at all or any kind of a living. What would happen was, somebody would distinguish themselves in a group as a particularly good player or something, and he might be poached by a show band who could offer stellar wages compared to what they were making. But there wasn't any great rivalry. Oddly enough, some of the groups went on to have long careers, but at that particular moment in time, the people who were making enormous money were the show bands. I mean, one of our show bands here, called The Royals, they were very, very big, and one of the support acts they had was the Beatles. Paul McCartney was incredibly impressed with them, with the bus and the van they used to drive around, and the luxurious standard of everything."

"But for Lizzy, money was so tight then; they were just scraping by," continues D'Ardis, arriving at the story of the b-side. "They didn't have the money to record a b-side. So actually, he just asked me then, in a casual way, if we could use the track that we recorded of mine for the b-side, and that was the b-side of the first single, 'I Need You'. But to be honest with you, it was reasonably a sort of Blood Sweat & Tears knock-off song. But it could have been 'How Much Is That Doggie In The Window?' because Philip didn't really care what it was, because it was the b-side. So they put the record out, and it didn't really do very much; it might've got a few plays. But then things went quiet and I didn't have much to do with them after that. And then the next thing that happened to them was 'Whisky In The Jar', which was maybe a year or two after that. But in terms of the group themselves, I was tremendously impressed with the group, and him. Eric Bell as a guitarist, was a young man of probably no more than about 18, with curly hair, and I never heard anybody play with such skill, at any age. He was astonishing, a virtuoso player, at that young age. And Gary Moore was in it as well, and Brian and somebody else on keyboard."

"Somebody might've had that impression," reiterates John, on the supposed stipulation of Lizzy recording one of his compositions. "But no, that's not the way it is. The two things were kind of separate. The only odd thing about it was, I had some spare studio time, if you like, and they were really working in the studio on a pro bono basis, or very small money, and I think then probably what happened was, his voice got put on the single, my song, at the end of one of those sessions. But really, it was because they were kind of an up-and-coming band, and had been in the studio, essentially, for promotion."

And the horn arrangement? "I would've put them on afterwards, yeah. Because at the time, it was never going to be a Lizzy track. It was really going to be just a demo for a song. It was only after he had actually done the single, and had some of the acoustic stuff in the can at that point as well... but obviously the record company, or themselves, didn't feel that what they had in the can was okay for a b-side. So that's the actual arrangement. To release that song as the b-side was really a last minute thing, when they arranged a record deal."

The fact that it was EMI, even the modest EMI Ireland, was a bit of a coup. "Basically, the company was owned by EMI UK," explains John, "but they would at times try and release records that weren't going to be generally available in the UK and would only be available in the Irish market. They did quite a lot of that sort of thing with ethnic stuff, ceilidh and accordion music. This was a very unusual record. Like I say, somebody was very persuasive to get them to put it out."

Besides 'The Farmer' and its b-side, 'I Need You', the "acoustic sessions" tracks recorded all at essentially the same time include the non-LP 'Mama And Papa' and 'It's Really Worthwhile', as well as early versions of debut LP songs 'The Friendly Ranger At Clontarf Castle' and 'Saga Of The Ageing Orphan', plus an early, slower, more plush version of 'Dublin', which would show up officially on the band's *New Day* EP.

'Mama And Papa' is a dramatic piece of baroque folk, woven through with a profusion of piano, Spanish guitar, flute, and Brian on bongos. Phil's singing is weary and low of octave – weirdly, both Ozzy Osbourne and Steven Tyler, on their very earliest recordings, would similarly sing in lower, more manly voices than they'd become famous for. There's almost a Nick Drake vibe to the song, although maybe it's more John Renbourn, who also springs to mind come 'It's Really Worthwhile', which also leans to hippie bluegrass. Interestingly, on the subject of lack of drums, or actually more so presence of bongos, note that Brian does mention playing bongos live with Phil on impromptu jams. Still, to confuse matters, Horslips drummer Eamonn Carr recalls playing bongos in the studio with Phil early on, but upon hearing these tracks, confirms that they are from a later date, and that it is not himself on beatnik percussion. Moving on, 'The Friendly Ranger At Clontarf Castle' is starkly medieval folk and quite effective, as is both 'Dublin' and 'Saga Of The Ageing Orphan'. All five, really, portraying Phil as a torrid folk troubadour outside of time, again, very much an Irish Nick Drake.

Examining this official first spot of actual product, 'The Farmer' stands in considerable full-band contrast, although it's still essentially a rootsy ballad, sounding very much like The Band, whose *Music From Big Pink* and self-titled second were regular plays at the band's hippie hangout in Clontarf, with The Band's songs also making it into Orphanage jams. B-side 'I Need You' is of a jazzy pop wholly uncharacteristic of Lizzy, replete with complex horn arrangements and old rock 'n' roll rhythms. Its saving grace, if there is one, comes with Eric's raw guitar solo and a general jump complexity to Downey's drumming. It's also interesting to hear Eric Wrixon's organ work spotlighted, here and there, amongst the song's hive of activity.

One can hear the clutch of demo tracks, and at fairly high quality, at the site of D'Ardis' company, Trend Digital Media (trenddigitalmedia.com, under About Us and then Thin Lizzy @ Trend). "Yes, well, I'd had those in the vault for quite a long time, maybe until about four years ago, because I didn't really want to do anything with them, with Phil being dead and everything. But then his mother was trying to create interest, and has done a lot here in Ireland and so on, so I contacted her and asked her if she would be interested in getting these tracks made available, because people really hadn't heard them at that point, in say 30 years. She was very keen, and then I contacted Niall Stokes, who runs a magazine called *Hot Press*. He was very interested in the whole project, and so then we pressed a small number, like 20,000 or 22,000 CDs of the five tracks, and actually they stand up quite well, because we remastered them and so on. And these are all Lizzy tracks, all written by Philip only. And this went on the cover-mount of the magazine, just a one-off; they're not really for sale or anything. It's just sort of a tribute to the band. And so that would've been the full extent of our recording, those five songs and the two that were the single."

It is of note that neither D'Ardis or O'Neill know precisely when the five non-issued tracks were recorded, O'Neill citing any time from late '69 to late '70, remarking that the band was at Trend on numerous occasions. Indeed to *Hot Press*'s Colm O'Hare, D'Ardis says they were done after 'The Farmer' and to this author, he leaned, with moderate certainly, toward before 'The Farmer', due to 'The Farmer's' full band presentation (John was also pretty sure that the tracks took about four days, although yet again, he had told O'Hare two days). That sense of certainty eroded further when placing the 'I Need You' b-side in the sequence of events, not to mention that no one is quite sure whether Gary Moore was there as a (casual) producer or a guitarist, even though it is definitely Eric Bell playing spirited and precise all over the place.

Upon the release of 'The Farmer', one Irish paper announced the band with the headline 'New Record', writing, "Rated as the third-best group in town at the moment, Thin Lizzy are certainly keeping their fans happy and their date book full. They are doing their 'Thing' at the Countdown tonight and tomorrow night at the Glasnevin Tennis Club. Bass guitarist Phil Lynott wrote the lyrics of 'The Farmer', the group's forthcoming disc for Parlophone. All of which only goes to show their hard work plus lots and lots of practice pays off in the end, and the boys have been doing more than a goodly share of both these past few weeks." Another early notice was not so cheery, a news piece entitled 'Festival Of Living Music In Wexford', citing that, "In the evening concert, Tin (sic) Lizzy was over-amplified, even allowing for pop conventions – the theatre is small and its acoustics are good. Their group acoustical numbers were very successful. Of the others, 'I Put A Spell On You' is a sophisticated construction with a good shape. Brian Downey (drums) is a technician to watch."

"There was so much opportunity that seemed to happen with Thin Lizzy, right from the very first night," muses Bell, asked about how the single deal had gone down. "These opportunities just seemed to attract themselves to us, or we would attract them. It's very strange. Again, just out of the blue, this guy had a record studio in Dublin. The guy who owned the studio somehow got in touch with us and said if we would record a song that he wrote, and put it on the b-side, he would let us record a single for nothing. And we heard about this and we approached him, and we went into the studio, and we were so naïve that we actually brought in a PA, like to sing through. And the guy said, 'Oh, you won't need these in here' (laughs). So anyway, he gave us a copy of his song, called 'I Need You', and we listened to it and said, 'What?! You want us to play on that?' And Phil said, 'No, let's do it man, because we can record our own single.' Why we recorded 'The Farmer', I don't know. I have no idea. I think Philip was going through his Band phase at that time, where it's all sort of cowboy songs, western songs. Anyway, we ended up doing 'The Farmer', and we released it. We couldn't give it away. There were only about 300 copies made or something, and now it's worth a fortune."

As the single was making its way into circulation, July 31 1970, the band, at the suggestion of O'Neill, sacked Wrixon, apparently due to the cost of running a four-piece as opposed to a trio. "We did have a fourth member," concurred Phil. "But because of financial reasons, the band couldn't run as a quartet, so he had to go." Adds Bell, "Eric Wrixon had come along with it. I wanted a three-piece band, but I didn't have the nerve (laughs), to say to Eric Wrixon, 'Oh, you're not in the group.' So he came in and he was with us for about four months." Wrixon had been thinking about leaving anyway. His father had just died and he had been going through a life reassessment. As well, the drama of being Thin Lizzy and the band's stressful communal living arrangements at Clontarf was beginning to wear on him.

It pretty much fell upon Terry O'Neill to deal the final blow. "Yeah, I had gone to rehearsal and I'd spoken about this with Philip and Eric and Brian first, and I just went to rehearsal I said, 'Look, we can't afford to keep going the way we are. We'll have to get rid of Phil.' And I said, 'So what if we did it without a bass player?' right? And nobody said anything, and then I said, 'Oh, I've got a great idea. What if we do it without Eric Bell?' And it was, 'No, why don't we do it without Brian Downey?' And then eventually Eric Wrixon said, 'I get it.' And he just started packing his gear and that was it. In rehearsal, you know? It was that simple. Because it was kind of obvious that we didn't actually need him at the time, and to be quite honest, you couldn't really hear him, at gigs. So it wasn't really that kind of a band. He accepted it fairly fast, you know? Except at the time there were one or two places that kind of said, 'We've heard you're now a three-piece and not a four-piece anymore,' and they wanted to reduce our money (laughs)."

"But yeah, every band that was cool wanted to sound like The Band at that time," continues O'Neill, thinking back on the pastoral track that got Thin Lizzy going, issued the same month as Eric Wrixon's sacking.

"You can hear it on 'The Farmer'. If you talk to anybody, everybody was blown away with The Band, right around that time, and had been for a year or two. Yet at the same time Eric and Philip wanted to be Jimi Hendrix – so did every other cool band at that time – and the Stones and the Beatles and Frank Zappa. There was incredible and innovative music being created all over the world and it was all getting picked up by all the cool young bands everywhere. The story about the b-side and the free session… I'd helped John D'Ardis and John Kane set up Trend which was originally in John D'Ardis' garage, in Shankhill, in County Dublin. Lizzy never recorded there; hardly anybody did. But I'd arranged for Skid Row to get loads of free time when Trend moved into Lad Lane in town. They needed a band to test the studio. There are great photos in *Hitsville* magazine of some of those recording sessions. I did the deal for the single with Parlophone/EMI's Irish A&R man, Tony Hanna. The single came out during the summer and we did some demos for Nick Tauber from Decca a few months later."

"I just remember that it was just a deal and we hated the song," laughs Terry, thinking back on the b-side. "That's the truth. We absolutely hated the song. Philip really hated the song, didn't want to sing it, didn't want to do it. Nobody wanted to do it, and I kind of said, 'Well, if we do it, we get the single,' do you know what I mean? When I went to get Thin Lizzy in, the studio was kind of establishing itself, and it wasn't quite as desperate as it had been with Skid Row. The deal was that yes, I could have it free, if John D'Ardis' song was the b-side, and we agreed, because we didn't really have the money to do it otherwise. And then I went to EMI in Ireland and they agreed to put it out because the band had been getting a bit of support."

And that horn arrangement? "I can't even remember who plays on it. I have a feeling, thinking back, that the horns went on afterwards, that we went away, and then the next time you heard it, the horn are on it." As for Eric's recollection of the horns, "Yeah, I was there; we were all there. I think that was a few show band guys that they got, that could read the dots, read music."

Legend has it that 500 copies of 'The Farmer' were pressed, with 283 sold, and the rest melted down to make more hopeful records. John D'Ardis doesn't buy it, simply citing the presence of a paper label, although he does remember talk of having records "ground" down.

By November 1970, however, O'Neill would be forced to sell out for £250, Brian Tuite then taking over the band along with Pete Bardon. "I'd just got 19," explains O'Neill, recounting the ousting of himself. "I'd managed the band from November 1969 and arranged rehearsals, publicity, gigs, recording etc. First gig was February or March - still can't find original diary. But I didn't have any money, blah blah blah, and

Brian Tuite was probably about 25, but he seemed like a man. We were just kids. And he had gone out with Clodagh Rodgers, Frank Rodgers' sister. She was this big blonde bird, kind of good-looking, and she had a hit record, or maybe more than one hit record, I don't know. But anyway, he got friendly then with Frank Rodgers, from Decca; I'm not sure if he was head of A&R or head of the company."

"So yes, I'd spoken to Decca's Nick Tauber first, sent him demos and he came to Dublin to see the band in rehearsal. He brought me out for dinner in The Russell Hotel on Stephen's Green, now closed but one of the best and most expensive restaurants in Dublin. I picked it! Played him more demos but Decca began to dilly-dally. As I say, I'd then heard that Brian went out with Clodagh Rodgers, Frank Rodgers, head of Decca's sister, and was well in with them and that Decca wanted him to manage the band. As I was just 19 without any money, I sold the management to them for £250."

"As far as I can remember," reiterates O'Neill, "I'd brought Nick around to a rehearsal, then we went out and had the dinner, the two of us, and then it was all kind of 'all systems go,' but it was vague, and then we had lots of telephone calls, and during one of these calls, he said to me, 'Really, if we're going to invest a lot of money, you need to get a partner. And we were thinking that Brian Tuite would be a good partner for you,' you know. 'Yeah, of course, I know him, blah blah blah.' So I went to see Brian. Because I had actually gone to see loads of other people, and they all said, 'No, it'll never happen and all this shit.' And Tuite says, 'Yeah, yeah, let's do something' and, 'Let's get all the band together for a meeting and we'll all talk about it.' So we got the band together. The band was just a three-piece at this point. Eric Wrixon had already gone, and this is probably in about October or November 1970."

Asked why he had approached Decca, O'Neill says, "Well, we had the single out, and then I started talking to record companies. And I don't know why. I think the reason I spoke to Decca first was because Granny's Intentions was on Deram, and they had a little bit of success, and I knew them. And I think they might've told me something. I can't remember. But anyway, that's when I got in touch with Nick. I never actually got any part of that deal or anything. I never looked for part of it, funnily enough. I should have kind of left that band with 1%, and I would've been happy for the rest of my life. But nobody even thought 1% of anything would be worth anything at that time. They were just starting, and the chances of somebody becoming famous outside of Ireland were beyond anything. The only people that had become successful were really straight middle-of-the-road people like Val Doonican and The Bachelors."

"I can't remember CBS being in the picture," continues O'Neill. "I remember when I met with Nick Tauber, which was just before I finished with the band. Nick probably thought I wasn't experienced enough, and I probably wasn't at the time. But he did kind of say he wanted to hear more, but Tuite had the in. But whatever label they were with, Decca, but he was the only one who showed any interest anyway, you know? Nick Tauber. No one was kind of chasing the band or talking with the band. And we hadn't talked to anybody. But back when I went to get the single out, I went to Irish Record Factors, who were the distributor. EMI were there, and Tony Hanna, the guy I spoke to first, he just immediately agreed. And then after that, I remember going to John Woods, who ran Philips Records, in Ireland, or Pye, I think they were called. He kind of said no, they wouldn't help them. There were a few people I went to – Irish kinds of labels – and nobody expressed any interest. But Nick was interested, and he came to Dublin, and he seemed to show some real interest. But I think Tuite was already sort of noodling away behind things."

"But we were really successful," continues O'Neill, back to examining the single. "You know, it didn't sell any copies, but it was on the radio quite a lot, and the band were getting kind of good money compared to other bands, but we still hadn't had any money. We really needed equipment, and this guy Brian Tuite owned an equipment shop, you know? And so we had a whole kind of wish list, new guitars, new amps, PA, every fucking thing, and go to play in London. And so anyway, we had a meeting, he went through the list and he said, 'Yes, I'll do that, I'll do that, I'll do that,' and we're going, 'Great, great, great,' right? And at the end of the whole thing, he says, 'Now, one thing, I don't want you as a partner. I want Peter Bardon.' Right? Who kind of walked into the room at that point. Tuite wanted him in, because he was kind of an establishment music business-type, show band-type. But it was a bit kind of like (laughs) serious, right? It was a bit of a freak-out. I mean, we went outside, and the band were genuinely up in arms about this, you know what I mean? And I was kind of... I don't know why I was taking the bullet, but I was saying, 'Listen, I can't do it anymore. These guys might be... because I know that Tuite will get you the deal with Decca, and the equipment.' And he used to drive American cars like Thunderbirds, or whatever the fuck."

"So I, and no one else, looked after the management of the band from the beginning until November 1970 when I left and Tuite and Bardon took over," offers O'Neill, as a helpful recap on the game of musical chairs that was Lizzy management. "In relation to management after me, as far as I know, it's Tuite and Bardon from November 1970. They got the Decca deal. Then Tuite, Bardon and Ted Carroll. Then maybe Ted on his own. Then Chris Morrison and Chris O'Donnell until the end.

They had no other managers to my knowledge but lots of jumped-up tour managers who pretended to be managers!"

And as Benny White from Elmer Fudd explains, the definition of manager was pretty fluid back in those casual days... "Yeah, well, Terry sort of worked for Brian Tuite, as far as I was aware. Brian Tuite would be like a cloud, I would say. How can I put it? He would be like a puppet master at the top, and there were all the strings coming out, and various other people would work for him at the end of the strings. Brian Tuite had a recording shop, sound gear and stuff like this, and that was his forte. But he did manage a couple of bands, like ourselves and Thin Lizzy, I think, at one stage. When I say managed, he got us gigs. There were no written contracts or nothing. He put us here and he put us there; that was about the scale of the management. We, in Fudd, we were out for a recording contract, with Decca Records, and I believe now – I believe; there's no proof of the matter – but they actually wanted us on board big time. They came and heard the band, and he wanted to get rid of his gear shop, so he said, 'Well look, if you take this off me as well, you can have Fudd,' and they refused. So that was the end of that. Again, it's hearsay, but that's what I heard, and pretty mad about it. You know, he had a couple of business interests that he wanted to offload along with Fudd; that was the story going around at the time. I'm not quite sure if it's true at all. But of course, Terry O'Neill, yeah, he would be a man that was involved – when you're involved with Brian Tuite, he did other things for Brian. Like he managed bands like ourselves, but really, it wasn't managing in the real sense of managing a band, where a manager takes care of his acts in every way. Most of the guys at that time just got gigs for bands, that's it. And took a little off the top."

"It was just accepted that that they managed Thin Lizzy," continues White, further on the subject of Brian and Terry. "That's all I knew about it. We were more interested in our band than Thin Lizzy, because we were trying and working very hard to get a name for ourselves. It was really about us. And actually, after we left those guys, we went to another fellow who said he'd take us on. Ollie Byrne was his name. Ollie ran a club called The Countdown; he said he would take us over, and he took out his diary, gave us about seven gigs for the next two or three months, and the first two we went to, never existed (laughs). He was just... Ollie's dead now, but again, going back to a manager: a guy that got you gigs."

Says John D'Ardis on Brian Tuite, "He had a shop that was renting out PAs and that sort of thing. I just remember Terry and the groups hanging out there and how they were involved together. But you really have to understand how casual everything was then. Nobody was thinking in terms of a career or anything like that. They were just happy to be doing what they were doing." And Ollie Byrne? "Well, he was, again, a bit of a character, mainly a promoter. He put on dances and so on and was also involved in clubs; he had an interest in some of the clubs. He would be hiring groups, if you like. He was a figure on the scene, but I don't think he was particularly involved with Thin Lizzy."

"The first album, I wasn't involved with," explains Ted Carroll, clarifying his early days experience with Thin Lizzy, which begins after the band's sophomore effort. "I had heard that album, and I was offered a joint management position with the band. I was impressed with Phil's songs and I knew Phil, because obviously I'd worked with him before in Skid Row; I managed Skid Row. But I hadn't been aware of his songwriting prior to that. I was impressed with his songs, and that's what made me decide to go to work with the band."

Inevitably, Elmer Fudd and Thin Lizzy played shows together, up and around Ireland in '71, one local notice relating that Thin Lizzy, *"fly home again next Friday (9th) for a whirlwind four-day tour including venues they missed during their last trip. Guest group with Lizzy on all four dates will be Elmer Fudd, the thudding Dublin group who now look as if they're the hottest property on the club scene in Ireland. Fudd are managed by the same team who launched Thin Lizzy, Terry O'Neill and Brian Tuite."*

"We did, yeah. We played Dublin with them on a few occasions. We would open for the band, and on a couple of occasions, we actually blew the house down; really, really went down well. So much, I think, to the annoyance of Philip Lynott. Yeah, Philip Donnelly, our guitar player and I were only talking awhile ago about when we used to get together, and he said he was in seeing Brian Tuite, and he's standing behind the door, and all of a sudden the door opened up, and it was Phil Lynott. He didn't see Philip Donnelly and he said to Brian Tuite, 'Never put us on with that fucking band again!' In other words, we were really blowing them off the stage. That's the impression that Philip got. And then he turned around and saw Philip Donelly and he said he was only joking."

Within this anecdote and through other examples, White could tell that Phil Lynott was destined to make it in rock 'n' roll. "Yeah, big time. To me, Phil's a real showman, and he looked good and he knew it. He knew it. He was posing all the time. As if there were a million comers around Philip. He was just posing all the time, the way he walked, the way he talked. Even the cigarette in his mouth became a prop, if you like. The way he put it into his mouth and all that. He's a really good-looking tall guy, and the women loved him. The women really loved him. But with the touring, there were crazy nights. We had very many strange, weird parties, not outlandish like Led Zeppelin, but drink and drugs. But none of us, thank God, ever got into it heavy like Philip did. There was great potential there for that to happen, but it didn't. And I went on later, actually after Fudd broke up, Philip took me on, into the band, at least into the Thin Lizzy show, and I'd done the lights for Thin Lizzy for about a month all around Ireland, which I really enjoyed. This was when Brian and Scott were already in the band."

Terry O'Neill heartily concurs that Phil could command a room... even at poetry readings. "Yes, well, Philip, even during the time of Thin Lizzy, he would go and read poetry at poetry sessions and everything. When I was managing the band, on Tuesdays and Wednesdays and Thursdays nights, there would be little things on in tiny little rooms, intellectuals reading poetry, reciting things and so on. And Philip got into that particular scene, if you like. He mixed very well with other people and he went into all sorts of circles. Also, I think it was a real advantage being black in Dublin at the time. There were just no black people in Dublin. It was really like, the opposite to racism. It's like everybody wanted to know a black person, and there weren't any around. So the minute we walked into a room, like probably there were 10% of the people who were racist and walked ten steps back, right? But nearly everybody else came forward to Philip. It was just a really serious advantage (laughs). We all wanted to be black, once we saw how well he was doing being black (laughs)."

"Philip, Eric and Brian, the original three-piece Thin Lizzy, have never been captured properly," sighs O'Neill in closing, "There have been too many assumptions. A lot of things are suggested that just aren't true. Met Jim Fitzpatrick on Burrow Beach in Sutton last week and asked him what did he think of the Philip Exhibition and he said, 'Not one woman in it – that's not the Philip I knew.' Philip had quite a reputation but it's never mentioned. And you know, people say that the rock 'n' roll lifestyle killed him. It didn't. He died from constant use and abuse of drink and drugs. If an accountant dies of drink and drugs no one ever says, 'Oh, it's the accountancy lifestyle that killed him.' Same with plumbers, doctors etc. Look at all the people involved in the music biz and how few die of drink and drugs. It's one of those clichés that I just can't stand. There's been enough shoddy Philip stuff out there. Whatever you do, try get it right."

2
THIN LIZZY
"One is to tell a story"

The profile for rock from Ireland was on the upswing as 1970 came to a close. In October, both Skid Row and Granny's Intentions had issued full-length debuts, the former for CBS, the latter for Deram, future Thin Lizzy member Gary Moore having been involved with both bands. The following month, Thin Lizzy themselves were signed, hooking up with Decca Records, after having impressed the label's aforementioned Frank Rodgers (also of Irish descent) during a session where they sat in as backing band for Decca hopeful Ditch Cassidy who was auditioning for signing, with Lizzy getting the nod instead. A more intentioned telling of the story has Brian Tuite setting up the audition, with Tuite pressing for a three-album and single deal including the covering of recording costs. Part of the audition process also found the band playing a second day-time gig at Dublin's Peacock Theatre for executive Dick Rowe and Scott English, who would end up producing the band's debut.

"I'd finished with the band at this stage," notes O'Neill, "but they came to see Ditch, at the Zhivago Club, which is kind of a nightclub. They came to see Ditch, and Thin Lizzy backed him for his kind of audition. Then Lizzy played a few songs, and Lizzy got the deal that night, I think. This would've been probably around middle of November 1970, or maybe December."

"Like I said earlier on, so many opportunities came our way," remembers Eric Bell. "Every time I talk about it and think about it, it convinces me more and more that Thin Lizzy was meant to be. Again, Ditch Cassidy's band had broken up, this particular week, and they had no band, no backing band. This guy from Decca was coming over from London to check out a few talents in Ireland, and Ditch was one of them. Somehow, I don't know how it happened, but we ended up in this club in Dublin with Ditch Cassidy, about three o'clock in the afternoon. And this guy came in. I think we had a sort of friend/manager-type bloke, and he stood beside the guy from Decca in the middle of this empty club, three o'clock in the afternoon, and Ditch is sort of singing all this soul stuff, and myself, Philip and Brian... I think we were just a three-piece then. I'm not sure. Yes, we'd just turned three-piece. So we were backing Ditch, and it went on for about 20 minutes, half an hour, and then we packed up our equipment. As we were packing it up, our friend/manager came over to us and said, 'Listen, the guy from Decca wants to have a talk with you, so we'll see you around the pub in about 20 minutes, but don't tell Ditch,' type thing. And we're going, okay. We had no idea. And so we went to the pub and the guy said, 'Listen, I'm very impressed with you as a band. Would you like to record an album for Decca?' And we looked at him, like, we couldn't believe it. It was unbelievable! Just like that."

Deal done, on January 4, 1971, Thin Lizzy boarded a flight in Dublin, tramped off the same flight in London and went straight into the studio that day to begin the recording of their debut album, finishing the job in five days (plus two days to mix), with Scott English producing, assisted by Peter Rynston. English, an American, was known more so as a songwriter, having co-penned 'Bend Me, Shape Me', a hit for both The American Breed and Amen Corner, as well as 'Help Me Girl' for Eric Burdon And The Animals and 'Hi Ho Silver Lining' for Jeff Beck.

But English was not to press those skills on his new charges as might have been expected as part of the deal. Indeed, Phil Lynott was to achieve convincingly, one of his long harboured goals, to become a performer of his own material. Of the ten tracks on what would become the band's self-titled debut, he co-wrote two, took sole credit on seven, with guitarist Eric Bell – guitarist in a trio! – taking credit on but one. Phil had indeed arrived, the day his first album hit the shelves, April 30 of 1971, four months after its recording and one month after the band's relocation to the music beehive that was London.

"My songwriting began when I was with the (Black) Eagles," said Phil, in conversation with Gun's Steve Bolger, "but I would say it became even more important to me, as opposed to singing, when I joined Skid Row. Brush and myself started to write numbers when I joined, and then I began to see the great potential in writing my own material and how important it would be in achieving success. There are three basic sorts of spheres I like to write in. One is to tell a story. Another is to give an impression whereby you take your own feelings from the lyrics. And then there's the type of song where I am trying to say something. For example, in 'Diddy Devine', I am trying to put across that everyone inherits something from somebody else. Likewise, in 'Honesty Is No Excuse', to be very honest is no excuse for what you actually do."

'Honesty Is No Excuse' is a highlight of the first Thin Lizzy album, featuring a prominent mellotron part courtesy of legendary classical and jazz pianist Ivor Raymonde, also a producer and composer, most notable for his work with Dusty Springfield. All told, 'Honesty Is No Excuse' is the first of many confessionals from Phil, a poignant expression of guilt (here for philandering, in later years for drugging), a gorgeous ballad blessed with tasteful and skilled drumming from Brian, whose fills are legion yet controlled. Busy Brian is an element that would distinguish the Eric Bell era of Thin Lizzy, this idea that percussion can bubble flamboyantly beneath the most delicate of melodies and arrangements. What's more, the production of the percussion is plush and sympathetic, like early Zeppelin at its best.

Asked to cite a favourite Eric Bell moment on the first record, Eric says, 'I like the solo on 'Honesty Is No Excuse'; it's a very melodic sort of approach. And that mellotron… this guy had come in. He was sort of like, what would you say, a '50s matinee idol (laughs), sort of look. Very, very professional, like no messing about. Just came in, did it, and left, I think. I don't know whose idea it was to put a mellotron on. It could've been Scott English."

Whether the goodly production job afforded the Thin Lizzy album was something captured by producer Scott English or re-mixer Nick Tauber is up for debate. The band readily admits they were smoking pot immediately upon arriving at the studio, Eric joking that he could barely even see Phil across the room. Then English showed up with his own big bag full, becoming legless himself upon short order

"When we met him," recalls Bell, "we found out that he had written 'Hi Ho Silver Lining' for Jeff Beck, and had also written a song called 'Brandy', I think. He was a huge American guy with a big black beard and so on. What actually happened was, he had this enormous bag of grass, and he sort of put it on the table and he said, 'okay guys, help yourselves' (laughs). And that was the end of it. I mean, I can't remember recording the first album, really. And I think Scott English got so out of it that he started mixing up the tracks, because I know he was losing some of my guitar solos, this, that and the other, and we got this other guy in, Nick Tauber, and Nick took over the final sort of mixing. And yeah, I haven't heard of Scott English since."

"I joined Decca Records as an assistant producer and A&R man," explains Nick, on rectifying the situation, "and then the first Thin Lizzy album came in, after being made, produced by a guy named Scott English, right? He wrote 'Mandy', that song by Barry Manilow (originally titled 'Brandy', as noted by Eric above). He co-wrote that afterward, but that came in, and the band and the A&R guy that signed Thin Lizzy, a guy called Frank Rodgers, they weren't happy with the mix."

"I don't know why he got the gig," says Nick, asked what he knew of English, who, after all, didn't actually produce much before or after Thin Lizzy. "All I know is that he was an American and he was a friend of Dick Rowe, the A&R manager, and that's how he got it. All I know is that I thought it was a bit of a strange choice, but those things happen. He made the record but he wasn't really a rock producer, and I think that's why the album came out a bit weird. It was strange, not what they were looking for. I don't think it was bad, but I didn't think it was hard enough and tough enough and big enough."

"I was young, really young, only 18, 19," continues Tauber. "I'd played drums in a band, I'd been an engineer at a studio called Regent Sound studio where I worked as an assistant for Black Sabbath, I engineered for Cat Stevens, people like that, and I was just the youngest guy. To be honest, I think I got it because I was the youngest guy in the flaming department, and they said, 'Look, go and see if you can remix it.' Basically, 'Do you think you can make a better job?' Well, I said, I think I can, but I'll give it go. So they said, 'okay, go off and do it.' So I went off and remixed the whole record. Phil Lynott, and Frank Rodgers the A&R man, thought it was much better, much better. And so they were really pleased and so I got to do the next record with them, which was the *New Day* EP."

And whoever deserves credit for the lucky sound of Thin Lizzy, it's indeed quite good given the record's vintage, and given the fact that it really does mix delicate guitar and vocals with an active, aggressive rhythm section. In fact the other track of which Phil speaks, 'Diddy Levine' (incidentally, yet another from the suite of guarded broken family lyrics from Phil), is a second example of this, again, Led Zeppelin coming to mind, as does The Who. Further on the mix, as good as it turned out, the band weren't even aware that it was happening, and in the process, Eric was quick to find out that they had used the wrong guitar tracks in places, leaving his preferred takes on the cutting room floor.

Not that there are signature Thin Lizzy dual guitar leads this early in the band's history, but indeed, while recording the album in London (at Decca, in Hampstead), the band had tripped down to the Lyceum, where they saw for the first time, this technique as performed by the legendary Wishbone Ash.

Also in this department, Lizzy managers ex- and present (Terry O'Neill and Brian Tuite) looked after Elmer Fudd who, like the Lizzy of the future, shared lead between two players. "Actually, yeah!" says Eric, upon mention of Elmer Fudd. "Some bands in Dublin had twin guitars, yeah. There was another one called Peggy's Leg, I think. They had lead guitar and rhythm guitar, but the rhythm guitar would sometimes double up leads with the lead guitarist. There was all that going on, yeah."

"I can see that," agrees Fudd vocalist Benny White. "But we weren't the first, because there was a band from England called Wishbone Ash. But I think we were the first band in Ireland to have it. They probably did get the idea from listening to us, because we played a lot together at the same shows and we were a serious guitar riff band. We did a lot of stuff by Purple, Mountain, Spirit, the original Byrds, and we had a really heavy version of 'Lucy In The Sky With Diamonds'. But we also did a lot of our own stuff. We wrote a lot of really, really good songs, which unfortunately, there are no good recordings of. There was one called 'Beautiful Death' and a 27-minute one called 'The Harpooner'. 'Beautiful Death' wasn't a suicide song, it was about somebody who is dead, and the person was really missing her. It was the sort of drug-fuelled music of 1969, you know?"

"And we'd done a couple of demos all right. Not great quality, quality demos, but certainly we got a couple and we were great live. This band was really, really great live, and we were very loud. I think at one stage in Ireland, we were probably the loudest band in Ireland; you know, the way that Deep Purple were reportedly the loudest band in the world, well we were certainly the loudest band in Ireland, I know that. And yeah, we did make a couple of demos, not of high quality, and where they are now, I have no idea. It really annoys me to think that they are out there somewhere. Because we wrote some cracking songs. And so we based our early stuff on two guitars and we introduced the twin guitars into our own originals as well. It was really, really good. But as I said, we did a lot of shows with Phil and the boys. It's more than likely that he did get the idea for twin guitars from us."

Brush Shiels figures the Elmer Fudd reference with respect to twin leads is way off base. "No way," laughs Shiels, "although Elmer Fudd were good. I'd say the Allman Brothers were the only real two-guitar band that any Irish band was really interested in. Even though the Lizzy thing didn't sound like the Allman Brothers, ultimately, but that two-guitar thing would be coming from them mainly; there weren't too many other people doing that. There were bands with two guitars, but the Allmans were playing the harmonies and in a particular way."

Despite Shiels' claim, it is Wishbone Ash that is cited most regularly as the earliest and best exemplars of twin lead harmonies (at least in terms of UK acts, and in a rockier environs), the band famously touted by the likes of Iron Maiden's Steve Harris and other Maiden members, indeed, more often it seems than the more likely Lizzies themselves.

Eric recalls distinctly taking in Wishbone Ash with Phil. "For us to record the first album for Decca, we were still living in Dublin, and we'd just came to London and stayed in a bed and breakfast for about ten days, and we got the underground, the tube train, to Decca studios every morning about nine o'clock in the morning to West Hampstead. So we weren't living in England. Anyway, we had one night off, and, because we'd never been in London before, well, not as three people together anyway, Phil said, 'Eric, let's go down to the Lyceum tonight; there's a big, huge gig in London. There's a few bands on, and there's a band called Wishbone Ash, man,' and so we said yeah, great, so we went back to the bed and breakfast and got all dressed up, and got the tube downtown, found out where the Lyceum was, absolutely amazing place. I mean, we couldn't believe it! We're just off the boat from Dublin, and it's like a fabulous big opera house and there's all these hippies and really weird-looking people, and the place is stuffed."

"Everybody was sitting on the floor and in the lotus position, rolling dope. That's just what it was like. And so we sat down as well and started rolling dope, and these bands who'd come on, really good bands, and then Wishbone Ash come on, and Phil says, 'Hey Eric, you see, if you close your eyes, I think the bands in Dublin are just as good, but what these bands have over here is, is look at their clothes.' You couldn't get those clothes in Dublin at that point. You know, they just weren't there. You got checked shirts and fucking farmer's jeans, type of stuff. And that was just starting to happen in Dublin; they started getting these clothes in Dublin. But you couldn't get them at this point."

"So Philip was very knocked out with the way the bands looked on stage, and also their poses," says Eric. "He said, 'You see the bands in Dublin, they stand with these wrinkled jeans on, playing the blues looking at the fucking stage with their heads down. But they're just as good a musician. But the musicians in England have got panache. You know, they can sell it.' And then he came out and said, 'Hey Eric, you fancy getting another guitar player in the band?' We're watching Wishbone Ash, with double playing guitars, leads, you know? And I said, 'No, Philip,' and he said, 'Oh, okay.' And he never mentioned it again. Ever. But that was obviously in his head, when he got Scott Gorman and Brian Robertson."

"What happens is, I come along and write the words, chords and melody line," says Phil, continuing his chat with Steve Bolger, twin leads still a mere twinkle in his eye at this early stage. "Then the boys have a free hand to give their ideas on how they feel it should go. If Brian and Eric change my concept of the number, or if I prefer their arrangement, then I share it with them. At all times, Thin Lizzy's numbers are basically a team effort with Brian supplying the drumming arrangements and Eric the guitar work. When I get a melody in my head, I work it out on the guitar, or I might play chords until it hits a mood that I feel. Sometimes I set out to write a particular type of number; like I want to write a fast beaty number, I sit down and keep working until I get out a fast song. Other times I might just pick up the guitar and while sitting there, it all flows out."

One of the more daring and creative numbers on the album is in fact psychedelic opener 'The Friendly Ranger At Clontarf Castle'. Immediately we get pure poetry from Phil, and after a time, the song collapses into a rudimentary yet choppy bass and drum groove over which Bell wafts wah-wah. The Clontarf of which Phil speaks, is named for an area on the north side of Dublin where he, Eric Wrixon Eric Bell and Eric's girlfriend took up residence, eventually joined by Gail Barber who moved into the house's glass conservatory room vacated by Eric Wrixon upon leaving the band for Sweden. Gail and Phil would become lovers and the relationship would last for six years, even to the point of engagement. Clontarf unsurprisingly became party central, to the point where the neighbours would petition, to no avail, to have the revolving cast of long-haired hippies cast out of the gentile environs. "It's like, there's a terminus in Las Vegas where all these people meet that you don't meet on the strip," laughs Brush Shiels, putting his finger on the vibe of the place. "You don't even know they're there. They're waiting to go to somewhere else and you don't even know them. So it was a bit like that, like either a halfway house or a terminus. But it was very exotic and erotic, an interesting place for eclectic existentialists (laughs)."

"Myself, I had my own flat," explains Eric, "which I shared with the drummer from the show band that I used to be in, and Philip has his own flat, at Donnybrook, I think. After about six weeks of meeting each other, Philip suggested one day, 'Hey Eric, do you fancy getting a house together, so that we can work on our music all the time? Like it won't just be once a week in a rehearsal room; we'll actually be living together, you know?' And he got that idea because there were lots of bands doing that in those days, commune living, lots of American bands plus Blind Faith and Traffic, and they would all get a house together and live together. So Philip asked me would I be interested, and I said yeah. So he went out one day, and he actually wore his suit and a tie, tidied himself up, and went to see an estate agent, and came back about two hours later, and he was jangling these keys in my face, and said, 'Got it. You wanna come out and see the place?' And it was out at a place called Clontarf, which is pretty upmarket, in Dublin; lots of pretty rich people live in that area. And so we got the bus and we stopped at this bus stop and walked up this street, Castle Avenue, and round about the first or second house, we had the apartment upstairs, and he took me up and it was amazing, really something. And that's where we ended up living.

And Clontarf Castle was up at the top of the street. It was actually sort of a small castle-type thing, and our street was called Castle Avenue."

Ever one to tap into myth, the song is more so inspired by the castle, rather than the band's party pad. Clontarf Castle was in fact a two-minute walk away, and the locale of a battle at which locals defeated Norman interlopers in 1014.

Gail's and Phil's relationship ran hot and cold due to Phil's philandering, but at this early stage, relations were intense enough that she was to be found centre stage on the album's 'Look What The Wind Blew In', a pressure cooker of a rocker, quite progressive, and stacked with novel note and chord choices out of Bell. It's an explosive and joyous song, acrobatic and reminiscent of Skid Row but clearly indicative of the hard rock talent latent in Phil's new band.

"I think it had to do with the times that we lived in," notes Eric, asked about the wide range of influence on the band. "I had my record collection. I'm from Belfast, and I moved to Dublin to join an Irish show band, so I brought my record collection with me. Then after Thin Lizzy formed, myself and Philip got a house and started living together, and so he brought his record collection and I had mine, and Brian Downey didn't live with us, but he brought some of his records. So we had this cross-section of music, you know? I had some very early Deep Purple albums and Jeff Beck's *Truth*, all that type of stuff, and Philip had things like Buffalo Springfield, the Byrds. I would listen to his record collection and hear some things that I hadn't heard before, and he would listen to my record collection as well. So there was all this type of music around, and like everybody else, you sort of pull bits and pieces from it."

Asked to what extent Skid Row had been an influence, Eric figures, "Skid Row was an absolutely incredible three-piece band, but we didn't copy any of their music because, to be honest, it was too technical for us. It was very, very intricate riffs and time changes that everyone was into. We had more of a melodic approach to music."

Terry O'Neill understands this sentiment all too well. "Quite recently, I was talking to Brush Shiels, just to give you an idea of Skid Row. We had done a tribute to Jimmy Faulkner, and Gary had died, and I was saying that we should do a gig for Gary, you know? And we'll get all the guitar players. And he said, 'Yeah… I can kind of see a problem there.' And I said, 'What I was thinking was, if you and Noel Bridgeman played, right, and all the guitar players got up and did a number, with you and Noel.' He said, 'First of all, me and Noel would have to practice for about three months to be able to do what Skid Row did, right? And secondly, the guitar players wouldn't be able to play it. Because, in truth, we wouldn't be able to play it' (laughs). He said, 'In fairness to Thin Lizzy, there are loads of Thin Lizzy tribute acts,' you know? Because you can play Thin Lizzy's music. You can't play Skid Row's music. It's a bit like when Dweezil Zappa does Zappa Does Zappa, but nobody else can attempt to play Zappa. And similarly, nobody can really play Skid Row, because the timings are all like 11/7, and 16/13 or something (laughs). Completely different from Thin Lizzy, you know? So nobody kind of tried to be Skid Row; nobody really tried to go there. But there were probably other acts like John Hiseman and people like that, where Skid Row were getting their influences from, who were playing this very kind of muso kind of music. Skid Row and Thin Lizzy each did it their own way. Skid Row were kind of like virtuosos, or they became virtuosos."

Brush himself realizes the inspiration Skid Row provided to Irish bands, but he's also refreshingly adamant that what was admirable in Skid Row wasn't necessarily a good set of ingredients for Thin Lizzy.

"Technically we would've been playing faster material than what the boys were doing. And the boys were thinking that they would have to take it to wherever we were, and then take it to wherever it would take them. But we were obviously the criteria on how to do it in a particular way. And obviously, the fact that there were things that would've been a bit more complicated that were on the records that we made, obviously Phil felt he wanted to improve all the time, and take it further. But at the same time, you have to stop trying to improve in the strict sense, and consolidate whatever you come up, which was the Lizzy way of doing it with two guitars. Phil didn't really need a bass style and all that. They had a way of doing things. Once he got there, there was no point to try to make it more complicated. They'd come up with a particular way of playing, and you stay there when you get to that point, instead of trying to make it more complicated. Which is what Skid Row was doing. We were trying to make it more complicated and at the same time we would be playing very simple country numbers, which people couldn't figure that out at all, that we would play both types of things on the same album. And I told Phil never to do that. I said, you know, don't confuse people by playing too many different types. Don't be playing country, for a start, anyway (laughs)."

"We had a country track on each album," continues Brush, "but when they did 'Cowboy Song', it wasn't really country, it was more Bob Seger, you know? Phil would've been very interested in country music, but that's not the way to do it. Once you get organized, like with the Lizzy thing and the two guitars, you stay with what you've got, which is basically blues-based."

No use drilling down and trying to compare drummers either, namely Noel Bridgeman up against Brian Downey. "There's really nothing you can say. You know, the boys brought their own energy. If you listen to the John Peel BBC sessions, where Skid Row was playing live, Gary, Noel and myself, we started off with a nine-minute drum solo. We actually opened with a drum solo. Never said anything, the drums just started playing and they went for nine minutes. Noel had his own style. Based on wonderful technique and energy, and Downey similarly. Again, both of the lads would've been coming out of the same era: have a listen to Ginger Baker, have a listen to the guy with Jimi Hendrix, go back, listen to Buddy Rich, all the different jazz drummers. And then you're developing your own persona, and then every little bit after that, that's the way you are. So the boys both came from the same backgrounds, both drummers doing fuckin' drum solos that sounded like an elephant stampede, or a wildebeest with a motorboat engine around his neck. Today, you don't hear it anymore in the same way. But if you listen to Brian on the live album or if you listen to Noel on the BBC tapes live, and you open with a nine minute drum solo, there wasn't too many bands doing that – that's how confident we were."

"Noel, he's my best pal to this day," adds Brush, asked specifically what he knew about rumours that Noel nearly ended up in Lizzy in later years, when Downey felt down about the band. "Noel could have very easily wound up in Thin Lizzy. But then, anybody could've wound up in Thin Lizzy, really. I think when you're down and things are happening, the lads are leaving every day, and then things changed. Noel is one of the great drummers of all time, but I think Brian was always Thin Lizzy's drummer; he was Phil's oldest pal, really. And obviously, they mightn't see eye-to-eye every so often, but it's all tied up in the folklore. It could happen, but it didn't happen, you know?"

"And Phil, more than anything, he became the bass player in Thin Lizzy," muses Brush, down a similar thought process. "That's always the most important thing. You're the bass player, and you're the only bass player for your band. That's the most important thing. It doesn't matter how technically gifted you are. It doesn't matter all the complicated stuff you can do. The most important thing, he came up with the ideas, he came up with a very solid way of playing. He wouldn't be one of the greatest bass players in the world, but he's the only bass player in Thin Lizzy, and between himself and Downey and the two guitar players, they got a sound together that went worldwide, and anybody else playing the bass, it wouldn't work. Phil knew what kind of bass he wanted to put to the songs he'd written, and that's really what it's all about. You have to be very careful; once you start complicating the bass, the band falls apart. Well, any band that I was ever in fell apart because of that, you know (laughs)."

But Phil also had to make a conscious decision not to be complicated because he had to sing as well... "Yes, you could say that, and at the same time you can say, as I've said on numerous occasions, there's no need to be more complicated than the early Jimi Hendrix. You know, keep it like that and you can't fail. That's how I felt about it anyway. The first couple of Jimi Hendrix albums, not where it got to where the boys are all jamming in the middle of it, but the early stuff. You only had to keep it like that, and add little bits and pieces to it. That would work forever, in my opinion."

"I was very lucky to have met Gary Moore when he first came over from Ireland with Skid Row," says Sweet guitarist Andy Scott, providing his own anecdote illustrative of Skid Row's impact on the scene. "Sweet… you would never believe this, we'd just entered the charts with our first record, and were put on the bill with Skid Row in a biggish club, but nevertheless a club, in the north of England. But we were playing on slightly different stages. You know, it was one of these clubs that had split levels and things. And I walked in the dressing room – because it was always a shared dressing room back then – and we had heard the Skid Row album. Mick Tucker and I had been trying to learn the riff to 'Mad Dog Woman' in the afternoon, which was extremely fast, not realizing that Skid Row had arrived, so that when we walked in the dressing room, Gary Moore is now playing 'The Lilt', our hit that is in the charts, on his guitar, but with a slightly bluesy feel. I went, 'Touché.' And ever since then, every time… And with Lizzy, sure, I used to go to Lizzy gigs all the time, and they were absolute gentleman. I loved Phil. I think immediately, you heard 'Whisky In The Jar', and I know that was a different band back then, but you knew that this was going to be a band to watch out for."

Elsewhere on the Thin Lizzy record, 'Clifton Grange Hotel' celebrates mum's lodging establishment for entertainment people and members of Manchester United (no "normals," says Philomena), informally known as The Showbiz or The Biz, or as Phil affectionately called it, "Me ma's." Again, the guitar work from Eric is exemplary and versatile; Bell hitting notes of fusion, of rock, of psych, effects everywhere, all upon a frame of flamenco. The soft and mystical Eire celebrates morosely the band's Irish roots, as does 'Remembering Part 1' (one of Eric's personal favourites), which alternates traditional folk with rumbling proto-metal and prog breaks, again, aggressive rhythms throbbed by upfront bass taking centre stage over guitar.

"There are a few little things I really like on the record," says Eric. "I liked the very first phrase of the guitar in 'Eire' – it sounds like a saxophone, like a tenor saxophone. It's very strange. It's amazing how your approach to the instrument changes over the years. Sometimes I think, God, I wish I was still thinking that way, you know what I mean? But at the time you don't realize that what you're doing is valid. You're just hoping for the best, that somebody out there likes it. And I liked

'Remembering', because it's like a big jam session somewhere, plus there's loads and loads of guitar work going on."

Also rocking hard is 'Return Of The Farmer's Son', which reminds one of early Budgie, a Welsh power trio also beaten and bruised from the bottom up. An amusing interplay occurs where Phil sings of being smacked on the ass, and Brian responds with a fierce lick personifying just that, although this whole sequence is wall-to-wall killer chops from the kit. Again, a triumphant Celtic melody rifles through another Thin Lizzy track, not that one can concentrate on it, given the tour de force that is Brian Downey and his powerful yet warmly recorded drums and bashed cymbals.

Finally, there's the not particularly Irish folk of 'Saga Of The Ageing Orphan', Downey using brushes on this resplendent acoustic track, and the Bell-composed 'Ray-Gun', a Zep-tinged Hendrix funk on which Bell again stomps wah-wah, texturing the track as he does so many others on the album, allowing for melody to arise from the composite rather than direct from chords. "Ray-Gun, I wrote the music for," remembers Eric. "I was just messing about one day. I had gotten all these riffs and all these bits and pieces and Philip said... Philip used to say to me, 'Is that yours?' And sometimes I would go no, because I'd been playing somebody else's song, and then he says, 'Is that yours? Ray-Gun?' And I said yes, and he sort of disappeared and came back with the lyrics, and that was that. But I love all that album. I think it's such a warm, quite original album. Each track that comes on (laughs), is sort of my favourite, as I listen to it."

All told, Thin Lizzy was an intriguing and sophisticated album, the sophistication coming from the song construction if not the arrangements, which were kept fairly basic to guitar, bass, drums and vocals, with minimum overdubs – one could imagine most of the album being played live without much loss of parts.

As noted, prior the album's release, the band had relocated to London (just like Skid Row, a year earlier), settling in West Hampstead, conveniently near Decca and also handy to the M1, each at separate addresses. Philip and Gail had to settle for the worst of accommodations, given landlords' reservations over renting to a shacked-up couple, and an inter-racial one at that, not to mention a general lack of appreciation for Phil's chosen line of work.

Moving to London was par for the course for many bands all up and down the UK, so it was a no-brainer for an ambitious band from Ireland, Thin Lizzy rightly citing the lack of radio stations, lack of places to gig anew, and the proliferation of show bands soaking up the entertainment dollar.

"It was the Irish kids who really held us together," explained Phil.

"They gave us work and accepted our music, until they voted us Ireland's top band. It was then that we got a recording contract and the chance to come to England. It had to come that we left Ireland because it's so easy to play yourself out of work over there, because the country so small."

Brian Downey also has intimated that the move had been partly encouraged by the airtime Kid Jensen had been giving the band at Radio Luxembourg, Kid and Phil becoming fast friends at this point, staying at each other's places, playing records and discussing them long into the night. Still, Ireland remained of vital importance to the band in the early years, given the good crowds and good pay the band could muster in a hurry, Irish dates being the modest cash cow the band found necessary to finance the often money-losing touring up and down the UK, where attendance and enthusiasm was often woefully lacking.

Asked about the set list in those days, in particular, covers that would have been tabled, Eric remembers, " 'If Six Was Nine' and 'Fire' by Hendrix. And we did 'Here Comes The Sun' by the Beatles. This was way back when Lizzy first started. And believe it or not, one day, we were actually rehearsing Roger Miller's 'Little Green Apples'. Yeah! Philip walked into rehearsal one day and says, 'I want to try this song,' and myself and Brian said, 'What's that?' 'God didn't make those little green apples' (sings it), and it was like. 'What?!' And he said, 'No man, the lyrics are fucking brilliant.' He wanted to do it because of the lyrics. Yeah, and we did a Deep Purple instrumental called 'Wring That Neck', off of the *Book Of Taliesyn* album; that's when Eric Wrixon was with us, the keyboard player. And we also did some Rod Stewart and the Faces."

And Eric fully concurs with this idea that Ireland kept the band afloat financially. "That's right, that's exactly right. Ireland, it's like, I don't know if it's the same in every country, but Ireland is such a small place. Thin Lizzy became probably the biggest band in Ireland, before we just recorded the first album for Decca, and so we played all the biggest places in Ireland. And if you keep playing them, well, they won't look at you. The big venues in Ireland, you can play there maybe once every six months at the very most. Otherwise, they want other acts as well. So you can overplay the big places if you turn up too many times. The audience will probably fade away because, 'Oh, we can see them anytime.' And so you have to play it a bit cool. So anyway, the very fact of us leaving Ireland, especially in those days, because the only people that had made any name for themselves in those days was Van Morrison and Rory Gallagher, and that was basically it. There was nobody else. So we were about the third sort of pioneer band, if you can call it that, who made it good in Ireland, and then we had to leave Ireland and live in England. And the very fact of doing that makes you much bigger in Ireland, you know, because you're living in England now. So they get the impression that, 'Wow, Thin Lizzy are living in London now.' And they don't see us playing that often, because we're not living in Ireland anymore. So anytime we come back, we're sort of a bigger name than we were. People will come out and they will pay more money and we'll get more people in and so on."

Radio play in Ireland, explains Elmer Fudd's Benny White, was a perennial problem as well. "Yes, because you see at the time in Ireland, all the shows on radio were sponsored by a company or sponsored by a management. So you actually had to pay money to get your record played on radio. You had to pay the company money, because they had to pay the radio stations money to get their product out on the radio, and there was a little bit of music in-between. But if you were a band with long hair and it wasn't a very poppy song, forget about it. Forget about it. It was purely pop and country and western, and maybe the Beatles, of course. But being an Irish band, even with a record, it wasn't to make you famous, because you never would be, nor would you make money; you never would. But still, you accepted that as being part of the business then. That's why London was much more exciting. Because all the big bands started from there. All these English acts were in London playing world-famous places like The Marquee. And that's why the Irish bands went to London. We thought maybe we could follow in those footsteps, and some of them did. It just didn't happen quick enough for Fudd. We eventually got fed up and quit."

Moving to London meant as well, leaving behind the aggravation caused by an embarrassing yet attention-grabbing show band scene. "Yeah," laughs White, "except after Fudd, in April '74, I joined a really great show band called The Plattermen with Rob Strong. Andrew Strong, coincidentally, who played the lead part in The Commitments, that's his son. Rob Strong was the singer and the bass player in The Plattermen, which was a really good show band. But you're right – if you were in a rock band or blues band, you hated show bands, because the show bands did all the pop music and the country and western music. We really hated them. But I ended up joining The Plattermen for a year, but they were doing Blood, Sweat & Tears numbers, so that was good. I was so desperate then, I joined a really clean image band called The Times, from Mullingar, and I started making real, real money. But all the fun was gone out of it. Once it became a very straight business, the fun went out of the playing. But yeah, there was a little thing between groups and show bands. Show band meaning a band that put on a show. It was like cabaret. It wasn't actually a big rock show. It was a cabaret show, very slick, six or seven guys on the stage all moving in exact time to the music, same direction, and very flashy suits. Always the same suits. Actually, the singer might've had a different coloured suit from the rest of the band, but it was very much a clean image and pop music, as opposed to the darker side of the rock music, which was much more fun."

In any event, well before Lizzy had done it, there had been a pattern emerging of Irish band's leaving for London. "Granny's Intentions were the first," figures White. "Yeah, Granny's Intentions, from Limerick, were the first band to go to England to try and make it, and they had minor success. There was also Skid Row, of course. Very serious riff band, pretty heavy and very popular."

John D'Ardis remembers the impact of Granny's Intentions as well. "They were the ones that everybody thought were going to break out of Ireland. They were also managed by Brian Tuite and were on the Decca label and were released in the UK, on a Decca subsidiary label called Deram, who also had Cat Stevens. They seemed to be very credible; they were the most prestigious of the groups."

Good friends to this day with Skid Row drummer Noel Bridgeman, Benny White nonetheless did not know future Thin Lizzy member Gary Moore all that well. "We had done some shows together, my band Fudd and The Gary Moore Band. We ended up in his hotel room with his girlfriend; we were all drinking and smoking and stuff. Never spoken for more than five minutes, so I could never get a really good picture of what he was like. It would be, 'How ya doing, Benny?' and it would be, 'How are you doing Gary?' and that's about it. Certainly shook us all up with his playing, though, that was for sure."

"Because there was no interest in what we were doing over here," is the reason Brush cites for taking Skid Row across the waters. "There was Van Morrison and Rory Gallagher, but there was never any real interest. That would've been the late '60s, although it never really caught on until '74, '75, and so in the interim, just to get a few gigs, you'd have to go to London and get to know people and meet people. But we went to London, and before we knew it, we were in America. The best way of doing it. But we went up very fast, and came down just as fast. It was worth the trip (laughs). Whatever deal we had with CBS… like, the people that signed us hadn't signed anyone for years; the lads that got us to sign, they weren't really that knowledgeable, and what we got was a half a percent in America. So out of 100%, all we got was half a percent. So even though we made the first album in a day and the second album in 34 hours, they're still selling and still reckon they've never recouped our money, CBS. And they never actually gave us any money. They never paid us any money. But we got a couple of tours of America, had a great time, and like I say, the ride up was as fast as the going down."

Still, peering further back than Granny's Intentions or Skid Row, one can't discount the impact of the aforementioned Van Morrison. "In Britain, people knew Them mainly for things like 'Here Comes The Night'," noted Phil back in 1973. "But in Ireland they were really big and we liked almost everything they did. When *Astral Weeks* first came out, I raved about it, only I didn't realize that it was the same guy who used to sing with Them. The album said so many things that had never been said before and musically it was so different – tight yet loose at the same time. Vocally, Van has influenced me more than anyone else; his phrasing and scat singing are particularly nice, and he has the power to add new meanings to words, rolling them around on his tongue and stretching them out." Of note here is Phil's mention of Van's "phrasing and scat singing" – compare Phil with Van and one rapidly and then repeatedly finds communion and comparison with the complex manner in which both singers placed their well-chosen words across chords and riffs, defiant of time and timing, on a slant.

Back in Dublin, Thin Lizzy had put together a farewell gig on March 16, with Ditch Cassidy and Gypsy Rock supporting, the day after a pretty big show with Status Quo and Freedom. On the return boat to England the following day, the guys got lucky and struck up an acquaintance with radio maven John Peel, who subsequently figured in the band's growing success. Also on the radio front, the Lizzy guys got in good with David "Kid" Jensen (another Clifton Grange Hotel guest), who vaulted the debut album to No.1 on Radio Luxembourg's Hot Heavy Top 20, over and above Paul McCartney's *Ram* album, although granted, this was more a reflection of Jensen's preferences than a result of democratic voting. At this point, Ted Carroll had joined Thin Lizzy's management team, making it a trio like the band. Thin Lizzy's first gigs in the UK were notched in late March and solid into April, Carroll figuring the very first being the 23rd at Ronnie Scott's, the band billed ignominiously as Tin Lizzie as they had been so many times before.

What impact did the Thin Lizzy album have upon the world? Well, the band were definitely getting themselves known around London, and folks back home in Ireland were celebrating the local boys done good. Over in North America, despite the album being dutifully issued (and with a completely different cover), it barely made a dent, no doubt due in part to lack of tour dates to go with it. Japan saw issue as well, on the same blue and silver London imprint as in North America, but it would be eight years and a lifetime of catalogue before the band would make it that far askance.

"Oh man, what was happening in those days was incredible," remembers Eric, asked about the business side of record-making. "Even our first album… around that time, we must've come over and started living in London, not too long after the first Thin Lizzy album was recorded. But I remember going back to do our first Irish tour, and we checked into the hotel in Dublin that day, and myself and Philip, I think we were sharing a room, I'm not sure. But Philip said, 'Hey Eric, I'm going down to Grafton Street,' like Dublin city centre, 'and I'm going to see if the album is in the shops.' Because that's what we were over for, to promote our first album, for the tour. He came back about an hour later and he was f'in and blindin', and he says, 'Fuck! I don't fucking believe it! Decca hasn't even got the fucking album in the shops, and that's why we're here! To promote the fucking thing! And I've been in fucking six record shops and they haven't got it.' And so he phoned up Decca and he went fucking mad on the phone. I remember him, 'What's the fucking point, man? What's the point of us being over here to promote the album and they can't fucking get it!' And so a lot of that stuff went on, and it still does."

Asked about the Thin Lizzy cover art (essentially a junky car reflected in the headlight of another junky car), Eric comments that, "The guy who took those photographs, I think it was the first week that he had this lens called a fisheye lens, and he took us down to, where was it, the markets in Dublin, the fruit and vegetable markets. That was the back shot, the one where he used the fisheye lens, like a circular three-dimensional-type shot. Pretty unusual. The front cover was done, if I'm not mistaken, where Philip's mother had a hotel in Manchester, called The Biz. It was sort of a car sitting around, and the guy took a few shots of that. But then there's another, like a German version of Thin Lizzy's first album, and it shows you this chick's thigh, and there's a little car going down it, like a Tin Lizzie Ford, you know?" Of note, this was the image used for the North American release as well.

In any event, before Lizzy could catch their breath and celebrate their first record, they found themselves working (at Decca No.1) once again with Nick Tauber on what would become "four great tracks in a colour fold-out sleeve' or, conversely, "four tracks on one great maxi-single." As it turns out, the label was set to dump the band, and an impasse with management was broken with the compromise of an EP, the compromise being between a second album and nothing at all.

"In those days, it was hard, a financial pressure," relates Nick. "They're always looking for results. So it's quite hard for bands. I don't think it was a compromise though. What it was, they made the first album, and obviously it was like a first album. It was good, but it only sold about 20,000 albums, which is not enough. Albums had to sell a lot more records to get in the charts. And so it sold very well in the clubs, it got good reviews, it got a lot of publicity, and they were working their asses off. But there's a lot of pressure coming from the company, not from Frank Rodgers, the head of A&R, but on him, from the old school.

Because you've got to remember, Decca was a bit of an archaic record company then. And even though they had the Rolling Stones, early on, and had a load of other bands, they were going through a very bad period of success, and so if the band wasn't immediately making money, they weren't interested. They'd look for a way of getting rid of them. So I think genuinely, there was a lot of pressure, but not much, to be honest, anyone could do about it. What we did was, we just carried on. I mean, considering there was a lot of pressure on them, they made three albums and the singles. Nowadays, you wouldn't get that sort of time."

So the *New Day* EP had to be cobbled together on the cheap, from art to recording to the pressing of it. It was to be tracked in four days ("about a week" says Tauber) commencing June 14th, with the material being song to song adventurous but in the aggregate, very much a fit to what the band had accomplished on the album. 'Dublin' was a ballad of dark passion, like Nick Drake with a Celtic touch, Phil not just celebrating Dublin, but lamenting the leaving of it, a true tale of an ambitious man who had to move on to find work in his chosen field.

As Phil explained to Harry Doherty, he had a very clear idea why he was writing these songs with so much Irish in them. "I mean, I don't play a fucking bodhran. I love the Chieftains, don't get me wrong, but their music is handed down father to son. Once the Chieftains go, everybody is going to have to learn it off records. Basically, we were a rock and roll band and the thing was to try and write Irish songs as they came. 'Dublin' was the first Irish piece I did, and then, I think 'Eire'. (It's) to write modern Irish songs as opposed to traditional Irish songs. That was the thing, so that people could look back and say, 'Ah well, there was a black Irishmen writer back in the '70s writing songs that went like this, that had strands of the Celtic thing but were also influenced by the Western society.'"

'Remembering Part 2' (*New Day*) came out a complicated rocker, proggy of rhythm, a Downey showcase to be sure, and once again, sent obscure through novel guitar work – it makes sense that the entire band is credited on this one. 'Old Moon Madness' was perhaps the least successful track, again proggy and rough and strange of rhythm, near to a very commercial Captain Beefheart song. Finally, 'Things Ain't Working Out Down At The Farm' paired up nicely with 'Remembering Part 2' (*New Day*) as a spirited rocker distinguished by a cascade of drumming behind not much of a performance or arrangement for everyone else. This of course would not be the legendary Thin Lizzy sound as it would be remembered and celebrated, but this was definitely a distinct, unique, considerably admirable characteristic of the band early on.

"I'm just a big Thin Lizzy fan and I liked everything they did," says

Tauber, asked for his assessment of the material. "But 'Things Ain't Working Out Down At The Farm' was my favourite because it was just really odd, very clever. Phil was a very clever young man, and that worked really well. It was very different from the album, let's put it that way, quite a big step in another direction. They were trying to find a slightly different direction, searching. I mean, I like the record now. It's a classic – did you know that? Very well sought after. You can't buy it on the Internet or anything. It's really rare and sought after. And it was a gatefold sleeve and everything, with very interesting artwork of the rising sun and stuff, and the lyrics. I just think what we needed... they were touring so much, and there wasn't time to make a complete album, so they wanted to keep the interest going, and it also kept the radio play going like John Peel and all the other radio stations. You can't keep going back to the first album, because those tracks are a year old. That was the theory behind it, that they wanted to keep the foot up. They had developed a lot after the first album, because they'd been on the road so much, and they were definitely a better band. So I think Philip's thinking was, let's do another record so people can see how we're progressing and I can see how my writing is going."

"All I know was I got called up to do it. Philip and I went over the songs, went in there, and I wasn't privy to a lot of the politics. I would hear it obviously; as the producer in the studio, you hear people talking, the managers, A&R people, but 1) they didn't ask your opinion and 2) you weren't really privy to what they were thinking. So I feel that it was part of keeping the old foot up and going. I think that has a lot to do with it. Once they start with the first album, they didn't want to have big gaps between them. Because Phil hadn't completely finished writing the second album yet, and because they were on tour and he didn't have time to finish it, I think the feeling from the A&R men and the managers was that an EP would be a good idea."

"I remember our management called us in one day for a meeting," notes Eric, "and it might've been that Decca was giving us a chance to redeem ourselves, I suppose. So instead of releasing a single, they came up with this idea for an EP, which I suppose had novelty value. Because EPs were on their way out then, if not disappeared altogether. So I suppose it was pretty unusual for a rock band to record an EP in those days. The artwork was fabulous, I thought – beautiful cover."

"I thought it was a pretty good job," concludes Tauber, "but I have to be honest, I had not quite got to grips with the band. But we did a pretty good job. And Brian, an exceptional drummer, incredible. Brian Downey is one of the finest rock drummers of the last four or five decades. He doesn't give himself enough credit. You know, he can play in any band. He could play in the Stones, he could play in U2, Foo Fighters – he could play with anyone and hold his own. Great feel, great sense of timing, great sense of taste. Incredible drummer. I wish I could work with people like Brian all the time."

No question Brian is prominently featured on the early material, while, as discussed, Eric spends much of his time adding colour. In between, it seems Phil had been often left to carry the tune, and after all, they are Phil's tunes. "The great thing about Philip," explains Nick, "which is the great thing about McCartney, those two people, Phil and Paul McCartney are bassists, but they write songs. So they write songs on piano, on acoustic guitar – that's why both of them are very melodic bass players. That's why when they put the bass tracks together, there's a lot of melody in it. If you listen to Philip or McCartney... I mean, Phil is much more of a rock approach, but it still has a lot of melody into it, and that's because he writes with acoustic guitar. He didn't write on bass; he wrote on an acoustic guitar, Philip."

"*On sale from last weekend is the new maxi-single from Thin Lizzy,*" related one local notice. "*Called* New Day *on the cover, the lead track is in fact, Philip Lynott's 'Dublin' – an acoustic song that has been receiving quite a lot of attention since its release. The English trade papers have given the four track record enthusiastic reviews and it could be a commercial hit for the group in Britain. Germany, meantime, has been concentrating on Lizzy's album and it has notched up considerable sales there, probably because of the massive exposure Philip received on the Kid Jensen show on (sic) Luxembourg.*"

In any event, emerging from the studio none too pleased with their schedule, Lizzy closed out June with club and TV dates in Germany, followed by a BBC session on July 7, and Irish tour in August and finally the release of the *New Day* EP on August 20, if only in the UK and Ireland. The date was also significant in that it marked Phil Lynott's 22nd birthday.

"The picture with Lizzy surrounded by water is Thin Lizzy playing a free gig in the 'Hollow' of Blackrock Park," relates photographer Raymond Wright, concerning one of the band's more interesting gigs that August. "Lots of groups played but Lizzy were the headliner. They had just played in our national stadium the night before. There was no mention of the gig as it was free and you had to pay into the stadium, of course. I had only a few shots left on my camera so I think I took three at best. The one you see has a girl jamming with them. I was thinking it was the lead singer from Mellow Candle (Alison O'Donnell), who were on the bill. But she said it wasn't her as she is in the background sitting on the ledge. It was a great gig with lots of people jumping into the water near the end. Yep, one of those Woodstock gigs (laughs)."

3

SHADES OF A
BLUE ORPHANAGE

"That's the end of Thin Lizzy"

izzy closed out 1971 with Eric Bell joining Skid Row to help make true a few London gigs, in jeopardy due to Gary Moore leaving the band just after release of the band's second album, *34 Hours*. Also on an extracurricular tack, rumours persisted that Ritchie Blackmore was fulminating over a new band configuration. The provisionally monikered Baby Face was to include Phil Lynott, Ian Paice and maybe Paul Rodgers. "Ritchie Blackmore came into the studio when we did our second album, *Shades Of A Blue Orphanage*," recalls Downey, "and he actually jammed in the studio, because he was in touch with Phil at that time, and he was going to start a new band – which I only found out later. I thought he had just come down to jam, but I think he was there to check Phil out, rather than just coming purely to jam."

"Yeah, that was weird," adds Eric. "We were just in this big pub one night. I think it was on the outskirts of London, and it was in the summer. We were making a little bit of a name for ourselves around the club circuit, and one night we played this pub. It must've been about 400 people, and I'd just seen Ritchie Blackmore, standing right in the middle of the crowd, and he was all dressed in black, as he does. And I said, 'Oh my god, fuck me, Ritchie Blackmore is here.' A little bit nervous, you know? And I don't know what happened. We did the gig and that was that and we all went our separate ways. And a week later… we used to rehearse in this pub in London, every week if we weren't gigging, and this particular day we all met at the pub and Philip walked in. Me and Brian were there, and he says, 'Listen, lads, I'd like to talk to you about something.' And we went, 'Yeah, what? What's up Philip?' And he said, 'Well, it's like this. Ritchie Blackmore's asked me to form a band with him.' So myself and Brian looked at each other and go, 'Oh, well, that's it then, that's the end of Thin Lizzy.' And he says, 'I don't know what to do.' And Brian and myself said, 'Well, it's up to you, mate. Good opportunity for you. And if you do it, best of luck to you. I won't feel bad about it. It's just an opportunity.' He says, 'Well, I don't know about it. Can I think about it for a few days and let you know?' And we said yeah. So a few days later we were going to gig, and he says, 'Listen, lads, I'm not going to take up Ritchie's offer. I'll stay with the band.'"

Break-up of Thin Lizzy narrowly averted, the lads got on with the job, again working with Nick Tauber, Thin Lizzy's second album emerging pretty much immediately, on March 10th 1972, although significantly, it would not see release in North America.

Like the debut, the front cover of *Shades Of A Blue Orphanage* was a bleak affair, featuring a vintage photo of three unfortunate looking street urchins, the proposed prompt presumably toward the three lads in Lizzy. "That was really nice," recalls Bell. "I think it was Philip's idea. He had, as I say, a very artistic side, and he had lots of different books of photographs and this, that and the other. I'm not sure whether he owned that particular book; he might've gotten it out of the library, but I remember looking through it one day, and that photo was in the book. And I think we got permission to use it. There was a copyright issue and I think our management sorted that out. And then the inside cover was us walking through St. Stephen's Green, that park in Dublin, in the pouring rain (laughs), which I thought turned out really nice as well."

"We did *Shades Of A Blue Orphanage* at De Lane Lea in Wembley, with an engineer called Louie Austin," explains producer Nick Tauber, picking up the tale. "It was good record, but to be honest, I don't think myself or Phil or the band were completely happy with the results. Some of the songs were stunning. I just don't think the sound was really that great, and I don't think we got to grips with the whole thing, really. I mean, it was getting better – they were getting better and I was getting better."

"I think Nick Tauber had discovered – or rather rediscovered – a lot of my guitar solos that went missing when Scott English was around," points out Eric, speaking favourably of Tauber's work. "He would sort of sit with me, and he would say, 'Now listen, I think you've got some good ideas on this track, on that solo, and some good ideas on that track and that solo. Why don't we try and splice them and take that part of the solo and then take that part of the other solo and put them in the song?' So he sat with me and listened for quite a long time, listening to all these guitar solos and sort of mixing them up and so on. The other thing that I liked about Nick was, I would get ideas, like if Philip was out there working on a vocal, the backing track would be playing over and over and over again as Philip is working on the vocal, and I would be sitting with my guitar in the studios with it up to my ear, making things up as I heard this backing track. And then I would say to Nick, after Philip had done the vocals, 'Oh, listen, I just got this idea; can I try this out?' And he would always say, 'Yes, go ahead.' It didn't matter how bizarre the idea was, he would let me go for it, you know? Very refreshing to have someone like that."

Manager Ted Carroll had said that the switch to De Lane Lea was because Martin Birch worked there and that Phil and the team was angling to have Birch to produce the tracks. Other than the Birch connection, the guys were hesitant. After the fact, Downey was negative on the results, ruing in particular his drum sound. It is said that the switch to De Lane Lea drove the costs of making the second album to £6000, ten times the bill for the self-titled debut. Carroll managed to get the bill down by a couple of thousand however, arguing against the hassles of equipment malfunctions at the newly born facility.

"Rings a bell," says Eric hazily, quizzed on the Martin Birch connection. "Again, that would've been Philip. At that time Philip was into, like as well as songwriting and things, he started realizing that producers played a big part in getting a band signed and so on. And I suppose, once we got our foot in the door, so to speak, like recording for Decca Records, Philip would be saying, 'Right, let's see what we can really do here.' So he would have meetings with the management, 'Hey, do you think you can get this guy down? Do you think you can get that guy down?' And sometimes it would work and sometimes it wouldn't."

Indeed *Shades Of A Blue Orphanage* (one of Eric's old bands was called Shades Of Blue, and you know about Orphanage) lacks the fire of the debut, with less rock and less high quality rock, even if the balladry on the record arguably exceeds that of the debut, namely in classics like 'Brought Down', 'Buffalo Gal' and 'Chatting Today', which is actually an Orphanage original. But Tauber's comment on sound rings true – the debut, in fact, is sharper of definition. Let's not forget, it was produced essentially by a non-producer and then remixed, it seems, very capably by Tauber. And in fact, Tauber's work on the *New Day* EP rises to the standard of the debut. Yet *Shades* is muddy, the floundering title track serving as microcosmic metaphor for the album's psychedelic faults.

"I think we just wanted to progress," opines Nick, asked as to the stated mission of the second record. "Because the first album, like any first album with a band, you've got all the songs you've built up over a few years and you just want to get them done and get them out. I mean, I don't think they suffered the classic disaster that most people suffer, because the songs were great, the playing was really good. I just don't think my production and the sound was great. And we went into De Lane Lea, which had a new Cadac desk, all sorts of problems, but that wasn't really the band's fault. There were all sorts of glitches on it, clicks on it, and all sorts of things going wrong with it, and I just think we struggled. And there was a lot of pressure on us as far as the budget was concerned. We were given a certain amount money, which they thought was a lot of money, which me or the band or the management didn't think was a lot of money. So we were under a lot of pressure. And that's one I think could have definitely done with a remix, and a little more time. It's played really well and the songs are really good; I just don't think it sounded great."

"They were under massive financial pressure – massive!" continues Nick. "Again, everyone was always moaning about the money we were spending, even though it was fuck all. They were giving us all a hard time about it. We were in a brand-new studio that had loads of teething problems. It wasn't the album it should have been, but it wasn't the band's fault at all – the band was trying really hard. But I hated the mix; it was all clouded. It's a much better record than the public gets; it deserves to be better."

"I thought that *Shades* didn't work out as well as we hoped it would," agrees Carroll. "I thought the songs were good, but it wasn't recorded under ideal conditions. I don't think the band really had enough time to work on the material. I liked it as an album, and I still do, but I think it could've been a bit better. And perhaps if we'd have had more time, you know, Phil might've had a chance to write a few more songs, and it might've been a little stronger."

Eric Bell prefers the debut to *Shades*, affirming the contours of the situation as expressed by Tauber. "All bands sort of did this. They get an album deal, and the first album, they put all their best songs on, and the songs that they'd played at gigs for a long time, so they're really tight, and loose at the same time. And you can go in with a certain amount of confidence, because you know the material so well. But our management was sort of getting us so much work in those days, that we were gigging all the time, and so we'd recorded the first album, and then the second album was just sort of looming up and our manager said one day, 'Right lads, the second album for Decca is coming up in about six weeks. Have you got any material for it?' And we went, 'What?!' We were still gigging, so we were writing songs in the changing room before going on onstage to play, at gigs and so on. And the album came quicker than we thought. So we had to go in, and we hadn't gotten material for the second album, so some of the songs are written in the studio. Like 'I Don't Want To Forget How To Jive' and all this, and there were only a few tracks that we sort of knew, that we were doing, really.

So it just happened so quickly, and we hadn't really gotten material for the second album."

"I think that the band were… not so much fishing, but like any band on the first couple of records, were trying to establish some form of identity," continues Tauber. "I never found working with them like hard work. I worked with other bands that were much harder work. Phil very much had his own vision for each record. Whether we succeeded, he would never say. He was very positive. Whenever we finished a record, he was very positive about it, very up; he would always go and do the press and do a good interview. He would always be very positive and up. Maybe upon reflection he had criticism, but at the time he was always being very positive and very up for it, and he would make it work."

Still, there's much not to like on *Shades*. We've talked abou the title track, but opener, 'The Rise And Dear Demise Of The Funky Nomadic Tribes'… it's a mouthful, and an unsuccessful evocation of the last album's opener, at least in terms of lyrical colour; it's not a favourite of Downey's as well, who called it weird and morbid. Musically, it's badly captured funk, lacking the inside-out innovation of this band at their hard best, say 'Return' or 'Remembering Part 1'. "I like the rhythm guitar work that I did on it," notes Bell. "In fact, there were a few guys from some of the music press here when it was released, and that's all they talked about was, 'How did you come up with that rhythm for 'The Rise And Dear Demise'?' (laughs)."

Elsewhere, 'I Don't Want To Forget How To Jive' is an amusing first taste of Phil's love of Elvis, even though its raw semi-rockabilly is a jarring fit for Lizzy or a Lizzy album. At 1:43 however, one is quite sure the hyper-aware Lynott was cognizant of this fact, even if Downey, brevity notwithstanding, has stated that it perhaps shouldn't have made the cut. "I think it was just done for fun," recalls Tauber. "Phil had quite a good sense of humour, even musically. They just put it on as a bit of a light-hearted thing."

Back into the ballad 'Sarah' (Version 1), written for Phil's grandmother, is a touch too sincere and surrendered, so incredibly mellow however that you'd have to applaud the band's bravery to be this delicate, this fragile. 'Sarah' is followed by the aforementioned 'Brought Down' which is a creative triumph all 'round. The song's flamenco intro gives way to Phil singing… not so much a capella but alone and in his cups, after which the band enters. Under debut circumstances, I might have said "the band explodes," but the production and mix is so intimate on this album, that there are no explosions. " 'Brought Down' contains probably one of my favourite guitar solos that I've played, ever," comments Eric. "It's just very bluesy, and done in phrases; I like the phrasing on it. But the rest of the album is a little bit weak."

Closest thing to an explosion on *Shades Of A Blue Orphanage* is next track cued, namely 'Baby Face', which, in another studio would have been a heavy metal track, a predecessor to 'Black Boys On The Corner' (more on that later). Producer Nick Tauber calls this his favourite track on the record. And check out the sublime, taut, intense break – this one indeed rumbles with a debut-era sense of urgency, and again, it's a pity that the electrics attempted for it sound so half-plugged.

The aforementioned 'Chatting Today'... well, that's prime balladeering Phil, vocalising and enunciating across a roil, singing quite energetically over a tight flamenco feel underscored by Downey on lots of high hat. Lyrically, this is a highlight of the album, an equal of 'Buffalo Gal', which mixes deftly Phil and women and Jesse James and the Friendly Ranger, Kid Jensen allusions notwithstanding. Says Eric, " 'Buffalo Gal' was a nice one, yeah. Very difficult to play, it really was. It took me forever to come up with stuff for that. It was just such strange timing, especially for a three-piece band."

As we near the close of this difficult, ragged record, we hit upon 'Call The Police', a rocker that starts promising enough but then descends into a confused funky hard rock that doesn't work. Things stay "diffused" (by mellotron?) for the closing title track ("amazing atmosphere on it," says Eric), even if the lyric artfully envelopes and sums up many of the Phil's themes, colourfully, obliquely... it's almost like a cryptic blueprint for the catalogue's literary milieu, at least through *Chinatown*.

"*It's very hard for second division bands to make an impact with an album when there is so much competition,*" wrote *Melody Maker*, reviewing the album. "*So it is to their credit they have attempted to put down their own thing and experiment. Brian is a fine drummer, with a nice turn of speed and great independence in his solo work. Eric plays good lead guitar and chooses a nice variety of tones and sounds. The overall recording sound is a bit 'British studio,' if you know what is meant... Competent, clear, but lacking in brilliance... a sturdy stepping stone in their development.*"

In conjunction with the release of *Shades Of A Blue Orphanage*, the band knuckled down and got to work promoting it, playing UK dates and Irish dates followed by more UK dates. February and March '72 found the band on an actual support tour rather than the usual haphazard club dates, support one day, headliner the next. This was an extensive UK leg, second on the bill to Liverpool pop band Arrival, supported by Barabbas. End of March, it was over to Ireland, however, said one news post, "*The boys, who were flying in at the end of an English tour, lost their plane tickets and missed their scheduled flight. Meanwhile, the Thin Lizzy van, waiting for them in Dublin, was towed away by the Irish police. Manager Ted Carroll got lost at the airport.*"

Lizzy finally arrived at Croke Park ten minutes before they were due to play. Needless to say, the concert was a resounding success."

"Croke Park was a monumental gig," relates the shooter of these shots, Raymond Wright. "Croker is our national GAA stadium. They were the first rock band to play it. As you can see from the experience, Croker knew nothing about a gig. They put Lizzy in the centre of the field and sold tickets to the four sides like a GAA match, resulting in Lizzy having to turn around all the time so all the people could see them. Sound was crap but still a good gig. I was lucky in that I got the seats facing them and the sound. Can just imagine what the other side was like? Also it rained pretty heavy. The stewards would not let us onto pitch as it would ruin the grass for the players!"

Back in the UK in April and May, one notice called the new record, *"one of the best out this year. Irish group with an immense following in that part of the world, just starting to crack the ice over here."* Also hopefully, the band were starting to headline more shows, even as their support slots continued to be with considerably obscure acts. Into the summer months, the band were back in Ireland including multiple dates in Northern Ireland.

Producer Nick Tauber found himself suitably impressed with how hard Phil was prepared to work the band. "Fuck me, mate! Sure (laughs). He was driven. That man was incredibly driven. That band would not have been successful without Phil. Phil was going to be successful. He was a driven person, very ambitious. But he would put the work in. He would go to every reception, every party, every launch, he would put himself out, he would make friends with the press, all the rock journalists loved him because he was a nice guy, he would go to everyone's birthday party, he would go into the record company and speak to the secretaries. He did what a good public relations person would do. People liked him because he knew how to deal with people in business, very well."

After dates around Europe in September of '72, as well as yet another management change (booking agent Chris Morrison joining the team, for the departing Brian Tuite), the band got 'round to recording a single, 'Whisky In The Jar' backed with 'Black Boys On The Corner', again Nick Tauber presiding.

"We weren't looking as far as America, to be honest, at that stage," explains Ted Carroll, asked whether Decca had been doing a good job for the band at this point. After all, *Shades* didn't even see release stateside. "We were focused... the way we looked at it, is that we wanted to achieve more success in England, and in Europe, and we felt that once the band got a higher level of fame and acknowledgement, that America would automatically follow. We weren't focused on America at all. The first album came out in America, but the second one didn't, and we weren't really too bothered about that, because we didn't really feel we were ready to take on America. We were focused purely on England."

"But no, we felt that Decca just didn't really have the clout and didn't do enough promotionally for the band in the UK. But to be fair, they didn't do a bad job. As background, what happened basically was I was managing the band with a friend of mine, called Brian Tuite, in Dublin. He was the guy who bought the management, originally from Terry O'Neill, for allegedly 500 quid (laughs). Brian is an ex-musician himself, and he managed other bands, Granny's Intentions and that, and he had a place called The Band Centre, which was an amplification hire business, so he also supplied amplification and public address systems and stuff, to clubs and to bands. So he was kind of embroiled with his business back in Ireland, and Thin Lizzy weren't really going anywhere fast. And I said to Brian, 'Look, I think I need to try and... I don't have enough contacts on my own. I need to bring somebody else in, in England, to help with this. And would you be prepared to bow out if I find the right person?'"

"He said okay, and so basically Chris Morrison came in to replace Brian, and at that stage we decided... this was on the back of *Shades Of A Blue Orphanage*. Nothing had happened, and there hadn't been much promotion, and the only thing that really marked it was Kid Jensen on Radio Luxembourg – he promoted it heavily. He was a big fan of the band, and it was No.1 on his hit parade, which was Jensen's Dimensions, which was quite good, but it didn't translate into sales. We were looking at maybe a couple thousand sales of the first album and less than that, maybe 1800 on the second one, at that stage."

"So we weren't getting anywhere fast. And so myself and Chris went to Frank Rodgers at Decca, who had signed the band, and said, 'Look, Decca doesn't really seem to be that committed. Will you let us... you know, we owe you an album, but it looks like the way things are going now, it looks like you might not even want to do that album. Will you let us out of the deal?' Because we needed to get some money. We need to find a record company who would invest in the band, both financially, in terms of investing some cash to help them carry on, and also get behind them in a more prominent way. And Frank said, 'Well, look, why don't you just do a single, and we'll see how it goes, and if that's not a hit, we can probably let you out of the deal.'"

"So that was the agreement. And so we'll do a single, but we didn't really think it had much chance of being a hit. Well, we had a good shot at it. That was the original idea. 'Black Boys On The Corner' was a song of Phil's. It was a kind of melodic, kind of rock sort of record that was in line with what was popular at the time. And we wanted to try. I mean, it was a deliberate attempt to get a single and get out of Decca with our best shot, and then of course the b-side, 'Whisky In The Jar' took us all by surprise. When I heard it, I thought this is a hit, we flipped it, and it became a hit, and that put a whole new kind of set of circumstances on the situation."

'Whisky In The Jar', a re-working of an Irish folk standard – it's been suggested there's a spot of 'Brennan On The Moor' to Thin Lizzy's slant as well – would indeed become a smash hit, whereas the b-side, 'Black Boys On The Corner' is more illustrative of where the band was going, into top-flight hard rock, hard rock with brains as well as brawn.

"You know, there's no bass guitar on 'Whisky In The Jar'?" mentions Tauber. "Right, well, when we put the tracks down, Phil played the acoustic guitars, Eric played the electric, and Brian played drums. Then we put lots of other acoustic guitars on, then Eric put more guitars on, and he put some harmonies on, and then Phil went and did the vocal and put some harmonies on, and we looked at it, 'Well, should we put the bass on?' And Phil said, 'Nah, leave it as it is – sounds great.' And you know, he really was such a great bass player, one who has the aggression of a rock bass player, and he also has the finesse and melody of a good songwriter. And that is very unusual, very unusual. And that's what stands him out from a lot of bass players. John Deacon from Queen is the same as well, and Paul McCartney, obviously, because they're great songwriters, but they're great songwriters and bass players. Being a songwriter and a bass player will naturally lead you to a melody when you play bass. That always happens. If you write a song but you're the bass player in a band, you can't help but lean towards melody, because you've written it. And that's what makes them really clever."

"We don't need bass on 'Whisky In The Jar'," blustered Phil to Pat Prentice back in '73. "Hell, I could've written a bass line but the song didn't need it, so I'm not there with it. It's something we started doing one day when we were bored. We all know folk songs so it was natural. It's just this poor guy who's drunk and kills somebody. He's telling all about the demon drink."

As regards 'Black Boys On The Corner'," explains Nick. "I did both of those songs. That's brilliant. And I'll tell you what went in – we went in to make a single. 'Whisky In The Jar' was going to be the b-side and 'Black Boys On The Corner' was going to be the a-side. That was the deal, the way we made that record. And what happened was (laughs), when it came out of the studio, the record company went, 'No, no, 'Whisky In The Jar' is a great record. Got to put 'Whisky In The Jar' out.' And Phil was a very… he was pragmatic. He went, 'Okay, okay, make the fucker a hit then.' He was like that. 'Okay, you guys wanna do it. You guys fucking go and make it a hit.' He was smart. He went, 'Right, you've chosen it. Now you fucking work on it.' Which is very clever, you know what I mean? And they were so convinced that 'Whisky' was going to be a hit, and they were right, actually, in the end. I have to say. I take my hat off to everyone. And I think the management company, Ted Carroll and Chris Morrison, also felt that it was going to be a hit, and I think that helped them as well. I mean, they had very good management in Chris Morrison, who was an amazing manager, fantastic, just perfect, as well as Ted Carroll – they were great. Chris took over from Brian Tuite, who was the band's second manager in Ireland, and so was Ted, but Ted went into partnership with Chris Morrison, and then it was Chris O'Donnell. Chris Morrison took Phil right along, and now looks after Damon Albarn with Blur and the Gorillas and everything. He's an incredible manager, and I think he did very well with Phil, very well. Chris Morrison had a lot to do with their eventual success."

"'Whisky In The Jar' was a total fluke," explains Bell, in his telling of the tale. "We were messing about in the rehearsal room one day trying to get some original stuff together, and it just wasn't happening. It was one of those days. Nothing seemed to work. So we were going to pack up and go home early, and Philip said, 'No man, we paid for the fucking place; we're going to stay till the end.' So we had about another hour and a half, and Philip, just out of boredom, picked up a second guitar, a Fender Telecaster, and started singing these songs on his own, through the microphone, just as a laugh. And he started singing these corny Irish songs (ed. Brendan Behan's 'The Auld Triangle', Ewan MacColl's 'Dirty Old Town'), and after 20 minutes of this, he eventually got onto 'Whisky In The Jar', which was just another thing that he was taking the mickey out of, really, you know. So at that point, myself and Brian, more out of boredom than anything else, started playing along with him. And at that point in time, our manager – there were two managers – started coming up the stairs and walked into this room as we were playing, and as soon as he came in, we stopped playing. And he had a new amplifier for me, and he said, 'Oh, let's look at this, let's try that, see what it's like.' And as we were doing this, he said, 'What was that song you were just playing, before I came in?' And we didn't even know. We said, 'What? We were just messing about.' And he said, 'Yeah, but what was that song?' And Phil said, 'Oh man, fucking, Whisky In The fucking Jar, right?' And Ted, our other manager said, 'Have you got an a-side for your first single with Decca? It's in six weeks. Do you have a song for it?' And we said, 'Yeah, 'Black Boys On The Corner'.' He said, 'okay, have you got a b-side?' And we said, 'Well, nothing really,' and they said, 'Why don't you record 'Whisky In The Jar'?' And we said, 'You've got to be kidding. Why would we want to record that? It's got nothing to do with what we're doing.' And he kept on with us, and anyway, we went into the studio and we recorded 'Black Boys On The Corner', and then we recorded 'Whisky In The Jar', and it came out, and it became a fucking massive hit. Much to our surprise. We just couldn't believe it. We're like, what?!"

Adds Brian Downey on seeing 'Whisky In The Jar' hit the charts, "Honestly with 'Whisky In The Jar', bands were singing that song in a much different way than we were doing. Our version was a much slower version. And so when we heard 'Whisky In The Jar', first it was a much faster tempo, and when we did it, we were doing it for just a bit of a laugh one day. Our manager had been walking in one day when we are playing it, and he said, 'You guys should go in and record this number because it sounds fantastic.' And we did, you know. We actually went into the studio, maybe a month later and recorded it as a b-side to a Phil Lynott track called 'Black Boys On The Corner'. 'Whisky In The Jar' was supposed to initially be the b-side until one of the guys from Decca heard our version of 'Whisky In The Jar' and decided there and then to make it an a-side. So we didn't really have much say in the matter. We just went along with it, and lucky enough, they were right, and it got into the charts all over Europe and in the UK and Ireland as well."

"With 'Black Boys On The Corner'," continues Brian, "Phil came up with the idea, again, with the intention of it being as commercial as possible. Which I didn't think it was. A lot of time changes, and not even slightly commercial, and like I say, what actually happened was, when we recorded both of those singles on the same day, it got to head office in Decca, and I think was Mr. Dick Rowe, who turned down the Beatles earlier, he decided to switch the tracks around. He wanted 'Black Boys', b-side, and 'Whisky In The Jar', a-side. The thing about it was, I mean, it's a great song to play, 'Black Boys On The Corner', really good, really in keeping with our album tracks, and I think it could've been an album track, and maybe we should've held onto it for that. Just keep it for our new album. I think it could've worked, in fact, on our third album, called *Vagabonds Of The Western World*. But unfortunately it was just put onto the b-side of 'Whisky In The Jar', and disappeared without a trace."

Final word on the genesis of Thin Lizzy's breakthrough hit goes to Ted Carroll, who in effect dispels some of the rounding off and myth-making of the above accounts, most pertinently, dispelling the idea that covering 'Whisky In The Jar' was anything near the "total fluke" that Eric says it was.

"Pre-hit Lizzy was a three-piece, struggling to make an impression," begins Carroll, "and at Phil's suggestion, 'Whisky' had been introduced into the set some months before it was recorded. The idea was to create a tiny bit of variety into the basic Lizzy set by breaking it up in the middle with 'Whisky'. This entailed Phil swapping his bass to play rhythm guitar for just this number and the changeover gave him the opportunity to engage the crowd in a little banter as he swapped instruments. 'Whisky' had a very different feel also, to the rest of Lizzy's set as Phil's rhythm guitar playing gave this song a very different sort of smoother rhythmic feel to the rest of the set, so it stood out a bit."

As we transition toward the studio version, Ted recalls that he, "went to the pub on York Way, near Kings Cross, where the band was rehearsing a couple of days prior to going into the studio. Phil said to me, 'I thought that we might use this, meaning 'Whisky', as the b-side of the single. We've been playing it live for a few months now and it's been going down quite well.' This is virtually a verbatim quote of what Phil said to me. After they had played 'Black Boys On The Corner', they played 'Whisky' and Phil looked at me and said, 'What do you think?' I immediately told them, 'I think that if you can go into the studio on Thursday and get that down, exactly like you have just played it, then I think that it could be a hit!'

"But yes, I think that they had developed the arrangement over the months on the road, with Eric's very catchy guitar intro and so on. Then they'd polished it some more in rehearsal and Eric had this brilliant solo in the middle, very melodic and it flowed effortlessly, beautifully constructed, with a great sound. The record was so catchy, it had an instant hook right at the beginning, with Eric's distinctive slow guitar intro, that then picks up as the rhythm comes in. I think that it's one of the most distinctive intros ever; it still stands out whenever the record gets played on the radio and it still gets played a lot!"

"Actually, adds Ted, "the solo in the middle was too long for a radio play single and Nick Tauber and Phil worked with Derek Varnals, the engineer at Tollington Park, to create an edit in the solo. Derek, although not much older than the band members at the time, was a very experienced 'old school' engineer, who had learned his trade with Decca. He had worked on hits with Lulu, Tom Jones and many others as well as engineering nearly all of the Moody Blues albums. This was the first time Lizzy had worked with him and his experience and skills played a big part in the success of Whisky as well as Lizzy's subsequent Decca recordings. So anyway, the promotional copies of 'Whisky In The Jar' featured the edited version with just a very short guitar break that actually worked really, so that the record would not have problems with radio play. A lot of rock singles at that time tended to be a bit long. The original version of 'Whisky' with Eric's full solo was over four minutes – too long for radio play. But Derek did a brilliant edit, although I'm pretty certain that the regular issued version of the record had Eric's full solo. We didn't want to short-change the punters."

Thin Lizzy got some mileage out of the smartly appointed 'Black

Boys On The Corner', the song showing up on the compilations Decca issued in '76 and '77, to capitalize on the band's considerable success at that point. The UK issue was called *Remembering - Part 1*, and is matched by a North American record from '77 called *Rocker (1971-1974)*, which switches out 'A Song For While I'm Away' for 'Honesty'. In Germany, the album was simply called *Remembering*, but it was issued as a 27 track double. In fact at one point, it hadn't been so cut and dried that 'Whisky' would be the a-side everywhere. Ted Carroll is on record, speaking to New Spotlight, as saying that the plan in the UK was 'Black Boys' first and 'Whisky' as the flip – until, that is, they heard how well the 'Whisky In The Jar' arrangement had turned out.

"Yeah, it was," agrees Eric, confronted with the idea that 'Black Boys On The Corner' – an empowering rocker about defiantly flaunting one's blackness through flash – just might have the Thin Lizzy's first hard rock masterpiece. 'I don't know… Philip had come up with the riff (sings it), and we sort of approached it like… like it went through a lot of changes musically, and in a way, we were still trying to find ourselves. Even though I thought, it's a funny old business. Some people want you to be this way and no other way, you know what I mean? Just play heavy rock, and end of story. Whereas the real Thin Lizzy, the original Thin Lizzy, we used 12 string guitars and acoustic guitars mixed in with electric. And looking back on it, I thought that was the original Thin Lizzy – it was the first album, basically. That's the true Thin Lizzy. Even though the other Thin Lizzy after was more successful, it was the original Thin Lizzy, the first album, definitely. But we started getting heavier, which is why we started recording stuff like 'Black Boys On The Corner', and the acoustic guitars disappeared."

Asked about 'Black Boys On The Corner' back in '73, Phil explained that, "We don't want people to get the impression that we are a folk rock band who do nothing but update old Irish drinking songs. The flipside is really much more reflective of what we play on stage. We do all our own material apart from one number, and it's all hard-driving rock. At one time I made a conscious effort not to sound like Hendrix, but it just happens I've got that kind of husky inflection, so I thought what the hell – people seem to like it. I wasn't consciously imitating him, although I've always thought his stage act was the perfect balance of showmanship and music."

In any event, the ersatz- a-side 'Whisky In The Jar' would wind up No.1 on the Irish charts as '72 came to a close, following a high profile tour on which Lizzy and Suzi Quatro blanketed the UK supporting Slade, Phil's mom in attendance as the troupe passed through Manchester on November 15th. The Slade tour came courtesy of Chris Morrison, new to Thin Lizzy's management team, who traded upon his connections with Mel Bush and Chas Chandler to get the job done. But the band couldn't rest on the success of landing the spot. Given the massive energy of the white-hot Slade at the time, contrasted with Phil's still quite introverted stage demeanour, Slade management actually threatened to kick Lizzy off the tour if they didn't turn up the intensity. On following nights, Phil and the boys responded, Phil demonstrating a recurring ability to assimilate new information and use it for the betterment of the band.

"That was another sort of opportunity thing," recalls Bell. "Again, we went down to have a meeting with our management, and he said, 'Right lads, I've got a fucking... I've got a tour with Slade,' and we went, 'What? Slade?!' We thought Slade was a little pop band. 'You've got to be kidding, what the fuck?! What do you want us to be on the Slade tour for?' It may as well be the Bay City Rollers or somebody, you know? And they're going, 'Well, no, no, no, they're the biggest band in fucking Britain at the moment.' Let's face it, which they were. They were just mega, absolutely biggest band in the whole of Britain. And they got us on this tour; I think it was about a ten day tour, whatever it might have been."

"Anyway, the very first gig, we got there, and Thin Lizzy at that point in time, we were used to playing pubs and clubs that held maybe 200 people? And this day, we arrived at this hall, and it's like a town hall somewhere and it holds 2000 people. And we were like, what?! And the stage was gigantic! There were balconies and big red curtains, a huge place. And we got there, Slade's equipment was on the stage, and it was absolutely massive. The amplifiers, Jesus, they were like monoliths, you know? Just these enormous amps and things, and we went, 'Fuck me! Slade isn't a little pop band,' you know (laughs). And Suzi Quatro was there, and then Slade came in, and they were some of the nicest guys you ever met in your life. You know, so friendly, really down-to-earth. Really nice guys, and they couldn't do enough for us. Really, such nice people."

"So the first night, Suzi Quatro went on, and this was the very first gig. And myself and Philip are standing in the corridor just outside our changing room, talking about something. And the next moment, Suzi Quatro comes running past in tears, with her bass. We're looking at her going, 'What's wrong?' And she just looked at us and disappeared into her change room. It's like, fuckin' 'ell. And 20 minutes later, we're on and the people just started going, 'We want Slade, we want Slade!' And Phil and me and Brian looked at each other, Jesus, what do we do now?! And they started throwing things at us, you know? And we just didn't know what to do. It was the first time we ever experienced this. And you're talking 2,000, 3,000 people. And they're up in the balconies and they're down below and all they want to do is see Slade. That's all they're there for. They're not interested in anybody else."

"So we walk off! And we come into the change room, and just freaked, couldn't believe it! And Chas Chandler walks in, who was their manager, you know, and he also managed Jimi Hendrix, who is Philip's idol. So Chas walks in and he looks at us and he says, 'What the fuck was all that about?!' And we're going, 'What?!' And he says, 'What the fuck was all that about?! You've got to get your act together. You're here to fucking wake up the crowd for Slade, not send them to sleep. So get it together or you're off the fucking tour.' And he slammed the door and walked out. And Philip actually turned sort of white, you know. Because this was his idol's manager, Hendrix's manager, talking to him. You know, get it together or fuck off. And it was, oh man, it was such a nightmare, that tour."

Perennial Thin Lizzy tour manager Frank Murray wasn't along for the nightmare, but recalls Phil telling him that, "Yes, Chas Chandler, the manager of Slade, told them to pull their socks up and do a show. But the funny thing is, Brush Shiels, who was in Skid Row with Phil, when Philip left Skid Row, and Brush came over with a version of Skid Row, Noddy Holder used to go and see Skid Row in Wolverhampton, and he was quite a fan, and he kind of liked the way Brush dressed, his image. And then he incorporated some of that into his own image later on with Slade. So it's funny to hear Noddy Holder's manager telling Philip, who had already been in a band before that Noddy liked, you know, get out there and get the crowd going, before Slade went on, because that's what you are paid to do. Not to be slouching about."

"So the next night we went down, same treatment," continues Bell. "We got sort of boo'ed off. I don't think that Suzi Quatro wanted to go on anymore. They just didn't want to know either Suzi Quatro or Thin Lizzy. And so about four nights into the tour, I would look over at Philip and he would be in one of his poses, sort of pointing the bass to the audience, which I never really saw him doing before. And so he was trying, sort of developing his showmanship, to save the tour. And he would throw little shapes and stand there and point the bass at the crowd and look sort of aggressive, and then about five seconds later he would go back to just standing there, you know (laughs). And then he would try something else. And then he would go back to standing there. And so he was trying, experimenting with stagecraft, and we would watch Slade every night, just stand in the wings, because they had such amazing stagecraft about them. And we would try to learn things. 'Eric, look at the way he's standing. Like, look at that pose Noddy Holder is throwing,' all the typical stuff. And that's when Philip started changing into his future sort of image."

How about yourself? Did you also adapt and start turning on the juice?

"Yeah, because we had to. I mean, actually in those days, I was out front more than Philip, which is hard to believe now. But Philip was pretty shy on stage at one point. A lot of guys used to be like that. Rod Stewart used to stand behind the amps, with Jeff Beck. And then he suddenly realized, wait a minute, it's okay to go on and ponce about a bit and have a bit of a laugh. Which, at that point in time, I wasn't interested in the entertainment side; I was just purely a musician. But I can see it now. I can see that a little bit of entertainment, as long as your music doesn't suffer, is fine – it sells it."

"I think she lasted until the end, yeah," answers Eric on the fate of poor Suzi. "But you just didn't know what way the crowd was going to react. I think the worst night we ever had was in Liverpool – Liverpool Boxing Stadium – and it was like, oh man. It was just horrendous. They started throwing cans of beer at us, and one of them hit Philip's bass, I remember, and he just went up to the mic and said, 'For fuck's sake, we're trying our fuckin' best. Give us a chance.' And the crowd sort of quieted down for a little while. It just takes one yobbo to start it, and they all join in."

Unsurprisingly, Thin Lizzy couldn't help but pick up a few visual tips from the uber-glam fashion disaster that was Slade. "Well, that was our manager," laughs Bell, deflecting blame. "It was glam rock at that point, and they took us out to Kensington, Kensington street markets, I remember, and we ran around the shops with our manager, and he picked out this friggin' chain mail waistcoat for me, which was made of little round discs that were hooked into each other, and it shone as the stage lights were on you – it would sparkle. I wore it on Top Of The Pops. But the funny thing was, as we walked off the stage sometimes, you would have to walk through a sort of aisle and there would be fans on either side who could... well, if they wanted to, they could touch you or touch your guitar as you walked past. And some of these girls just grabbed my chain mail jacket that I wore and the whole thing just went "ffttt,' and it started getting shorter and shorter each gig out, because these girls would just grab some of the discs off it. They were hooked onto each other, and so one guy would probably get about six discs, and then on the other side some girl would get about 12, and then our roadies would have to work on the jacket (laughs) to get it even again. Each time it would get shorter and shorter. So yeah, and they got Brian Downey to get sort of grey, silver streaks in his hair, and Philip was wearing these gigantic platform shoes."

"They tinkered with the glam thing, but you really didn't have to twist Phil's arm to get him to dress up for the stage," laughs Thin Lizzy road manager Frank Murray, cohort of Phil's since they were 16 together. "But someone like Eric Bell, that would be tough, to get Eric to wear stuff. Him and Brian would not be the dress-up types, if you know what I mean. That would take some encouraging."

As Eric recalls, Lizzy also learned about mirrors from the mighty Slade. "That's right. Noddy Holder used to wear a top hat with mirrors all the way around it, and myself and Philip, especially, we would go up to the balcony after we did our set and watch Slade from the balcony. And Philip would be mesmerized by the spotlight shining on Noddy Holder's hats, because it just created this incredible effect, on the roof of the building, as they are playing the stage. So we got to do an Irish tour about three weeks after the Slade tour finished, and we flew over to tour Ireland. We had a rehearsal one day in this club in Dublin, during the day, when it was empty, and Philip went out for a while, and he came back and he had this little paper bag. And I said, 'What's that?' And he brought out this... it was a budgie mirror, you know, that you can put in a budgie's cage. He had bought one in a pet shop, and he put it in-between the bass strings on the machine head of his guitar, sort of slotted it in, and it stayed there, and he said, 'Listen, Eric, I got this idea from Noddy Holder's hats. I'm gonna shine it in a chick's eyes, whenever we're on stage. I'll pick out some chick and I'll shine it in her eyes.' I said yeah, great. So anyway, he went one a step further, and he got, as you know, a mirror scratch pick on his bass, in later years, and that was the idea behind this, to sort of communicate to the women with this mirror."

"I think they're really doing something worthwhile," reflected Phil to Tony Norman, shortly after the shock treatment of the Slade tour. "They're taking young boppers off the street and teaching them to enjoy music. There's nothing wrong with that. Eric Clapton and those guys aren't out there doing it for the kids, but Slade are. They're a good bunch of guys too. We had a good laugh. They're four real characters. They'd drink anyone under the table. We thought we could drink until we met them!"

"We learned quite a lot from Slade about stage presentation," said Eric, to Keith Altham. "We were a bit cool and laid back until we saw how uninhibited they were – really natural blokes, both onstage and off; Phil got a bit fed up with Dave Hill nicking his birds but..." "I told him he couldn't do it to me in Dublin," added Phil. "I'm very big in Dublin."

Discussing Slade's hit 'Mama Weer All Crazee Now' with the illustrious NME, also in '73, Phil notes that, "We toured with Slade when this was No.1. It reminds me of when I first heard Steppenwolf's 'Born To Be Wild'. You can knock Slade as musicians if you want, but you can't deny their energy or the crowd response they get. They keep it simple and rocking."

Back in record land, in an Irish version of ginning up support for 'Whisky In The Jar' (a No.1 hit in Ireland but stalled in the UK), management re-promoted the single to English DJs along with a small bottle of Powers Whisky, special labels printed up for the boozy bribe. Whatever the cause, the single, after being ignored by Radio 1 for six weeks, worked its way to No.6 in the UK, the success of it prompting the London label in the US to issue the single even though they had passed on the recent full-length offering.

"For the first time in the history of the Irish charts an Irish group has made the No. 1 position," read one report. *"Thin Lizzy, the London-based Irish group who recently toured with Slade, are at the top with their current single, 'Whisky In The Jar'. For the three lads this is the best 'welcome home' present they could wish for."*

"It's come as a complete shock to find that we're in the charts," said Phil at the time. "From being nothing to something is a transformation that takes time to accept, because you're then in a position to make all your dreams come true." Added a wary Eric Bell, "We try and have as wide a spectrum of music and songs in our repertoire as is possible. But people might think we just play 'Whisky In The Jar'-type songs, and that's just not so. Our music has all kinds of influences from solid rock to traditional Irish music. At the moment, we'll only play about three gigs a week. The rest of the time will be spent recording and thinking about our position. We've also got to get a lot of material together. Philip is the main writer although we all make contributions. Our position at the moment is a difficult one because we don't want to be one-hit wonders. We'll record another single, which will be representative of our music, but it won't be produced strictly with the aim of getting into the charts."

Nick Tauber verifies that Phil was having the same reservations as Eric. "We had a big hit with 'Whisky In The Jar', and what he didn't want to do was be associated with a chart act. He didn't want to be like a pop band. He wanted to be a rock band. He wanted to have hits, but on the same level as The Who or Queen or the Stones had hits. He didn't want to be a pop band. He wanted to establish himself as a quality rock band that has good singles, you know what I mean? And so consequently – and playing live, they were a tougher, rougher rock band than the records were – I think he just wanted to make sure the records sounded more that way."

"We are still exploring the three-piece idiom," mused Phil in conversation with Disc's Brian Southall. "We want to get even more out of the sound and share some of it with the audiences. We don't expect everybody to like us, but we want to share our music with those who do. I can see the band becoming even more melodic, but we don't want to be restricted to one style. I'll probably still do most of the writing, along with Eric, but we will still do old Irish songs like 'Whisky In The Jar' if they come along and we feel they're right at the time. The follow-up single will be one of our numbers though."

Still manager at the time, Ted Carroll, while acknowledging the good fortune afforded to the band by 'Whisky', reinforced this sense of unfinished business as concerned the fine art of album-making. In an interview prefaced by the assertion that 'Whisky' had just sold 16,000 copies in the UK in a mere week, he said that, "While they've never had poor crowds, they are now putting up the House Full sign almost everywhere. They are making a lot more money and they have been greatly encouraged by the recognition the single has brought them."

As regards the full-length records, Carroll added that, "It must be remembered that they had just arrived in Britain when they were rushed into the studio to do the first one. They were raw and not really ready and they did the lot in five days. They did their very best, of course, but they weren't happy with the way it turned out. Neither were they knocked out with *Shades*. That was also done in a great hurry because they had to fit it in before a college tour on which they were to promote it. That's why they are looking so keenly to the third one which they will take the time and care they feel necessary."

So being a singles band was out, but a covers act? No problem. For January also found Thin Lizzy in the strange happenstance of recording at De Lane Lea an album of five Deep Purple covers and four instrumentals, the line-up for the project augmented by singer Benny White and keyboardist Dave "Mojo" Lennox, both hailing from aforementioned old Lizzy cohorts Elmer Fudd. The band name for the project, cooked up by German businessman Leo Muller, was Funky Junction, and the album was called *Funky Junction Play A Tribute To Deep Purple* (a German edition was also issued, with the group billed as The Rock Machine). The band were not credited on the album, which was recorded in one day, the hard-up Lizzy boys receiving, according to Eric, £500 for their services, with other sources citing the fee as double that.

"The Funky Junction album... I recall we were really stuck for money," laughs Downey, "and it was put to us, 'Do you guys want to do a tribute to Deep Purple? For some good cash?' And I said, 'Well, yeah.' It was put to us that we didn't have to tell who we were, Thin Lizzy. We went under the moniker of Funky Junction, and we got a guy called Benny White to sing on it, and we got a keyboard player called Mojo from Dublin, who played quite well – he played like Jon Lord. And we put this album together in dedication to Deep Purple. We got paid like a session fee and that was it. We thought it was going to be forgotten about, but years later, 'Oh, this is Thin Lizzy playing this.' You know, I used to just love listening to *In Rock* and *The Book Of Taliesyn* and the very first Deep Purple album, which we had in our flat that we used to have in Dublin. Eric Bell, actually, was a big Ritchie Blackmore fan, so he got *The Book Of Taliesyn*, and when I heard that, I just loved Ian Paice's feel. He's a very tasteful drummer. And then I went on to listen to *In Rock*, which was always on the turntable back in those days. I found Ian to be a really tasty player and a really good soloist as well, in the later years. He's a favourite drummer of mine. I always thought Black Sabbath were a little bit overrated in those days. I liked Bill Ward and I like those guys but I just saw Deep Purple in a different league. I got that feeling every time I went to see them live – they were just great on stage, always a great show, spot-on musically."

"That's another thing that was really strange," recalls Eric. "I think we were in the office one day, with our manager for a meeting of some discussion. And he said, 'Oh, by the way, this American guy come into the office the other day, and he's got a proposition to us. He said, would Thin Lizzy record an album of Deep Purple hits?' And we're going, 'What?! What are you fucking talking about?' And he said, 'Well the thing is, he's offered us X amount of money, and to be honest with you, we need money to keep the office afloat and to pay for the secretaries and pay for the phone bills and so on, and it would be very handy. It would be helping us and yourselves in the long run, to keep the office going. So I think it would be a good idea to do it.' And he sort of talked us into it and we said, well, okay."

"And the American guy had given him a list of songs that he wanted us to play, but the thing was Philip couldn't sing like that guy, Ian Gillan. His voice wasn't high enough. He just hadn't had that kind of voice. And there was also a Hammond – Purple very heavily featured Jon Lord – and we were a three-piece band. So we end up sending to Dublin for two guys, actually out of that band Elmer Fudd, and we got the singer, Benny White, and a guy called Mojo who played Hammond organ, and they flew over and we went in the studio and rehearsed for a few hours and then recorded the album. We released it and nobody knew who the fuck it was. And then when they found out years later that it was Thin Lizzy, it became a collector's item."

"Fudd were living in England," begins Benny White, giving his version of the strange Funky Junction tale. 'We had done the Old Cricket Ground in 1972, for the Melody Maker's poll winners concert. We supported Emerson Lake & Palmer, Wishbone Ash, Genesis, Focus, and we were on the bill also, which was great for us. So we were living over there, and the guys just had 'Whisky In The Jar' out. I think it'd just been released. This was the summer of 1972, or maybe it was into 1973. But they were living in London and so were Fudd. And Ted Carroll, the London manager with Thin Lizzy, came up to where we lived and asked me would I be interested in singing on an album of Deep Purple numbers with Thin Lizzy? And I said why? And he says, well Phil doesn't believe he has an Ian Gillan voice. I used to do Deep Purple songs in the band and I was probably the best at it at the time, in doing it the way Ian actually sang the songs. So he said, 'Would you be interested in singing on this album?' I said, 'Yes, how much?' Big bucks, £35. Which, to us, at the time, you know, it was a good day's wages; let's put it that way. And as I said, Thin Lizzy had very little money and we had less. And I said yeah sure. And he said, 'What about Mojo?' Or Dave Lennox, who was the keyboard player in the band. We'd got rid of the twin lead guitars and we had a keyboard player. Because we had a lot of stuff we wanted to do using keyboards, including Yes numbers."

"And so Mojo took the part of Jon Lord," continues White. "Great. He said we're getting £35 each. The rest of the boys in Fudd went back to Dublin; it was Christmas, maybe something like that. So I stayed with Phil Lynott in his apartment for three days, and that was funny, very funny. He was staying with a beautiful girl at the time, I think from the North of Ireland; gorgeous girl. This is way before he got married, a different girl altogether. But it was decided that Dave Lennox stay with the guitar player, Eric Bell, and I stayed with Philip, during the making of this album. And the reason it was funny was because Phil and I were stoned all the time, totally stoned, in his apartment. And he had this tiny little kitten. And when you're smoking away and this cat is doing what a little kitten does, you know, playing all around the place and jumping up on the phonograph, we were totally in bits the whole three days, looking at the cat (laughs). Really, really funny. I have vivid memories of the two of us nearly getting sick with laughter because of the smoke we had, and because of his cat's actions. It was so funny, yeah. So we got together and I think we rehearsed for two days learning all these numbers – where, I can't remember. But I do know that we went into the studio after two days rehearsal, and did this album in another two days."

"And Mojo and I each got our £35," laughs Benny. "I remember Eric Bell was slagging us, in a nice way, saying, 'You guys got more than we did.' So I mean, it was pretty basic. It paid for my flight home, put it that way. Well half of it. I think it was about 14 or £15 to fly back."

Telling Benny that I'd heard two stories on the total pay: £500 and £1000, White figures, "Well, the £500 wouldn't surprise me. The £1000 would, unless Ted Carroll or somebody else took a large chunk out of it. But I know I got 35 and I know that Dave Lennox, or Mojo, got 35 as well, and Eric Bell, as I said, I heard him saying one night that we got more than he did."

German businessman or American businessman? "German businessman, yeah – Leo Muller. But it's funny, during the tracks as well, when we were recording them, the guys had put down all the backing first, guitars and drums, and I remember somebody saying, 'Oh, time is moving on; we have to rush here.' So I'd say, 'okay, I'll have a run through this.' And I would run through, let's say, 'Fireball', and they would say, 'That's fine, Benny.' 'No, wait, wait, that was only a run-through.' 'No, sounds great. Onto the next song.' Then I would have another run-through, a warm-up. And they were actually recording the warm-ups and using those as the final vocal tracks (laughs). I couldn't believe it, because it takes time to get into that stuff, to warm up your voice, especially if you're out of bed or you're up and you've had two hours sleep and you're into a studio. But because time was so short, they were using the warm-up tracks as the actual finished product. Terrible. Looking back on it, it was funny."

As regards the (casual) non-Purple tracks on the album ('Dan', 'Corina', 'Rising Sun' and 'Palamatoon') Benny says, "That was all decided before Dave and I actually went into the studio, either with Leo Muller or the boys in Lizzy. We didn't have a say in any of that, because they were clearly instrumentals. I know that Dave was shown what to play on the keyboards for that really strange number, with the Moog synthesizer, 'Palamatoon'. He was told what to play there but I can't remember who told him. But it was certainly not Deep Purple, and neither was 'Danny Boy', and neither was 'Corina'. I think that's an old country and western song that Philip asked me to sing. In fact, if you listen closely to the album, you'll hear Philip doing backing vocals on it. He's doing harmonies; you can actually make out his voice there. It was a funny time. And then at the end of that we got our £35, and then onto the plane, 'Good luck lads; see you again,' and the next time I saw the band, they had Brian and Scott in there."

"I thought that Brian was probably the best drummer in the world," muses Benny, recalling the chops of the Lizzy band at hand. "I thought that Eric was really way up there, seriously way up there, very, very fine with his playing. I mean, the stuff he's playing, even on that horrible album that we'd done, it's so good, it's so well rehearsed. None of it is actually cut live at all; he really did listen to those Deep Purple tracks. Philip, to me, he wasn't a great bass player, but he was a magnificent songwriter and showman. Brilliant. You couldn't be better. He was so good, and he had it down to a tee. He knew how to rock, and he looked the part. He was the part. He was great, no doubt about it. You know (laughs), there's a photograph of myself and Terry O'Neill, Phil Lynott and Jody Pollard, taken in Galway, I think in 1971. My brother actually colourised it; the original is black-and-white. And I remember at that particular time, Philip also took a photograph of all of us. Philip is in one of the shots, okay? You can see him posing. But we stood in a line and Philip said, 'I'll take one of you, mates.' So even when he was taking the shot of us, he was posing, because people were walking by. It's hard to explain, but he put his legs in such a way so that the women could see his balls, you know? It's really, really strange (laughs). Thinking back it's so funny. I said, 'Gee, this guy, he loves himself.' But, he had it. You know, if you have it, flaunt it."

Touring with Lizzy in '71, singing away with Funky Junction, light man for the classic line-up in Dublin... there'd be one last encounter for Benny with Phil.

"I met Philip a few years later, probably around 1980, and we were all in a club in town, the Pink Elephant, and word was going around that Phil was coming down. And I said, well, I haven't seen Phil in years. I'll say hello to him. And he came down all right, and he was standing in the corner with some people and he is totally out of his head, he's gone, and I went over to him, 'Hi Phil, how are you? Benny, Benny White.' And he goes, 'Oh man, Funky Junction, yeah, gotta go, man,' and that's the last I saw of him. He died fairly soon after that. And I said, that's not right, man. That's not nice. You're totally out of it. You could see it in his eyes. This is a few of years before he died."

Funky Junction cut, dried and in a flash tried, for the boys in Thin Lizzy it was quickly back to... another single, and another novelty track to boot. 'Randolph's Tango' was light and airy like 'Whisky In The Jar', an acoustic tango with timbales, backed with non-LP track 'Broken Dreams', a rote blues comparable to early ZZ Top but frankly not as crafted or crafty, despite an intriguing solo section with three tracks of guitar, one, Eric's piercing, bluesy solo, a second, the leaden bluesy riff, a third, garagey, jazzy chords.

"I really liked 'Randolph's Tango'," says producer Nick Tauber. "Very interesting rhythm, but I think because everything else was a straight-ahead beat, it didn't get the same reception as 'Whisky'. It was a tough call. I thought it was an amazing song, but I think they should've gone for a slightly rockier thing, a pretty straight-ahead thing. But 'Randolph' was always going to be the a-side – there was no question. Went in there, did it, that was the a-side, as opposed to when we did 'Black Boys On The Corner' and 'Whisky' and flipped them. It wasn't like that for this one."

" 'Randolph's Tango' was a deliberate attempt to get away from 'Whisky In The Jar'," figures Carroll, "and release something that reflected where the band was at, which was melodic rock but not too heavy. Actually, believe it or not (laughs), I still think that if we would've gotten enough airplay, that could've been a hit. We all thought it was a good song and we all thought it was the best shot at a hit. That's what we were looking for."

Adds Eric, "Our management and our agency and Decca Records all said, 'Right, your second single has to be another Irish song, like 'Whisky In The Jar', part 2, because we want another hit.' And we said, 'No, man.' You know, no matter what we recorded, it was going to be hit. This is what we thought. Anyway, we recorded 'Randolph's Tango' and it did bugger all, absolutely nothing. So we sort of went 'Wha...?!' and 'But, but, but... where's the hit?!' And they say, 'We told you. You should have done 'Whisky In The Jar', part 2. It was all there for you.' We didn't play the fucking game."

'Randolph's Tango' was issued on May 4, 1973 with a launch party at the Shelbourne Hotel in Dublin. Wrote one reviewer, "That nice Mr. Lynott has something of the spirit of Hendrix in him in that he cannot easily be predicted – and that is a rare virtue. Here he sings a languidly Latin song over a backcloth of swirling wah-wah guitar. There are a lot of words and a fair amount of going ooooh-la-la-la too. With his voice in no little echo, the band sound not unlike Medicine Head at times. There's a break for some appropriately Spanish guitar playing. Not perhaps as instantly attractive as 'Whisky', but a handsome work for all that."

'Randolph's Tango' as a commercial property subsequently stalled at No.14 in Ireland and failed to chart at all in the UK. Not only did the band compromise their integrity with another single, but the ruse didn't even work. Thin Lizzy were running out of money and needed a follow-up hit fast.

4

VAGABONDS OF THE WESTERN WORLD

"You see the guitar hovering, just on its descent"

Thin Lizzy entered 1973 broke and watching every penny. The only bright spot was that the band's new press agent, Tony Brainsby, had succeeded as he had so many times before, for the likes of The Strawbs, Paul McCartney, Mott The Hoople and The Small Faces, in getting the band into the music newspapers and magazines 'round England regularly, often playing with the truth for dramatic effect as rock PR was wont to do back in the day.

The band in fact was finding it hard to get choice gigs for a spell, but luckily, this corresponded with work on what was to be the band's third album, *Vagabonds Of The Western World*, a protracted affair in the birthing. In the meantime, they adopted a deliberate strategy of taking lower paying gigs to raise exposure in prime clubs up and down the UK, as well as continued exposure in England's influential music newspapers. This was at the behest of a young Chris O'Donnell, the latest addition to the management team circa July of '73. And it persisted that the band was finding 'Whisky In The Jar' a bit of an albatross.

"All very true," notes Eric. "In fact, I think at one point, I'm nearly convinced that we went into the office, and we were basically saying to the manager, we've had enough. And he said, 'You can't afford to split up. You owe so much money.' You know (laughs), you actually have to stay together, because we owe money, for this, that and the other. Clothes, phone bills, equipment, roadies' wages, all that type of stuff. Yeah, so we actually had to stay together for another four or five months."

"There was tension because you had to pay wages," agrees road manager Frank Murray, "and time was running out for management with the banks and those guys (laughs). And also, you need success, like a single or whatever, and remember at that time, everything was very single-orientated, with David Bowie, T. Rex, Slade, and Sweet. So you had to be taking in some money from your shows."

"They always needed another hit," sighs Tauber. "But then again Phil never, ever moaned about money. As long as he had enough drink and something to eat, he never worried about money. Because Phil was such a domineering sort of person and quite forceful, he got most of the things he wanted. All the boys were great, but yes, money was tight. Because even though they had the hit 'Whisky', they had spent a lot of money making previous records, and they had to pay that money back, and I think it was quite hard. But they did get advances. I have to say this for Decca. They did help them out by giving them advances. But again, it's not my field. I don't know the actual facts. I mean, until they really make it, bands are always fucking broke. Every band I've ever worked with has always been broke – it's a standard thing, isn't it? But I don't remember any desperation, that's for sure."

Noted Phil, hitting the press rounds at the time, "People now expect us to play 'Whisky' and traditional Irish numbers all the time. We are really a heavier album-type band, although singles are nice for the money if nothing else. Everything we earned from 'Whisky' went straight back into the band, with new equipment and now any money we get goes towards a lighting system and a new set of drums."

"Vagabonds took nearly nine months," explains Nick Tauber now producing a second full-length album for the band. "But we weren't there all the time; we were in and out all the time. But you just felt you were making a great record, and I really didn't give a monkey's... And they had a new studio in Tollington Park, just around the corner from the Rainbow, which was very big at the time. Everyone played it; it was the new rock venue. We went in there, and they just gave us as much time as we wanted, and because it was their own studio, they weren't stressed out about the cost like they were when we were at De Lane Lea. So we just took as long as we liked. And I mean, that is such a great record. I put it along with *Johnny The Fox* and *Jailbreak* and *Bad Reputation*. I think that is the first proper great Lizzy record."

March found Nick and the guys in Air Studios, with later sessions taking place back at the aforementioned Decca No.4, Tollington Park, in May and in July. "I loved working at Air," muses Nick. "That's when it was in Oxford Circus; not the one now in Haverstock Hill, but the original. I liked Air Studios. As I said, De Lane Lea, when we went in there, it'd only be going for three or four months and you had loads of technical problems. It eventually became CTS. But yeah, I found the studio very cold, to be honest. I didn't hate it, it worked, but it had a Cadac desk, and it had lots of clicks and stuff on it. When things go wrong in the studio technically, it gets in the way of being creative. If you have to sit around while they mend things all the time, or when they de-click… we got lots of click on the tape, on the multi-track, when we were recording, and you had to de-click it and all that rubbish, and that just gets in the way being creative. I'm not interested in technology. I want to pull up the faders, I want all the outboard gear to work, I want the microphones to sound cool, I want to think about the music. I can't stand all the technical rubbish. I mean, I've learned to be patience, because you have to. If you don't have patience, you'll go mad in the studio, but I found De Lane Lea tough because there were teething problems in the studio, and we were one of the first ones in there. It made it tough to get through that crap, to get what I wanted out. What I wanted to go into was making a great record."

To clarify, "*Shades Of A Blue Orphanage* was recorded at De Lane Lea, and *Vagabonds* was record at Tollington Park," says Nick. "Tollington Park was the new Decca studio, just behind the Rainbow, and this was called Decca No.4, in Kensington. Decca's main studio was in a place called Broadhurst Gardens. Decca No.1, the Moody Blues rented that studio and they turned it into their own studio. They called it Threshold, after we had been in there. But we used it very early on. Decca No.4 is where 'Whisky' was recorded and 'Vagabonds', and 'Little Darling'."

And Air Studios? How does that enter the mix?

"We did some of the drums at Air, and for the rest, we went back to Decca 4. Because we spent a long time on that record. And the reason they allowed the time was because it was a Decca studio – it was internal money, so they didn't mind. I mean, it was a good studio, because it was brand-new, brand-new Neve, brand-new deck, brand-new machines, so they weren't being short-changed, that's for sure. I think the reason we went to Air first was because we were waiting for Decca 4 to be finished, and it was late, and we need to start the record."

Recalls, Frank Murray, "Decca Records had a studio in north London, over near the Hollaway Road, I think it was, and they were in a house, and some people lived above the studio. And so we could only record at a certain volume and at a certain time. It was a weird set-up, now that I remember. We had to stop making noise by a certain time, because I think the people upstairs had some children. So we had to get the loud stuff going during the day."

"The difference between *Shades* and *Vagabonds* was enormous," continues Tauber, switching stream to the results of all of this sporadic recording. "The *Vagabonds* record is a great record. We were really sure where the band was going, especially Philip. His writing and his sound and his approach to everything... that, for me, was the first proper Thin Lizzy record, where you could say you can hear Thin Lizzy, you know what I mean?"

"The thing about *Vagabonds* was, I wanted to have a better guitar sound than I did on the first two albums," notes Eric. 'And I sort of made it a point; I sort of had a talk with myself, so to speak. I said right, first day you go into the studios, don't forget, you're the guitar player; what goes down on plastic is going to stay there forever, so give it your best shot, you know? So anyway, we turned up, we came into the studio, and there were a few guys on the desk and so on, and I went out and started messing about with the guitar amps and my guitar, and this, that and the other, and I spent about half an hour, 40 minutes, trying to get a tone that I liked. And then I went in the studio and I said, 'okay, I'm going to go out and play guitar for about 30 seconds. Could you tape it for me so that I can kind of hear it?' The guy says yeah. So I went out and played a bit, and came back in, and he put it on, and I said, 'That's not me.' He said, 'Yes, that's you, man; that's just what you played.' And I said, 'Well, it fucking doesn't sound like it sounds outside.' And he said, 'Well, that's what it sounds like.' And I said, 'No, I don't think so.' I wasn't going to back down this time. And I said, 'No, that's not what it sounds like outside. Come on and listen with me, and you'll hear it.' And so he was one of these world-weary engineers, 'okay, man,' and actually came out, and I put the guitar on and I played a bit, and he says, 'Sounds the same to me.' And I said, 'It's not the fucking same, man. It's not the same! It's cleaner,' and I said, 'That setting that you have in there, the guitars all distorted and fuzzy. That's not what's happening here.' So he sort of looked at me and he walked in again, and I stood behind him, and I said, 'Right, let's try and get that sound.' And I just wasn't taking no for an answer. This was our third album, and I wanted to be as good as I could, you know? And it was quite a bit of time went on, and he eventually started twisting knobs, and I said, 'Now that's more like it.' And he says , 'Oh, if you think so.' And I said, 'I do think so.' And so that was the approach I had on that album, nearly the whole way through."

So exactly what sound were you going for?

"I was going for more of a powerful but cleaner sound, a cleaner tone. Like the sound on 'Little Girl In Bloom', when I join in with the bass, (sings it) - it's very clean. That type of thing, and even the solo in 'The Rocker' – it's loud but it's clean. So that was the sound I was trying to get out, and also the sound on the title track, 'Vagabonds Of The Western World' – it's powerful but it's clean; it's not too distorted. But it was just a constant fight all the way through the album to try and get it. But yeah, personally speaking, I like a lot of my own playing on that album. I wasn't as stoned as I usually was (laughs)."

"It was a good album overall," continues Bell. "I thought the songs were very strong, and like I say, we really took it more serious this time. Philip would be experimenting with different bass guitars to get a better sound. The whole thing was based on getting a better sound. That's what it was about, and Brian Downey, he had lots of problems with his drum sound, sometimes in the studio. Especially if it was a strange studio we'd never used before. They would mic up the drums and he'd say, 'No, no, don't like that sound.' And we would try everything. And what it would come to would be him sending out for a complete set of drum skins and taking off all his old drum skins and putting on all new ones, and then they would be too ringy, and they would have to tape them up to stop them ringing. I remember it took hours and hours to get the drum sound. It would be like three hours before we played. That's what it was like."

"I'm not sure how long it took, but I just remember it was our sort of our stand, our serious stand. Like the first album, we were just all stoned out of our fucking heads (laughs), and it was all our sort of live stuff, and then the second album, sort of took us by surprise. We weren't really ready for it. A lot of people like it now, but at the time it was slagged off quite a bit. So we came to the third album, and I think we all thought collectively, right, this is it, let's try to make a good bloody album here. Yeah, I like all of them, and personally speaking, on Vagabonds, my own guitar playing, I quite like. I can put it on today and not sort of cringe (laughs)."

Vagabonds Of The Western World, perhaps as a result of all this elbow grease put into it, is quite a beloved album among the Lizzy faithful. The biggest point of contrast with the first two, one supposes is indeed the brightness, aggression and immediacy Eric was seeking and had somewhat obtained, even if there is still an element of weirdness and lack of commerciality that the band hasn't quite shaken yet.

And it's not exactly modern sounding either. *Vagabonds* saw issue in September of 1973, yet it still ran roughshod and shotgun with the blues and even psychedelia, with very few flash, succinct riffs on display outside of perhaps 'Gonna Creep Up On You', a smart hard rocker built innovatively. And the title Vagabonds Of The Western World? Phil likely had in mind consciously or subconsciously an Irish film called *Playboy Of The Western World*, issued in 1962 and filmed primarily on Inch Strand in County Kerry.

"Philip would come down to the rehearsals," says Eric, asked about the writing of the *Vagabonds* album, "and he would say, 'I've got this idea.' So myself and Brian, we wouldn't play a thing, not one note, not one drum beat, and we'd let him play the whole song on his own and hear it with fresh ears. And like sometimes, I would try little things and Philip would say yes, and then some other times he would say no. He would say, 'No, it's too jazzy.' So I would try a different approach, 'No, it's too bluesy.' And then I would try something. 'No, Eric, it's too this,' and I said, 'Well, what the fuck do you want, man?! I've played everything I know!' And he would say, 'Right, now this is where we start.' So I would really, really, really start using my imagination, because I'd played everything I knew, you know? So I would have to really scrape the barrel and saying, Jesus, what am I going to put in this? And it was great. It was really good for me as a guitar player."

"Some nights I've been out and I've been pissed," quipped Phil, back in '73, on the subject of idea-gathering. "I've been unable to get a taxi home and consequently got in late. But there's been a great idea for a song in my mind so I put it all down on tape, whispering everything into the mic so that I don't wake up any neighbours. Then next morning I play back the previous night's recording and all I hear is this drunken fool mumbling and strumming on the guitar and I wonder where all the marvellous song went."

"Phil and Eric were very, very big Hendrix fans," explains Nick, "and also Philip was a big fan of Steve Miller, not his Mercury days, but the early psychedelic stuff he did on Capitol the first time around. We talked about it and I was saying, 'Your lyrics are very good Phil; how did you get that?' And he said, 'Well, I listen to a lot of records from the '60s, especially Steve Miller.' He never said he copied them, but Steve Miller's early tracks on the Capitol catalogue, they're cool. And Phil got a lot of inspiration from that. I mean, Phil was a very good poet. He had a poetry book out. He was genuinely one of those very few people, writers, not many of them out there, rockers, who you can say had a good literal poetry thing in them. A lot of them are just blaggers. Phil was genuinely poetic in a lyrical sense."

Indeed that is a quality on display here. Not to say he wasn't intense and eloquent on the earlier two and a half records, but perhaps *Vagabonds* displays more focus, more of an edit. "Oh yes," agrees Nick. "He would come in with the first draft. We would do the backing tracks, we would put the backing tracks down, he would do a guide vocal, because that would be like 'print one,' and then he would take a rough away and he would re-jig the vocals and re-jig this and re-do that, maybe change it around, maybe move the melody around and come back and try it again, and keep coming back until he felt he got something he was really happy with – then we would do the vocal. I mean, Phil was very, very good and very particular about ad-libs. He was brilliant on ad-libs, absolutely brilliant. He really knew where to put them and how to make them sound real."

Another element helping draw listeners into the evolving Lizzy was the slight conceptual nature of the album, accentuated by the lengthy Legend Of The Vagabond as printed on the back sleeve, plus the explosion of colour that was the front cover fantasy artwork. *Vagabonds Of The Western World* would mark the beginning of the band's relationship with Irish illustrator Jim Fitzpatrick, who would cook up many of the distinctive art pieces for the band during their golden run through to the end of the '70s. Jim and Philip had met way back, for the first time in Neery's pub, Philip coming over to Jim to compliment him on an illustration he had done for Capella magazine, which had featured contribution from the likes of John Lennon, David Bowie and Marc Bolan.

"Philip had lots of different friends in Dublin," explains Eric, asked about Jim. 'You see, I didn't know them, because I was from Belfast. So Philip had known a lot of people before he ever met me. And over the months and over the years, I would meet these people that Philip knew, like Jim Fitzpatrick, an artist. Philip had lots of different friends like that, poets and songwriters and artists – all very artistic type of people; that was his circle. And so he knew some of these guys from way back, and then whenever we started doing better, he would ask, sort of friends, to help them out as well."

"Obviously he got the idea from *Axis: Bold As Love*, the Hendrix album, with the three heads," ventures Bell, critiquing the cover. "And also, he seemed very influenced by – like we were all influenced by people – but the guy who did the Yes albums, Roger Dean. Which isn't a bad thing. And sort of comic books. Philip was very much into comics; he was into Marvel and Silver Surfer, all these type of DC American colour comics, and Philip would actually look at some of these, the small drawings they have, frame by frame, in the Marvel comics. Philip would look at some of these guys like the Silver Surfer or the Green Lantern, and he would see them on top of a hill posing, in an incredible, dramatic, heroic pose. And he would actually work on that to get that onstage, to copy those poses from the comics. Yeah, Jim Fitzpatrick, I mean, he did a great cover."

Confirms Frank, 'Phil, all of us, we used to collect Marvel comics, action comics and things like that. Silver Surfer, Green Lantern, the Sherlock Holmes novels. We grew up watching American culture, all the time, whether it was cowboy movies, gangster movies, American shows. Irish television bought an awful lot of American TV, things like My Three Sons, The Honeymooners, I Love Lucy, Dragnet. So we watched all of them and then all the American movies. American culture was, in a way, embedded in us, particularly the Westerns, and then of course there was rock 'n' roll (laughs). But we would've wanted to go to North America, even without being in a band."

"Philip had a very loose idea," recalls Fitzpatrick, on the brief for the *Vagabonds* sleeve. "I sat down with him and then mocked up some roughs. It's supposed be a double spread gatefold, and I did a gatefold, and it was in the Philip Lynott Exhibition in town. He loved the gatefold, but the record company wouldn't let me use it, so we only used the top half of it, and then I had a sort of moonscape in the foreground. He wanted all sorts of little bits and pieces. I put in the stones from Newgrange, megalithic stones with the oldest carvings in the world on them, and he loved all that kind of stuff. I don't know who came up with the phrase 'cosmic cowboy,' but that's the phrase they used in all the publicity at the time. It was a successful album as well."

"Jim captured that Celtic mythology long before anybody else," notes Brush Shiels, "long before Riverdance, years and years before it. And then of course, he got together with Phil and together they came up with these covers that are still out there and have stood the test of time. And still have that Irish... whatever they had done, it was very original, and that's all you can ask for."

Asking Eric about "cosmic cowboy," he figures, "as I say, Philip was into these comics. We would be going to gigs and we would stop at a garage for a piss or a cup of coffee or something and Philip would go and buy an armful of Marvel comics, and we would look at them as we were going to gigs, and he would be pointing, 'Hey Eric, look at this guy here.' And I would look at the little square, and it would be The Joker or Green Lantern or someone standing on top of a skyscraper, in this really dramatic pose. So while that was going on... as you say, the cosmic cowboy-type of thing, I think Philip even got the lyrics for the very first track on the first album, 'The Friendly Ranger', that's right, Philip got that quote from one of those DC comics, 'The Friendly Ranger' paused and scooping a bowl of beans, spreading them like stars'... I think he got that from one of the DC comics."

Vagabonds is where we also see more of a pronounced Thin Lizzy logo, although not the one that came to dominate beginning one record hence. Explains Fitzpatrick, "The original Thin Lizzy logo, designed as kind of a Cadillac version, was designed by Tim Booth. And Philip and him sent me a tracing. Tim did a beautiful sketch of it and I adapted that for *Vagabonds Of The Western World*. But then, to move on a bit, I did a beautiful black-and-white poster, one of my favourites, for the song 'The Rocker', which to me is the ultimate Lizzy song. It's always been my favourite. I love 'The Boys Are Back In Town', an anthem, but 'The Rocker' was where I was coming from; that song always appealed to me. And if you look at the lettering for the single, 'The Rocker', you'll see the Thin Lizzy Cadillac logo I adapted from Tim Booth's version, but if you look at the lettering for 'The Rocker', you see the prototype Thin Lizzy logo there. And to be fair, I didn't spot that, Philip did. He said, 'I like that lettering,' and he did take that "T" and "H", and turned that whole thing into Thin Lizzy, and I thought, that's a brilliant idea, which is what I did. A very creative man, Philip. Once he was on the same wavelength as me and I got on his wavelength, we worked superbly together, because he could see things that I couldn't, and I could see things that he couldn't."

No question, relates Jim, that Phil was ambitious about all aspects of the band. "Yes, absolutely. Philip... you have to remember, there are two Philips, one is Philip before drugs, and one is Philip after drugs. Philip before drugs, very shy, quiet, gentle character, very well brought up. He was raised by Sarah, his grandmother, and she was very strict, not a disciplinarian – from what Philip told me, she never hit him or anything. But like any mother... I was raised by my aunts and my grandmother. You did what you were told. If you weren't back by a certain hour, all hell broke loose. You have to be back by six for dinner. It was simple, there was no messing. And Philip was like that. He was brought up like that, so it was just his nature for him to always be on time, to make sure things got done his way, and the only time he didn't give me an awful lot of time was on *Johnny The Fox*. The rest of the time he'd have me well in advance, and so it gave me plenty of time to do a nice piece of artwork, and he was always constantly refining his own work, his own recordings. I loved it. And then it all went haywire toward the end, but that's another story."

As Nick Tauber relates, Phil completely earned his Associate Producer credit as well. "Yes, which he should do. He had a lot to do with the way the production sounds. I've never had a problem with that. I'm not one of those guys... I've made a lot of records, with Marillion, all over the world, and I'm not insecure about production. I know what I do and know what I do very well, and people want to be co-producer or associate producer, I don't have a problem. I know a lot of producers are very careful of their territory. It's only a bloody name. I know what I do (laughs). I've never been one of those persons who has that sort of insecurity thing where, if you don't have your name all on its own in big letters you get a bit weird about it. I want credit, written on the record, but that's enough. As long as it's somewhere, I don't mind. As for Jim, that was always Philip's thing. Philip found Jim. Phil had a whole vision. Jim came down to the studio, we had a talk and a cup of tea together, talked about tracks and the way they went down and listened to the tracks, but the band, the way they were presented, the artwork, that was very much Phil's thing."

Phil, predictably perhaps, told *Trouser Press* that *Vagabonds* was, "the best album we did with Eric Bell in the band. I liked the songs and it was the first time I'd co-produced. I finally got around to knowing how to record in the studio and the band had been in England long enough; we'd gotten through the 'Whisky In The Jar' thing, and we'd finally gotten a direction we wanted to go in."

To reiterate, the sum total of *Vagabonds Of The Western World* was not that drastically out of step with the hippie music that band had been creating thus far. Opener 'Mama Nature Said' was a rollicking barroom blues straight out of the British blues boom, although freshly, it housed an environmental morality tale. 'The Hero And The Madman' found Phil poetic and epic like the generally denigrated 'Clontarf'. Musically, it's a funky track with spoken word, Eric Bell relegated to fragile Hendrix-style wah-wah. And the recited, spoken word bit? "That's Kid Jensen, very famous Luxembourg DJ," says Tauber. "Jensen was the first person to help break Thin Lizzy. He hammered the shit out of it. I'm telling you, absolutely hammered it. He was a huge fan – huge. He's called David now because he's a lot older – no more Kid – but is a lovely guy. A Canadian DJ working in Luxembourg, at Luxembourg radio. I went to Luxembourg with Phil and with the manager to meet Jensen, and Phil went on to do an interview and they played the new record and everything." Jensen pales when he remembers how hard Phil worked him in the studio to get the part right, also noticing that it wasn't only himself that was put through rigorous paces.

Moving on, 'Slow Blues' is another stab at old musics, albeit with an intriguing funk that would rear its head again next record. Closing the first side of the album is 'The Rocker', a song and a single that would be the saving grace of the album, a lifeline as it were, a live anthem and a hit single all in one. Still, despite its verve and its slashing chords from Eric, it's a bit old school, say, in comparison to side two's 'Gonna Creep Up On You' for example, or even 'Black Boys On The Corner'. As well, for all its aggression, the song does expose a bit of a fault with the drum mix on the album, this idea that the percussion, especially the cymbals, are sometimes a bit red-lined and distorted. Eric's guitar is a bit too "hot" as well on here, making for a garagey delivery where impressive heavy metal power might have sent the track even further into the punk-rocking moshpits.

'The Rocker' would be issued as the follow-up single to 'Randolph's Tango' on November 9th, '73, following the album's issue on Sept. 21st. "Right, and so the third single came along, and we still didn't play the game!" says Eric. "We recorded 'The Rocker', thinking this is definitely a hit. And it got to about #40 or something in the charts and then it just disappeared. Even our manager thought, that's a really strong song. And I think, probably to save money, to save recording time and so on, well, we've got a single on the album, let's use that. And it became very popular, but as part of an underground, as sort of cult song, at that time. People in the pubs and clubs we were playing it but it didn't make it as a single."

Adds Ted Carroll, " 'The Rocker' was of course one of their biggest numbers live; it just went down extremely well when they played live. And at that stage, we were looking for a hit, and we just thought it was worth a stab. And we put it out, and again we were disappointed it wasn't a hit."

In fact, a people-powered petition of sorts was in the offing to get 'The Rocker' issued as a single, one press notice entitled We Want Lizzy explaining that, "*Although 'Whisky In The Jar' was a big hit for Thin Lizzy, they haven't had a lot of success with their singles. Pity – they've deserved it. But all that should be put right if Decca Records give in to the thousands of Lizzy fans who've been bombarding them with letters. Everybody who's heard their latest LP,* Vagabonds Of The Western World, *wants one of the tracks released as a single. And we at Music Star are no exception. The song's called 'Rocker' and it's about the finest piece of music since Conway Twitty wrote 'The Flight Of The Bumblebee'! So come on, Decca – do us a favour!*"

"Mind you, as far as we're concerned, our best work is definitely on the albums," countered Phil, to Tony Norman, again, trying to steer the band away from its association singles, especially Whisky. "The singles only show a small part of us. Albums reveal much more. We're really gonna put some sweat into the next one; we want it to be good. I don't think it will be out until June. We're not going to be rushed into pushing out an album quickly. We'll release one when we think the time is right."

"At last the campaign to have this released has been successful," wrote one reviewer, plumping for the track's success. "It's a great rocker, with some really mean vocals from Phil – the words certainly bear listening to. It's much more in the real Thin Lizzy vein, and it'd be nice to see this one in the charts. A very amusing song, too."

B-side in the UK would be the non-album 'Here I Go Again', an ambitious, well-dressed top quality ballad, with the Germans getting the non-LP 'A Ride In The Lizzy Mobile', an infectious funk and a place to hear Eric sing a bit. Neither track, again, sounds particularly modern for 1973, although each indeed perpetuates the idea that the Thin Lizzy of the day was relentlessly versatile, as well as prolific.

"They were outtakes of the *Vagabonds* album, I believe," remembers Tauber. "They were songs that didn't make the *Vagabonds* album. 'Lizzy Mobile' was a cool song. Phil used to come up with things like that. Lyrically he's very descriptive. Phil didn't want to give people b-sides they already had. He always thought that was a bit of a rip-off when you gave somebody a single, maybe an a-side and a b-side that are from the album. Even if it's 90p or 75 cents, they're buying it, so it's nice to have a couple tracks you haven't already got if you're a real fan."

Over to side two of *Vagabonds*, and the title track arguably upstages 'The Rocker', given its prescient blueprint, this idea of combining complicated hard rock with Irish melody, not to mention the outlaw and outcast element, plus, specifically, this idea that the Irish are the vagabonds of the western world – essentially, that's all the sights and sounds of Thin Lizzy, on display right there, if perhaps a bit raw and clunky.

"Well you see, again, you have to get into Irish education," begins Fitzpatrick, asked about this crucial element of Phil's lyrical canon. "When we were being educated, we were educated to admire rebels, in other words, all the different people who had fought the British over centuries, right? Then we'd also be told about Ned Kelly and all the different Irish people that fought the British right across the Empire. We loved the idea of outlaws, of being outside the mainstream. And I still do. I still regard myself as outside the mainstream. And Philip never wanted to be part of any mainstream any more than I did. But that outlaw thing comes from, I reckon, a reading of Irish history. Now, it's all tamer because we realize that that can lead people up the wrong path and they're lopping heads off of people, but in those days it was much more innocent. And the whole outlaw thing, like, Pancho Villa, it was in films, it was in cowboy comics, cowboy movies, it was always there, and Philip loved being the outsider. You have to remember too, we were both six-foot, six-foot-two. I'm six-foot-two, and Phil was about the same. And he looked different. He was an outsider. I had red hair down to my back, and I regarded myself an outcast, very much an outsider. And we were both raised, not by our mothers, not by our fathers, but by our extended family. And I suppose we learned to be very independent. Philip was an only child, I was an only child, and we regarded ourselves as very apart from everybody else. The Philip when he was with me was a very different person from the Philip that you read about. Very intense, very interesting. He loved being challenged. Philip really loved interesting discussions about Cuchulan and Irish mythology. I wrote a book myself called *The Book Of Conquests* and a second one called *The Silver Arm* and Philip loved them, devoured them. I remember buying a leather-bound book called *The Cowboys* that I knew he'd loved and I gave that to him as well. If I found interesting stuff, I would give it to him, to feed his imagination. He gave me a lovely book on Duke Ellington – that's what he was into."

The gem within *Vagabonds Of The Western World* down a lighter tack is 'Little Girl In Bloom', a ballad yet full band, presented the way some of the sympathetic numbers on the first two albums were arranged. In fact, this one may have struck an even deeper chord without this much window dressing, the beat from Brian perhaps holding it back a bit, as well as the prominence of the bass and lack of inventive guitar, although there's a hint of twin lead, Eric performing both parts. It's still a melodic and lyrical triumph however, on a record starved for great ballads, the only other true try at the form being closer, 'A Song For While I'm Away', again, somehow not the greatest arrangement, a little old school and psychedelic.

"I've heard it so many times, it's difficult to be enthusiastic about it all over again," offered Brian Downey, hitting the press trail back in the day. "But I'm pleased with it. It sounds much different to the other two, although it reminds me of the first one. The second album was rushed; we didn't have a lot of time, but with this one we made the time and it's worked out well. We are definitely an album band, and each track shows the various directions the band can go in."

Added Phil, on the topic of being associate producer on *Vagabonds*, "It's the best sounding album we've done; the material's a lot stronger, but there's still a lot to be done on record. I'm pleased with the production of it though. I'm learning a lot from Nick and maybe in a few years hopefully I'll be producing other people's albums. That'll be something to look forward to in me old age." Interestingly, in the same 1973 interview, Philip talks about solo albums: "I'd like to do one, and there's talk of it coming off. I think I'd do a weird one. You know, using all the slower melodic songs I've got written which the band don't want, and really get some strange arrangements. I might even get somebody else to sing them. I'd still use Brian and Eric of course, and probably a lot of strings."

A weird happenstance concerning Downey… on the initial tour dates for the album, the varnish from his drumsticks had reacted with his skin, causing a blister that then went septic. On the Irish tour dates, he would actually share the stool, so to speak, with Pearce Kelly from the Gary Moore Band, with Downey performing the easy stuff and Pearce rattling in with the fills.

And back to June of '73, the band curiously found themselves having to lip-synch an outdoor show. "Right, this is a good one," relates Ray Wright, who took the associated shots shown here. "This was the RTE show billed as "Lizzie on the Lawn," Tuesday, June 12, 1973. Yes, they couldn't even get the name right. It was a televised show for RTE, with invited guests only. Rang up RTE and read the riot act to them about tickets and so they sent me two tickets. Now guess what? The show was mimed! They were playing in Amsterdam and flew in for the show, but as they say, their equipment never made it. So it was good crack anyway.

Eric was wearing virginal white at the time, so most of my pictures were crap. But the televised version was quite good."

Thin Lizzy's presence in the music papers seemed almost commonplace now, and usually what was written was cheery, hopeful. A reviewer signing as B.S., in a four star review of the *Vagabonds* album wrote, "*Now here's a fine band with a great potential who had their direction changed a little by having a hit single in transit as it were. Lizzy are that rare breed of a heavish (sic) rock band but with very definite melodic overtones – what I mean is that they do songs with choruses, riffs and melodies you can hum, sing or tap. Following their 'Whisky In The Jar' hit, they have opted to go back to the heavier album road and this, their third album, is a very big step forward for them at least, if not for mankind. Phil Lynott, chief writer, has the feel of good songs and can vary his style quite simply to create a set that is nicely varied in itself. For instance, side one has a highly original tale called 'The Hero And The Madman' and also a really sleazy blues thing called 'Snow Blues' (sic) which bursts straight into 'The Rocker', showcasing Eric Bell's fine guitar style, Phil's Hendrix-style voice and Brian Downey's efficient and complimentary drum style. A very, very good album that surpassed even my high expectations.*"

"Phil was great," muses Ted Carroll, recalling Lynott's ability to handle the increased press the band was getting. "Phil worked his balls off and he was always available for any interviews or whatever. He was the spokesperson of the band. I mean, occasionally, perhaps around the time of 'Whisky In The Jar', Eric and Brian did one or two interviews, but at that time, when it was the three-piece, Eric and Brian weren't really interested in that. It was automatically assumed that Phil would do it, and it was absolutely his band. I mean, on one level, I suppose it was a band and they were all equal, but on another level, because Phil wrote most of the songs and was the front-piece of the band, it was his band and that's who the journalists wanted to speak to. And also, he had a personality, he was charismatic. People wanted to know him. He was dressed really well, he looked great and he was very striking. And so he was kind of a star before the band really became famous, although it wasn't big-time or anything like that. But Phil had a great personality, good sense of humour, the chicks loved him, and the guys as well; he just got on extremely well with everybody."

Adding to the press pile, he NME chimed in with its own measured thumbs-up. "*Before their single hit 'Whisky In The Jar', Thin Lizzy had the image of being something of an albums band – even a progressive band. Since then, they have suddenly been labelled as a pop band, pure and simple. Vagabonds Of The Western World should set matters right and get Lizzy a reputation as a rock band clean and neat. While their* material isn't exactly devastating and their musical expertise overpowering, Thin Lizzy do have in their ranks a very powerful guitarist in Eric Bell who once played with Them. And they have Phil Lynott who possesses a good-ish bluesy voice and gets a fine tone out of his bass although his actual playing isn't particularly inventive. Thin Lizzy would probably have done really well in the blues boom and Eric Bell might have even made it to guitar hero status. But there's more to Thin Lizzy than blues."

Interestingly but perhaps unsurprisingly, the foreign territory for Lizzy that was the Rolling Stone news rag called *Vagabonds* the band's second album, also brandishing it (and way late), "*a record that explodes with the raucous energy normally reserved for rocket launchings. This is a band that understands electricity and uses it to its advantage in a way untried since the Hendrix Experience, thereby forging their playing into something that eclipses mere music and become sheer sound. These guys manage to hit the note and mash it at the same time. Easy to play along with, as energetic as a hard-chargin' bull,* Vagabonds Of The Western World *is an utter delight.*"

"I thought *Vagabonds* was probably the strongest album to date," concurs Carroll. "Generally, the standard of songs on that was excellent. I thought the playing, the whole thing, reflected excellently the band in the shape they were in at that time. They were doing very well. They had gained confidence from having had 'Whisky In The Jar', and they were finally at a point where they were making enough money to be able to carry on without financial pressures."

But things were not good in Lizzy land. First off, initial orders for the album were heavier than expected and a strange cardboard shortage had caused a shortage of album sleeves, delaying production for a few days. This logically caused lack of availability of the album, most pertinently felt in Ireland. Wouldn't have mattered much had all sorts of money not been spent on ads, effectively letting the cat out of the bag. And then, barely three months after the issuance of the band's long-form statement of intent, their intimate trio of a line-up would be gutted, Eric Bell wrenching himself out of the band on New Year's Eve 1973.

"I was going through a very bad period in my life, personally," explains Eric. "With drugs and drink, and all sorts of personal issues with my girlfriend and so on and so on. It was a lot of bad stuff going on at that point in time, and around the time of *Vagabonds*, as we were actually recording it in the studio, I was getting these doubts in my mind about, you know, I don't know whether I can handle this anymore. It's getting too... like the favourite word today is dark, but it's getting too heavy, you know? It's just a lot of bad things going on all at the same time. And I wasn't getting any support from anybody, you know what I mean? I had to sort of fend for myself, and it just started getting more and more difficult, so I started drinking more; it was like a downward spiral. And that's one of the reasons why I left."

Do you remember your very last gig?

"Unfortunately, yes. It was in Belfast. Very strange, because, I played with Van Morrison in the early days. I was with Van for about three months. We only did a handful of gigs, in Ireland, but the last one, the last one I played, was Queen's University in Belfast. I got very drunk, and I started playing the guitar too loud, and then he told the bass player to tell me to turn down. And I did. And Van was playing guitar then as well, and I noticed he turned up. But I'd turned down, so I said, well, fuck this (laughs), so I turned up as well. And it was quite an embarrassing gig. And at the end of it, everybody had gone home, and we were all sitting about waiting for taxis to take us to our various houses in Belfast. And I just went over to Van and said, 'Listen, Van, I'm leaving the band.' And he just looked at me and said, 'Here's your money, man.' And that was all he said. That was it."

"So years later, I'm playing the same gig, the same place, with Thin Lizzy. And I'm just out of my tree, completely. I don't know what fucking day of the week it is, I don't know what time… and then halfway through the show I just said, 'Right, that's it,' and I threw my guitar up in the air, and I kicked all the amplifiers off, and that was it. And that was the same gig, in my hometown. I don't know what it is…"

Despite Bell's growing unease with how big Lizzy was growing, how many hangers-on there were, how many new rules were being put in place every day as the band's fortunes increased, the fateful day – and the fateful day's amount of drink – had started fairly innocuously. Eric had planned to spend the day with family, but slowly, starting with wine and whisky at a neighbour's and then more booze with an aunt, he found himself in rough shape for the evening's duties. Next on the day, Eric arrived by taxi at the gig. Finding the dressing room empty but the rider generously filled, he tippled some more, followed by a trip to the bar where he commiserated with old friends from the old town.

Continues Eric, "There was a voice in my head, because I was still going through that very bad time in my life, that I couldn't sort of shake off. And Thin Lizzy, we were playing more and more, bigger gigs, lots more pressure, this, that, and the other, lots more drink, lots more drugs, and I was getting more and more, leaving the planet Earth (laughs), and I started to get a bit afraid of it all; it started becoming a bit messy, and I just thought, listen, you've got to get out of here. You've got to get out of this environment and sort of clean yourself up. Otherwise I don't know what's going to happen. And this sort of voice, halfway through the show that night, this voice sort of said, listen, let's fucking… let's call it a day, while we still can, and threw the guitar up in the air, kicked the amps off, make a final statement and bow out. So I just got the guitar, and took it off, and I threw it about 15 feet up in the air, and it was too late. You can't change your mind, because you see the guitar hovering, just on its descent, you know what I mean? And I'd actually seen that, like in slow motion. I saw the guitar, just before it came down, and then it hit the stage, and I just went over and I had these two 4 x 12 cabinets and I just kicked them, and the whole thing just toppled backwards and fell, and that was it, I just walked off the stage, completely out of my head."

Eric, having collapsed side stage at this point, was slapped to his senses and actually returned to sloppily finish the show, having been threatened by Frank Murray to get out and do just that. "Eric had kind of walked out of the band in the middle of a set," recalls Murray. "And I had to plead with him. What happened was, originally he kind of walked off the stage and Philip and Brian kept on playing. It would've been an early version of drum 'n' bass (laughs). And Philip was singing away, and I was there to talk Eric back onto the stage. And it took me a while to get Eric back on, I think. He was asking for a couple of pints of Guinness. It was a very strange request. Eric did seem like he was in some kind of trauma. Now, we eventually got him back on the stage just to finish the set, and that was it."

"There had been a bit of tension, I suppose, coming up to that," adds Frank, asked why he figured Eric was unhappy. "Eric, if my memory serves me right, there was a petrol shortage going on at that time around the world, a world petrol shortage. So petrol was being rationed, and Eric was travelling in a car with his then girlfriend, and myself and Brian and Philip were travelling in another car, a little tiny Fiat, and we were using that because you could get about 100 miles to the gallon in it. So we could get around Ireland, as opposed to a big car that would've been a gas guzzler. So we were driving around in this tiny car. Eric was travelling with his girlfriend, and so that was the start of the breakdown in communications between us as well. I think Eric was just feeling that at that time he'd had enough. He had been touring too long and I think he wanted to spend time with her, the woman, really. That's the way I see it."

"I mean, Eric was allowed to play whatever he wanted to play," muses Frank. "And we were under pressure to have another hit single, but Lizzy has some classic songs as singles. There's nothing to be ashamed of. Things like 'Randolph's Tango' and stuff like that were brilliant songs. 'Little Girl In Bloom' is a masterpiece; his guitar playing on that is so sublime, so understated, it's brilliant. I don't know why the vibe came up, but the vibe had come up, and Eric felt under pressure. Maybe he was under pressure from his girlfriend. And I don't think Eric realized how in debt we were. I think he thought that if he left the band, he would've copped a large sum of money, which wasn't the case. In fact, all he copped was a large sum of debt (laughs). And now he wasn't earning money, because all of a sudden he wasn't in the band anymore.

"Manager Ted Carroll chimes in with his take on what went down, adding that he was not at the gig, but rather at a New Year's Eve party back in Dublin. "What can I say? Eric is really nice guy, great guitar player, one of those kinds of musicians who is very focused on his music and not as aware as say Phil would be of the importance of the band's image. I mean, since the break-up and over the years, Eric has said various things about how he was getting depressed with the direction of the band and having to do all this promotional stuff for 'Whisky In The Jar' and so on, but at the time, that didn't seem to bother him. I remember when it started; it was when 'Whisky' became a hit and they were doing things like Top Of The Pops. We had to kind of pressurize Eric a little bit, to kind of dress up, wear some sort of gaudy sort of clothes. You know, he likes to dress smartly, but he was a guy who thought the music should speak for itself, and he felt that image and all the rest of it... he wasn't really aware of image. So he was very focused on the music."

"Anyway, he got involved with a woman, a girl; I can't remember her name. I think he did eventually marry her, but he was involved with his girlfriend, who... they were pretty tight together, and there was kind of an unwritten rule – well, yeah, it was an unwritten rule, but it was a definite rule – that girls didn't come on the road with the band and they kept low profiles because the band was on the road to work. So what happened basically was that the band were playing Belfast, which was Eric's hometown, and I think Eric wanted to bring his girlfriend in the car up from Dublin to Belfast, and they didn't want her to come with him. They wanted it separate, so he and his girlfriend travelled by train, and he had a few drinks, and it was just... it was a lot to do with the fact that he was probably under a bit of pressure from her to be around at the gigs, and he was under the pressure from the band for her not to be there. And also, probably, she might have been meeting his family."

"I don't think there was a great deal of psychological stuff involved in it. I think it was just pressure that had built up at the time, and he just had too much to drink and lost it on stage, and because they were a three-piece... I mean, there had been some dissatisfaction for a few months before hand, because Eric wouldn't always be the most cooperative. I mean, he's a really nice guy and he was a great player and did everything he was asked to do, but sometimes, he wouldn't be... at the same time, he mightn't have been that cooperative. But there was nothing going on before the split that would have been reason for him to leave the band or to be pressured to leave the band or whatever. Basically, there was a certain amount of tension between him and Phil at times, I guess, so when he walked off stage and left Phil and Brian on their own, it was kind of considered to be the deepest treachery, if you like. It was a spur of the moment thing, and it came down to, 'We're not going to play with him again.'"

"And immediately, first thing the following morning," continues Ted, "Phil rang Chris in London, and asked to get hold of Gary and get him over to step in. I think if there had been a couple of days between that gig and the next gig, and some time to think it over and for people to cool down and stuff, then perhaps it mightn't have happened and Eric might have stayed. Because clearly, to get kicked out for one major mistake is perhaps a bit gross, really. But I talked to Phil and I talked to Brian on the day after it happened, and they were both adamant that they didn't want to play with Eric anymore, that he was out."

"Oh, no, no, no, it was deadly," continues Eric, recounting with a shudder the events of the following day. "I stayed at my family's house that night in Belfast (note: actually his uncle's, as well as the aunt who was part of the party much earlier that day). And luckily, everybody was in bed when I went home. Somebody got a taxi, because I was getting so obnoxious. They said, 'Get this guy out of here.' I'm in the change room f'ing, and blinding everybody (laughs). Very embarrassing. And they got my address from somebody who knew where I lived, and they got me a taxi home, and I sort of staggered out of the taxi, and it took me about ten minutes to find the keyhole. I kept missing it – so out of it I couldn't put the key in the door. But anyway, I eventually got the door open, and luckily my folks were in bed. Otherwise, I don't know what they would've thought of me. I was in a bad state."

"And so I eventually got to bed, and then the next day, I got a phone call saying that they wanted to see me up in the hotel, where Philip and Brian were staying. So I got a taxi up to the hotel. I had just the worst hangover you can ever imagine, I mean, just blinding hangover. And I got to the hotel, and I walked through the front doors into the foyer, and Philip and Brian were sitting there, and about five roadies, and they just all looked at me. Like daggers, you know? Just looked at me as if I was a leper. And one of the roadies come over and said, 'Oh, listen, Chris Morrison is going to phone you in about ten minutes.' That was our manager in London. So I said okay. So I sat down on my own. Nobody came near me. I just sat in the seat on my own. It was pretty weird. They're all looking at me. And then the phone rang, 'Oh, Mr. Eric Bell is wanted on the phone.' So I went over, and he says, 'Eric, what the fuck is happening, man?!' And I said, 'I left the band, Chris.' 'You fucking what?!' I said, 'I've left the band.' And he said, 'Do you not realize you're halfway through an Irish tour?!' And I said, 'I know, I can't handle it anymore. It's just... I've had it. I'm burned-out.' And he says, 'Is that your final word?' I said yes, and he says, 'Right, then, we're going to get Gary fucking Moore to finish it,' and he put the phone down. And that was that. I just got a taxi home again."

And nothing more was said by Phil or Brian? Before you left?

"Oh no, no, not a thing. Nothing. Not a word. I mean, the thing was, everybody in the band knew I was going through a really bad personal time in my life as well. But they just didn't give a shit. They didn't care less. They didn't talk to me about it or discuss it as a friend. It was just, 'Oh yeah, big deal, so fucking what. Let's do the next gig.' It really surprised me, in a way. I mean, we were very close. Like Brian Downey was one of my best friends, and myself and Philip, we were great friends. We lived together in a house and so on. So we were very close. And I couldn't understand, and in fact, some of the road managers, I was very close with."

"But it's just, nobody gave a shit. They just couldn't fucking care less. And I just sort of felt on my own, travelling to the gigs and so on, like we were travelling by car, and I would be sitting there, and I'm sort of, pretty messed up, you know? And nobody took a blind bit of notice at all. It's like yeah, so fucking what? Which, looking back on it, is a bit strange. But that's what it was like. If I'd have had a bit of support, it might've pulled me through and I would've stayed with the band. But oh well, that's the way it goes. I mean, that was then."

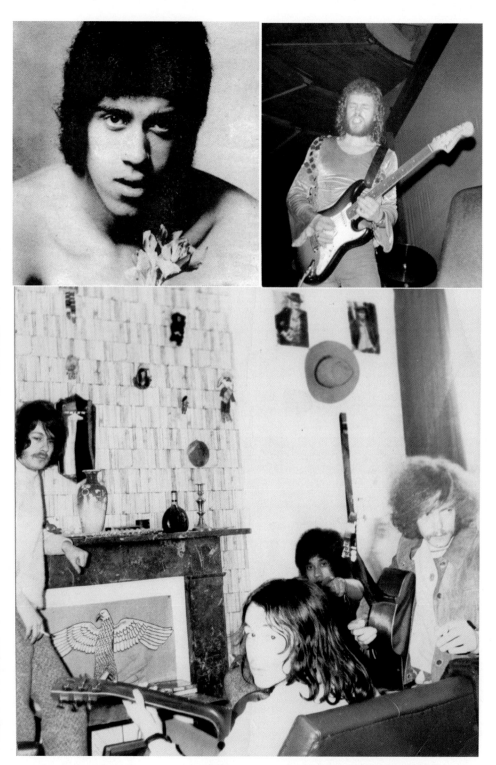

Top: (left) Phil, 19th July 1969 *(Gerry Gallagher)*, (right), Eric Bell
Above: The four-man first line-up at 28 Castle Avenue, Clontarf, 1970
L to R: Wrixon, Downey, Lynott, Bell *(courtesy Eric Bell)*

Above: The four-man first line-up. L to R: Phil, Brian, Eric Bell and Eric Wrixon
(*Gerry Gallagher*)

Phil and Eric Bell on stage circa 1970.
(*courtesy Eric Bell*)

A very unique situation. Eric and Phil on stage with Johnny Fean circa 1970.
(*courtesy Eric Bell*)

At London's prestigious Marquee Club in 1973.
This shot was used as a publicity photo.
(*Nick Sharp)*

Above: Skid Row guitarist and long-time friend Gary Moore (left) stepped in briefly following Eric Bell's departure.

Below: Lizzy's brief, first twin guitar line-up following Gary Moore's first, short time with the band: John Du Cann (left) and Andy Gee (right) with Brian Downey. (*courtesy Andy Gee*)

Vertigo Records publicity shot of
Scott Gorham, Brian Robertson, Phil Lynott and Brian Downey.
The line-up that produced the albums *Fighting*, *Jailbreak* and *Johnny The Fox* is
considered by most Lizzy fans as the classic incarnation of the band.
(*Nick Sharp*)

Above: Scott Gorham and Brian Robertson during a US tour at Electric Ballroom,
Atlanta, Georgia, 26th April 1976.

Both guitarists contributed enormously to Lizzy's success. Their twin guitar attack
became one of the main hallmarks of Lizzy's music.
Below: The full band in overdrive during the same gig.
(*Michael Mastro)*

Above: Phil Lynott during a US tour at Electric Ballroom, Atlanta, Georgia, 26th April 1976. Lynott was the driving force behind Lizzy. The charismatic frontman became one of the most instantly recognisable figures in rock and left a great legacy of songs for generations to come. Note, the Fender had a reflective scratch plate so it would beam light back to the audience. An idea he got from Slade's Noddy Holder who had a hat covered in mirrors.
(*Michael Mastro*)

Below: Another Vertigo publicity photo of the classic line-up with Robertson and Gorham playing their trademark Gibsons, and Lynott with his Rickenbacker compared to the Fender as depicted in the shot above.
(*Nick Sharp*)

5

NIGHTLIFE

"Plus he's got good hair"

With six hours to rehearse, Gary Moore found himself on stage with familiar friends, playing Thin Lizzy songs to an Irish crowd at Red Island, Skerries on January 4th, kicking off 1974 with a chaotic clang. By this point, Phil and his gal Gail had their new apartment in West Hampstead, along with a cat named Pippin, the aforementioned feline that had entertained Benny and Phil to the point of tears during the Funky Junction experience. Pippin would of course become immortalized in the name of Phil's song publishing company, Pippin The Friendly Ranger.

On 16th January, it becomes clear that there would be no patching things up with Eric, and Moore is ensconced as an official member of Thin Lizzy, two weeks later, touring Britain. Come April 4th, Gary's 20th birthday, the band would find themselves recording a Peel session, working up 'It's Only Money', 'Little Darling', 'Sitamoia', 'Still In Love With You', and an alternative version of the previously issued 'Black Boys On The Corner'.

In barely four months' time however, with one Thin Lizzy single to his credit, Moore would rethink his decision and bolt. Moore, like Bell before him, required hasty replacement, with Atomic Rooster's John Du Cann and Steve Ellis Band's Andy Gee hired in time for scheduled May tour dates through Germany. Du Cann's days with the guys instantly became numbered due to a prima donna disposition exacerbated by a Ritchie Blackmore complex. Things got so bad that Brian Downey had even quit the band for about six weeks, needing to be coaxed back by manager Chris Morrison, who found another £50 a week to pay the drummer. In a strange twist of fate, Du Cann already had a Lizzy connection, showing up on the front cover of the Funky Junction album. It utilised a live shot of Purple Records rockers Hard Stuff, in keeping with the spirit of artifice surrounding the project.

"In the early days, Gary would get incredibly uptight about his own guitar playing," explains Eric, providing a bit of a psychological profile of his long-time pal, the since deceased Gary Moore, Thin Lizzy member twice. "I remember seeing him one night in Dublin, with Skid Row. I went along to see them, and I'm in the changing room after to see him. He was sitting in the corner drinking this bottle of wine and just really, really depressed. I said, 'Hi Gary, how are you doing?' He says, 'Oh, okay, Eric. What a load of fucking shit that was.' I said, 'What do you mean? The gig?' He said yeah. And I said, 'Jesus man, you're playing some amazing stuff.' 'No, it's all fucking speed and fucking noise.' And I said, 'No, man, you're playing some amazing stuff.' He was a really, really exceptional, very serious guitar player. He played all the time. I've never seen anybody play the guitar as much as Gary. He would just be playing all day. That's how deeply he was into it, and so he was very sort of serious about it all in those days."

"Gary was a really nice bloke. I've known him for a long, long time. He went through... in fact, after I left Thin Lizzy, they got Gary to finish the tour, as you know. And Gary only stayed with Thin Lizzy for about four months, and he started developing a drink problem. That shows you what the band was like. It was pretty hard to keep up with. And Gary came in... like the day I left, Gary flew over the next day, finished the tour, stayed with them for a while, about four months, and he had to leave, because he was becoming a fucking alcoholic. So he left and joined John Hiseman's Colosseum."

For his part, Gary took the opportunity to cut loose somewhat deliberately. Having said that, previous to joining Lizzy, he hadn't had a drink for two years, given how hard he had to work trying to embark on a solo career at 19 years of age. Moore had in fact issued a solo album in May of the previous year. *Grinding Stone*, issued on Skid Row's label CBS, had been a ragged, bluesy affair, despite production by Martin Birch. It had not been well received, and the response to it plus dealing with the business without a manager had worn on Moore. Subsequently, he took the attitude that live dates with Lizzy was the opportunity to chuck a lot of booze down his throat and go wild every night.

Curiously, Brush Shiels intimates that no matter how much one likes the blues, the format itself can cause frustration, due to its tried and true rules. "The reason Gary left Skid Row was I was telling him how to play," laughs Shiels. "No, I wasn't telling him how to play; I was telling him what to play. It's a very different thing. He could play anything, but I wanted him to play in a particular way, and he didn't want to be dictated to, and that's why he quit the band. He wanted to play the blues, and I wanted him to play what I'm playing at the moment, which is 40 years later (laughs). And basically what happened, when he left the band, we found it impossible to replace him. But he found it impossible to replace us. And so if it wasn't for Lizzy giving him the odd gig now and again, he was in big trouble. Because he did do a few albums on his own, you know, Gary Moore albums. But I found them very derivative. You know, *Grinding Stone* was a forced album he'd done; it was a poor man's album of us, you know what I mean?"

"If you look at all the Gary Moore albums towards the end, the blues albums, there'd be an awful lot of Peter Green in there. But if you go back to the original Skid Row, that's where he made his name. He didn't make his name with Thin Lizzy. All the people who knew him, he was only like 16, 17, it was from playing with Skid Row. And so basically, he made his name playing in a particular style, but when he went into Lizzy, Lizzy had their own style, and so you know, when you go in there, it would've have the same kind of originality, for want of a better word. If you play the blues for long enough, which is what it was – that's how he made his living towards the end there, for a long time. You can only play in that particular style, and whether you like it or not, you never would've had Buddy Guy play in any other style, or BB King playing in any other style, or Peter Green. It meant that you'd be playing less than you could all the time, basically, because the blues, the last thing you want to be doing is overdoing it. So there were many players playing the blues that maybe would've liked to stretch out a bit more, but you make those decisions and you go with it."

"Gary was always a standby for Philip," muses Frank Murray. "It's like, 'Oh, Eric is not playing; let's bring Gary in. We know Gary from old, Gary is a great guitar player, it's not going to take him an awful long time to learn the set.' And if he didn't learn the set anyway, he could cover up with his great playing. So we had no fears on that. But Gary was drinking a lot then, and Gary... let's say, he wasn't a good drunk. So I guess coming with us... It wasn't like we were guzzling back beer all the time or anything like that. But we were packing out places because it was Ireland, and so there was a kind of excitement there. And also it was exciting because we were back in our home country, so on days off, we would probably go drinking around Dublin and meeting up with old friends. So there might've been a little more drink than usual taken."

"Gary joined just to fill in for Eric, for the Irish tour in January, and then at the end of January we asked him to join," recalls Carroll. "So he joined the band, and he was literally only in the band for just over two months the first time, and at that stage we were out of the Decca deal. We were looking for a deal, and we had some demos which we'd recorded. 'Little Darling' was obviously recorded at the Decca Studios. And again, we thought it was a good stab at a single and it just didn't happen; that came out just literally before Gary left. The reason Gary left the band... he joined the band but he didn't want to stay. I guess he was happy, probably, to stay in the band for a year, year and a half or whatever. But his long-term goal was not as being a member of Thin Lizzy. He wanted to do his own thing, which was in fact what he ended up going on to do, jazz-rock, technical stuff. And the problem was, we were looking for a deal for Thin Lizzy. We were out of the Decca deal, and so he realized that we were signing a new deal, and that he would be obliged to sign as a member of the band, and it would look weird if he didn't. People are coming to see the band with Gary in it, and he's not going to sign a contract. So he thought it was best if he left. So he came to me and said that, and I said yes, you're right, and so we bit the bullet and he left, and we started rehearsing, looking for replacement musicians. Gary had told me that he was leaving just after the Pebble Beach sessions, which included an early version of 'Still In Love With You'. Gary's solo from this session was used when the track was re-recorded and eventually stuck on *Nightlife*."

So to recap, Gary was about to fail with *Grinding Stone*, nor was he to wind up staying with Thin Lizzy. Nor was returning to Skid Row an option, says Brush. "It couldn't really happen, because, you know, my problem is that I can't get involved in a committee. Like, I can only just run the band. So basically, everybody would sort of have to... like, in most bands, everybody has the same say, kind of thing. But I would rather just go play to nobody on my own, than playing things I don't want to play, just for the sake of it. I mean, you have to remember, no matter how big Phil got, no matter how big Gary Moore was, if I ever was talking to the lads, they would've told you that I always treated them like they were in my band (laughs). Like that never changed. When I was talking to them, I still talked to them the same way, no matter how big they were. I would still talk to them as if I was in charge. That's the way it is, really."

"The most important thing," continues Brush, "is that there are a couple of Skid Row albums there, and if anybody wants to hear Gary Moore at his best, listen to *Skid* and *34 Hours*. I can't really say any more than that. They were great days, and we could never have done it as well again, because we would be trying to copy ourselves, if you know what I mean. Basically plagiarize myself. The albums are great albums, and it's always been a terrible disappointment that both of the boys had to head for the promised land prematurely, Philo and Gary, and I would love to have them around. But here we are – all we can do is just keep fuckin' trucking on."

Back to Lizzy's world, producer Nick Tauber, who would not be involved on the band's next album, was however around for the only spot of product for Decca involving Moore, namely the 'Little Darling'

/ 'Buffalo Gal' single, as well as the other unreleased recordings.

"Phil had this vision of moving up and forward," notes Tauber, addressing the change in Thin Lizzy guitarists. "Not only commercially, but he wanted to appeal to a big audience, and he saw no problem in doing things a certain way. Whereas Eric, Eric is a purist, and I think Eric was tired, because they were working a hell of a lot. But I just think Eric is very purist, and he likes the blues, he's a very good blues player, but Phil wanted to go down this rock route, which, granted, included blues, because some of the later records have a lot of blues influence. But he still wanted to pursue that thing, and I think Eric didn't want to go that way. And I also think that on the lifestyle front it was harrowing. They were on the road a lot. When they were making it, they did a lot of work on the road to get where they were going."

"I always got on very, very well with Gary Moore," continues Nick. "He was always really kind to me, but yeah, he did have a bit of a tough rap, you're right. He could be quite dark and moody sometimes, and sometimes he could make life very difficult for people. I don't know quite why he was like that. But I have to say, from my own personal experience, I've never had a problem with him. But you're right, there were lots of stories about Gary, all over the place."

Couple this aspect of being hard on himself with the fact that he was a bit of a conflicted hard rocker... you could see why his days in Lizzy would have been numbered. "You're right; his heart was in blues, same as Eric," comments Tauber. "And when you go to Brian Robertson and Scott Gorham, they're pure rockers. They could've been in Aerosmith, you know what I mean? They could've been in Guns N' Roses; they are pure rockers, those two, and they're very good at it, both of them. I mean, they are absolute classic rockers, of the new kind. Like an Aerosmith and like a Guns N' Roses. They are an absolute classic pair of rock guitarists and they really get it and they enjoy it. They don't have any conflict in their heads, to do something or yearning to do other things. Even though they can do other things and have tried other things, they're very happy in that environment. You have to be happy to do well, I think."

"It wasn't until Brian Robertson and Scott really got settled in, that they were there," reflects Nick, assessing a period in the band that would run a bit fallow. "That's when it started to gel. For me, the classic line-ups of Thin Lizzy were Eric Bell, Brian Downey and Philip, obviously, and then when Eric left, they didn't get back to the classic line-up until Brian Robertson and Scott Gorham got in. Those were the two great line-ups. And every other one was struggling. When Gary Moore was in the band, and he did 'Little Darling', they sounded great, but you always got the feeling that he was only there to help Phil out and he was never going to stay. Not because he didn't like it or because he didn't like the band, but he was one of those people that had other things he wanted to do."

The unsung song of the Moore sessions was a complicated, rhythmic, double lead-infused heavy number called 'Sitamoia', a Brian Downey composition, in fact. "Great song," enthuses Nick. "Phil used to always take the piss out of me, because I used to say, 'Well, what does that mean?' And he'd come up with a different version every time and piss himself laughing. I don't really know what it meant, but that was a great song."

Technically, there's supposed to be a dot over the "s" in the title, which causes the pronunciation to be "shit," very much deliberately so, as Phil related to *Melody Maker's* Harry Doherty in 1977. "At the time, we were with Decca, and we were doing this flipside called 'Here I Go Again', and at the end of it, I used the word fuck; I was screaming it out, and it was all very sincere. John Lennon had just used the word on a record ('Working Class Hero'), and I thought that for art's sake, I must use this word. It was real integrity. But when it came to mixing the thing, the guy said, 'You're not serious about using that,' and I said I was and there were wars over it, me saying, 'Can't you understand it's art? I'm an artist. I have the right to use whatever I want.' But they wouldn't let me use it and they faded the song out early. I'd also written 'Eire' for the first album completely in Irish, and they wouldn't let me put that down because they said the kids wouldn't understand it, so I had to translate it into English. Decca were a real crazy company."

"So there was that and... I wanted to use the word shit," laughs Phil. "Decca were gettin' a bit used to us at this time so I had to be sly, so I dreamed this title up, 'Sitamoia', which sounds nice in Irish, but when it's pronounced, it comes out as shitmoia, and I was able to use the word after all without them realizing it. But I did use one real Irish word, 'airgead,' in the song, which means money, and money is always the root of people starving and injustices, which is what the song is all about."

Upon Doherty pointing out the African musical influence in the song, Phil says, "I used to share a flat with an African fella from Lagos, and he used to play African sounds all the time. What really freaked me out was that I had all my Irish albums, my Sean O'Riarda's and that, and the one connection between the Celts and the African man was the tempo 6/8. It really freaked me that they were continents apart but had the same rhythms. They were better percussionists in Africa because they have much more feel, but the Irish had better melody. The Irish had stronger melody and the Africans had stronger rhythm sections and I thought it would be a good idea if I could link the two."

Like 'Sitamoia', 'Little Darling' (issued in early April b/w the original recording of 'Buffalo Gal'), is quite the aggressive number as well, reminiscent of 'The Rocker', written heavy but played through a non-metal arrangement, most notably not much guitar and a strange guitar sound to boot.

"Phil wrote it," recalls Nick, and the great thing about that was, I remember really distinctly, the Echoplex had just come out, the Echoplex delay line, and Gary had two Fender Twin Reverbs and two Echoplexes, and he put his guitar through both, and it sounded fucking amazing, totally amazing. That was the first time I'd seen an Echoplex; he had it imported from America; they were great – really cool sound. I love the rhythm and what Brian and Phil played, the rhythm section. I mean, I think it's one of the best tracks they ever played. It also showed you where they were going as well, as a band. For me, that was the closest thing to 'Black Boys On The Corner', 'Bad Reputation', 'Jailbreak', 'The Boys Are Back In Town'. It had all that really good commercial thing going for it. But yeah, those were the only tracks Gary recorded with me. Because he joined Lizzy right at the end of their contracts, where they had to do one more single before they left, which was 'Little Darling'. Gary plays great. I love 'Little Darling'. I absolutely adore that one."

'Sitamoia' would surface on the *Remembering/Rocker* compilation situation a few years hence, with the band and Tauber also working on versions of 'Still In Love With You', 'It's Only Money' and 'Showdown' (actually in the band's live set), all at Tollington Park. Famed Lizzy ballad 'Still In Love With You', despite being credited to Phil alone, originated, according to Gary, as a song of Phil's called just that plus a tune of Moore's called 'I'll Help You See It Through', the two compositions being of the same chord sequence and subsequently blended together.

As previously mentioned, Thin Lizzy had indeed replaced Gary Moore, before the coming of Brian Robertson and Scott Gorham, with Andy Gee and John Du Cann.

"I'd spent two-and-a-half years with Steve Ellis and Zoot Money in a band called Ellis, and Zoot was leaving, and we'd done a couple of albums," begins Andy Gee, offering a wealth of detail on this interesting wrinkle in the Lizzy saga. "And Steve and I went to a party at Notting Hill Gate, where I met Phil and Brian. Phil sort of took me aside and said hello, and Gary has left the band, and if I was interested to have a jam with them. We met a week later or something, in Hampstead where they were living, and there was a nightclub that they used as a rehearsal room, and we just jammed on a couple of tracks. And I think at that time, John wasn't actually involved. I think it was just the two guys, and me and we got on really well. Peter Green had told me about Gary years previously when he was still in Skid Row, so I knew a little bit about the band, but not a lot. Phil did mention that he wanted to have another rehearsal a little bit closer to where I was at the time, in the Kings Road in the Furniture Cave, and I met up with the guys there. I think that's where I met John the first time."

"Phil gave me a tape with a whole load of Lizzy songs on it, which I took home with me and I worked out all the parts. He said, 'We would like to do these tracks and would like to try it as a four-piece.' Previously on the recordings, it was really easy to do the double tracking for the guitars. I mean, both Eric and Gary had double-tracked the guitars on the recordings. I mean, it was no great deal. You went back in and did a harmony on what you did before, kind of thing. So I really liked the tunes. When I listened to it, I thought well, this could really go somewhere… really punchy chords, great riffs, lots of energy. We hit it off really well, and John was very enthusiastic as well."

"So the next rehearsal we had at the Furniture Cave. I just learned all the parts, because I didn't know what melodies or harmonies John was going to play. Whatever he wanted to play was cool with me. And there was talk of a possible German tour at the time. Phil and Brian were obviously very well played-in. Phil was very energetic, but Brian… originally, he was a bit doubtful whether it was going to be any good. But once we had the jam, it sounded great. And obviously, it was the first time that they'd tried it with the two guitars, and it was a good sound."

That's a chief point, as is the preceding view that Brian Downey had been a bit apprehensive. Problem solved though, says Andy.

"Yes, as I said, initially he was a little bit dubious about whether he was going to sort of join in, whether it was going to work. But I think once we played together, his worries disappeared and he was quite positive about it. I mean, I would have said Phil was definitely the driving force. There's no doubt about it. But you could tell that they'd played together for a while. They knew obviously everything inside and out. So as long as we got our stuff together, it was really no problem."

"From there, Phil asked me to go meet Chris O'Donnell, who was the manager, in Putney. I had a meeting with him and I had to explain to him that I had a contract with CBS. Zoot and Steve didn't get on too well, and he wanted to do other things, call it a day. I thought CBS would actually welcome me joining Thin Lizzy, because obviously there was a little bit of noise about the band – I couldn't see any problems. But then the reaction from CBS was actually quite different. They had other plans for me. They wanted me to join Rod Argent, who'd had had a hit with 'Hold Your Head Up'. I'd said well, no, I'm not too keen on doing that. Can't we just say if I do any recording with Thin Lizzy, 'Courtesy of CBS,' as was normal, when somebody is signed to a different label? I mean, Thin Lizzy were at the time with PolyGram, and stayed with them right to the end. And they said well no, we don't want that."

More on that later. First it's off to Germany, with a set list that would go comprise, essentially, 'It's Only Money', 'Little Darling', 'Slow Blues', 'Little Girl In Bloom', 'Gonna Creep Up On You', 'Rock 'n' Roll With You', 'Whisky In The Jar', 'The Rocker', 'Sitamoia', 'Hard Drivin' Man' and 'Talk To Your Daughter', as demonstrated on a bootleg CD memorialising this obscure line-up of the band.

"I just wish I would've had a look at the contract before we went," chuckles Andy, a native German until the age of 17, when he moved to the UK to advance his career as a rocker. "Because, if I would've looked at the cities that we were about to play, it was obvious that there were massive distances between each one. I mean, we arrived in Hamburg, we went to the PolyGram office, had some breakfast there, and then drove on to a hotel, and then we had a gig the following night, I think. I believe I did a radio interview with them as well, sort of voting on new records that were being released, something like that."

"The gigs, generally, would hold about 500. One of them was an ex-railway station, which was turned into a club. We did Stuttgart, which was probably about 800 to a thousand. Düsseldorf... to me it looked like a college gig, although I don't think it was a college. It looked like a sort of canteen that was made into a makeshift stage. Every gig we did was totally packed. We had to do encores everywhere; I mean, we almost did half of the set again. This small town where we played, it was almost like the shutters would closed when we came to town, you know, these longhairs coming in. And the promoter came out and said, 'Listen, you gotta do another set!' I mean, we were absolutely done in. We had done encore after encore, and he says, 'Look, you gotta do another set. If you just play for 20 minutes, I'll pay you another 1000 Deutsches.' Well, John and I were only getting 200 quid for the whole tour (laughs), so John and I said, 'Hey, we can have an extra 1000? Yeah Let's do it!' And we did. Because he says, 'They're going to smash up my place if you don't.' Not much choice."

Listening to recordings from the German jaunt however, one can hear a lack of chemistry, and confusion with respect to picking of parts. Two guitars sound more like a problem, not a blessing, or certainly not the blessing that the classic line-up was about to breathe into the band. As it would turn out, the case was that these were not the right two guitarists, even if it very likely would have worked with Andy and a different man than Du Cann...

"Yes, well, we worked really hard in the beginning," explains Gee. "John was making an effort as well. But as the gigs went on, I think he expected larger venues. He sort of expected open air, you know, big concerts. John said to me, 'Oh, I've been doing sessions in London. I get a hundred quid a session. I play for a couple hours in the studio, I get a hundred quid,' and he had his girlfriend back home. I mean, I did too. But as the gigs progressed, he was getting more and more withdrawn. Also we had this incident with his cases, when we arrived at the hotel, the first night. He asks Frankie, the driver, to carry his cases for him. And Frankie turned around and told him to fuck off (laughs). He said, 'We're no super band, man; you've got to carry your own cases.' We were all witnesses to that and we did laugh about it, but he took it a bit the wrong way, really."

"Now, John had been part of a band," laughs Frank, diplomatically. "I mean, he played with Atomic Rooster, and then he was also playing with a band who were managed by Deep Purple's management at the time, Hard Stuff. And John would walk around like, I mean, he wanted somebody to carry his guitar everywhere like a butler. So him and me had issues (laughs). So he had one issue with me, until I told him, told him straight. But I wouldn't want to speak badly about those guys. We're all too old now; we still had fun times, you know what I mean? The tour was crazy, like all Thin Lizzy tours. They were all these great characters. And Andy and John were good guys, doing their best. It just wasn't working out."

"As the gigs progressed," continues Andy, "John was getting more and more withdrawn. And to be honest, the last gig we did, it was almost like a three-piece again (laughs), because his solos became stranger and stranger, and he wasn't really doing any backing harmonies either. I mean, I was the only one who was really backing up. Phil was working extremely hard, I was, and so was Brian. And in the end, John was almost like not present. It became strange. So after the last gig…. I mean, we did five or six or seven; I'm not exactly sure. But Brian, at the end of it all, said, 'I've had enough of this.' He said, 'Look, we did a tour with Eric in Germany last year, and they were exactly the same gigs we're doing now. It's not getting any better.' So it's not what Brian expected either – he expected to do bigger venues as well. And he said, 'Look, I've had enough. Because John obviously wants to go back home, he's not happy, he's not really pulling his weight. But we'll contact you when we get back to London and try with somebody else."

Some good times were had, however - Andy re-connecting with family - and proud to bring the lads round the house as well (a home Gee has returned to all these years later, saying all the contents from the '70s are still there, as if from time machine).

"I was born in Berlin," explains Gee. "I went to school here in Frankfurt. My parents were German; they didn't speak any English. And of course I brought Ellis home, eight guys, three roadies, five in the band, and this time I just called them up out of the blue and said, 'Hey, I'm doing another tour, with Thin Lizzy; I'll bring them home as well' (laughs). But I'm 100% German. And my parents… we had a great time here. I brought them all home, and my dad bought lots of wine and stuff and we were partying like crazy. My mother made some food. Phil had a chance to call his mom in Ireland. My dad had to run into the cellar a few times to get out a few more bottles, because we were drinking them out of house and home (laughs). And they went through my record collection and stuff, and we had a right laugh. It was quite a highlight, really."

"Phil was a bit surprised because my mom had bought some Pink Floyd records and stuff," recalls Gee, with a laugh. "Plus I had an acetate single of McCartney's Wings, of C Moon, and he begged me for it. He absolutely begged me for it, and I actually gave it to him. I mean, Linda was a bit out of tune on it and they were all laughing their heads off because they thought it was so funny. And you know, my God, Linda was sort of thrown in at the deep end. She didn't want to have anything to do with the band. And it was actually Paul McCartney who turned around and said, 'Look, if you're not in the band, I'm not doing any more gigs.' So she ended up doing a bit of piano and doing some backing harmonies. And because this demo was like an acetate that I got from one of the roadies, he said, 'Oh, I've got to have this; you gotta give this to me.' And I said, 'I can't, I can't let this go. This is not meant to be heard by anybody.' And he said, 'No, no, I gotta have it,' and I gave it to him."

"But all my records got scratched and everything, because we were so wasted. We were really laying into it. And at the end we still didn't have enough, and we went into Frankfurt, to a club run by guy named Cookie, who I've known since I was 15. And I said, 'Listen guys, you gotta be a bit careful. Because all these good-looking women in here, you can end up with a thousand Deutsches bill, because they're all hookers.' So nothing happened there. We just had a good time, talked to a few girls, and onto the next gig, kind of thing."

"But they just kept winding me up," remembers Andy, about an undercurrent that found him constantly dealing with the hijinx of the road crew. "They knew I had a girlfriend back in London. Because she came up to Hampstead, you know; she was really nice. And Chris kept saying, 'Oh, are you gay or something? This girl really wants to sleep with you,' after a gig. And I said, 'Well, great, but I'm not really into it.' And it's, 'Oh, you must be gay.' And they kept on and kept on, and then four or five in the morning, knock on my hotel room door. I'm asleep, I get up and open the door, and this girl walks in with nothing but a shirt on (laughs). I heard some giggling in the background, but I was just so whacked-out, I was so tired, I just couldn't argue with her or throw her out, or anything, and she just came into my bed and I just thought well, fucking 'ell. She was nice and warm, she was a nice girl (laughs), and you know, after that, they left me alone."

Through the strange vagaries of online technology, combined with the presence of the full concert captured from the German tour, one supposes, there wafts and drifts this impression that the Du Cann/Gee line-up were substandard. The aforementioned personality dynamic somewhat explains why one might arrive at this conclusion, but Andy says there's more to the line-up's, ahem, bad reputation...

"The only cover we did was J. Geils, 'Hard Drivin' Man', and that was only because we played the whole set again (laughs). We absolutely had nothing left to play. You know, Phil just called it out and I think we maybe played it once previously, and during a rehearsal we might've played it once. We didn't do any covers – that was like the last resort. You know, we've got to do something else. So Phil won't let us go; okay, well we'll do 'Hard Drivin' Man'. Unfortunately, that ended up on YouTube, and I got slagged off left, right and centre, because people say, oh, it's terrible sound. I think my guitar may have been out of tune. I'm not sure if it's me or John, even – I can't tell. It could've been me, because it was like, we played for over an hour and we were completely done in. It was very energetic stuff and the only time we had any break was during 'Sitamoia', when Brian had a drum solo."

As it turns out, Andy's fluent German became an asset as well on the short jaunt. "Yes, well, Phil asked me to do all the announcements in German, which was really embarrassing for me. I mean, I'd never done that before, and to be honest, apart from the Ellis tour I did previously, and visiting my parents over Christmas and New Year, I hadn't been back in Germany in six years (laughs). And now here, suddenly, he's, 'Now talk to them in German.' And I said, 'Look, they don't want to listen... they're all keyed up to listen to English. They don't want to hear German.' So I felt a bit awkward and embarrassed, to be honest. In Stuttgart, I remember, 'Oh, tell them so and so just scored.' I said, 'Oh, by the way...' You know, I was always used to the singer doing it, gift of the gab and all that. It's his job, and they always did. But Phil thought it would be a great if I spoke to them in German. And they looked at me like I was from Mars (laughs)."

"And initially when we got there, I had to do all the translating, get them to the hotels," continues Andy. "I spoke the language, so I had to translate the menu, order everything – it was like double the job. And I said, 'Listen guys, if I didn't speak German, Frank would be doing all this. You got on all right last year. If there's any problems, I'll help you out, but don't make me do everything.' And because I did that, along with the girlfriend thing, I think, they started sort of needling me and said, 'Oh, you must be gay or something; what's wrong with you?' But they didn't get involved with anything! I mean, that was really the only time. I wasn't sorry. I mean, I was sorry a couple of weeks later (laughs). But you know, no big deal – you get a jab, take a pill, take some pills for a couple of weeks, put everything back together, which you can't do these days (laughs)."

But as alluded to, this version of Thin Lizzy was not going anywhere. 'Whisky In The Jar' had frankly shone brighter than all of the band's albums so far, and the drummer was grumbling.

"For sure. Brian was saying, 'Look, we'd done the same thing last year, and I really don't feel like it's going anywhere.' Once Brian sort of went, 'Look, we'll go back to London, we'll call you up, we'll try somebody else as a replacement for John...' We were motoring away, heading for Amsterdam, spending a couple of nights overnight, and then taking the ferry from there instead of Hamburg. We were driving past a huge concert and we could hear it in the car. We were on the motorway driving past the stadium and you could hear there was a band playing. Phil actually turned around and said, 'We were supposed to play there.' And that was the only time I saw John actually really quite upset (laughs). So of course, the van had already left. They had to leave earlier than all of us, and they were already on their way to the ferry to get back to London. There was no way we could just turn up and play there. And to be honest, I just looked at Phil and laughed, because I could tell that John was really taken aback by that. He didn't expect it."

What do you mean you were supposed to play there?

"We were actually to play there, but Brian called it a day, the day previously or a couple of days before the last gig. The one where John was really like, in a different band kind of thing, where it felt like hey, we're back to a three-piece, but we've got four on stage. That's when Brian turned around and said, 'I've had enough. I want to go back to London and we'll see if we can sort something out in London, with a replacement for John.' And Phil turned around to me and said, 'Look, it's got nothing to do with you.' From what I've heard, Brian has confirmed that in a book as well. He said no, there was no problem with me, but he didn't really feel that John had fitted in."

Andy thinks Brian might have put the brakes on a couple of gigs that had been booked on this tumultuous tour. "I don't know how many there were, because I'd never did see the contract. But as I said, we had to be 500 kms away from the next gig, so we wouldn't draw a crowd... let's say, if we were playing Stuttgart, then it had to be all in the south, and the next one had to be all the way up north. So we were spending five or six hours on the motorway every day, just so we wouldn't pull the crowds from the next gig, so to speak. Which was a hell of a strain on everybody, driving on the motorway. It was constantly north, south, north, south; that's the way it was booked. But I never did see the contract, so I didn't know what was still booked afterwards or what was coming. It was just… when we drove past and heard this band playing, you could hear the vocals and you could tell it was a stadium with a big gig. And you know, John looked a bit put out at that point, because he obviously didn't expect that."

"I thought it was kind of strange," recalls Frank, "because we were near the end of the tour. We had a few more shows to do, and in fact, I think we were heading into Holland for a festival and one other show in Amsterdam or something. And I remember after a show, Brian called Philip outside the dressing room, and had a chat outside, and they called me out, and they said, 'BD wants to stop the whole thing. He doesn't want to go on.' And I tried to go, 'Well look, we only have two or three more shows,' but Brian was adamant. He didn't want to get back on stage with the band, in that form. We couldn't do anything and we couldn't talk to management until the following morning. There were no mobile phones in those days. Nobody would be picking up a phone. And so we spoke to management the next morning and they arranged for us… truth be told, I think we invented some kind of illness; we said Brian Downey caught the flu or something. I know we made up some kind of excuse and then we high-tailed it out of there, and I remember driving through Holland actually, and seeing posters for us at the festival (laughs), and driving by, knowing we were never going to turn up there because we were heading for the ferry down in Belgium."

"I don't think they quite got Lizzy," muses Frank with respect to Andy and John. "It was a strange thing; they were trying to replace Eric Bell, who is a very unique guitar player. And the songs they had at that time were also unique, in a certain way. And I think they came from a different background, musically; they wouldn't have had the subtleties of Eric, let's say. It wasn't working out the way it should've, or up to the standard we wanted it to be at. We were just trying to get through a tour. Again, we were doing a German tour that we'd been contracted to do. Also Philip wasn't the kind of guy who wanted to knock the road. He would just be like, 'Well, let's just audition some guitar players.' So we started auditioning, and ended up with John and Andy. But it was a very, very, weird tour as well. We went to all kinds of, I suppose, one-horse towns around Germany, the strangest towns, probably towns the Germans, people who live in Germany all their life, never got to. And maybe that wasn't helping things either. We were getting good crowds and things like that, but things just weren't working out down on the farm (laughs)."

Back in London, victory not exactly having taken place and if so, definitely not enjoyed, it didn't look like Thin Lizzy would be retaining the services of Andy Gee.

"There was obviously no problem in terms of playing live," explains Gee, "but as far as recording was concerned, CBS weren't really giving their permission. Now, what had happened was, Ellis had had an advance. There were five in the band. We ran the band for two-and-a-half years on the advance. It wasn't that much, but they just said look, there are five guys in the band, so you're liable for 1/5 of the advance. If Chris and the management would have paid them money at that moment in time, it wouldn't have been a problem. Even if they would've let me join and I said, 'Look, I'll pay back the advance,' there wouldn't have been a problem. But they certainly didn't have the money to buy me out, so to speak. Because that would have been another alternative. If they said look, we'll give you the grand, the few grand that he owes you, that would've been the end of my agreement with CBS. But obviously at that moment in time, it was really a low point as far as Thin Lizzy and money was concerned."

"And I think that's why the German tour was sort of put on the table, almost immediately. I mean, I read later that somebody had to fly to Hamburg to pick up the advance for us to even do the tour, and bring back some money from PolyGram in Hamburg, as an advance, to actually be able to pay for the petrol and everything else. I mean obviously, O'Donnell must've been paying rent for Phil and Brian. They lived in Hampstead, which probably cost them money every week, and they wanted to have some money coming in. And they certainly couldn't afford for any money to go out."

There seems to be more to the story as well. Andy had done some work with Paul McCartney and Wings at this time, but the main driving force behind his drift from the Lizzy camp seems to be an element that is captured in the grooves of the ensuing album, *Nightlife*: this idea that the band was tired and rudderless.

After jamming with Cosmo Vinyl, an Irish slide guitarist considered for the Lizzy spot, Gee had briefly played alongside fresh hire, one Brian Robertson. "It was a whole lot of people standing around," says Gee, cryptically, about the strange session. "I felt a bit awkward, really. It didn't really have the same energy as we did when we played it. It was more for show, to the fans who were sort of hanging around, the hangers-on. I was either just about to, or had just come back from, a Wings tour for a few days in Paris. But the main thing was it just didn't sort of feel right to me."

"I don't recall there ever being any discussions over buying Andy out of his CBS deal," recalls Ted Carroll, giving the management side of the

German tour tale. "It was never on the agenda. We could barely pay the hire on our rehearsal hall, which was The Iroko Country Club in Haverstock Hill. We had no money, but had a German tour on offer, so we got O'Donnell to confirm the tour, he flew to Hamburg met the promoter at the airport, picked up a deposit in cash – I think that it might have been two or three thousand pounds – flew straight back and that bankrolled the rehearsals with Andy, John Du Cann and others. There was some progress being made with this line-up, but we had to delay the tour and eventually Phil decided, let's take the band with Andy and John to Germany and see how it works out on the road."

"It didn't," continues Ted. "Brian was unhappy with the progress, so Lizzy cancelled the final gig, a spot on a festival in Holland, that would have earned about three times as much as any of the other dates on the tour. I got a call from Frank saying they were coming home and Brian was leaving (or had left). When they got home, I saw Brian, who said that he'd had enough and wanted to leave."

"As tactfully as possible, I explained to Brian, that if he left now, he wouldn't even have a drum kit to take with him, as it would probably have to be sold to help pay off the band's debts. His original kit had been stolen from the van outside the Marquee club three years earlier. Brian wasn't into bread at that time. As long as his rent was paid and he had new cymbals, skins and sticks when they were needed, plus a modest weekly allowance to live off, he was satisfied, at least until the band enjoyed some major success. He was not a happy camper; in fact he was dumbstruck. It had never occurred to him that he didn't own the kit. He was not interested in the overall financial situation. I guess he assumed that this was my and Chris Morrison's problem – it was too! Anyway, I managed to talk him 'round and asked him to stay for a few months, 'just 'til we get a new line-up sorted out.' I said, 'You'll get paid and I promise that if you still want to leave, then you will be able to take your kit with you'."

During this transitional period, Thin Lizzy had left Decca and was looking for a record deal, eventually moving over to Vertigo, at that point quite moribund, known for taking (mostly bad) bets on wild progressive rock and hard rock non-entities, most notable rare successes being Black Sabbath and for a brief, early spell, Uriah Heep. Decca had in fact, withdrawn their offer to continue with the band, causing an eagerly anticipated £20,000 pound advance to disappear into thin air. Being £20,000 in debt, they also found themselves turned down by Island and RCA, although RCA indeed offered the band a deal, but refused to pay a £20,000 advance in addition to recording costs.

Explains Brian Downey, "From Decca, what happened was, when Eric Bell left, we were still under contract to Decca, and obviously Gary

Moore came in to take his place, and we had a year or two to go on our contract, so eventually, when Gary left, we decided to hold auditions for the guitar players, and we came up, after a good while, with Rob and Scott. At that particular period, the Decca contract was just about to be renegotiated, and our manager, in fact, went into the meeting, wasn't pleased with the outcome. So he decided to look around. And some record companies were looking at us as well. Vertigo was one of those labels, and they gave us the best deal. It was as simple as that. It was purely a business thing. So our manager negotiated a better deal."

Asked whether he perceived Lizzy to fit the progressive nature of Vertigo, Downey says, "Well, we did. We realized that with this new line-up that this was going to be the challenge. And we had this view in mind that new band, new label, more progressive. But unfortunately, it took us a while to get it to gel, because our first album wasn't... of course, a lot of people like it, but I was kind of disappointed with *Nightlife*. But again, you know, the label had that progressive feel to it and we knew that, and that was a good incentive as well to get going, to raise the quality of our music as well. So we were up against it – we knew that. We just wanted to get into the studio with the two new guys and prove the point. So we'd came up with the best album we could at the time, which was *Nightlife*. A lot of people still like it, but I was slightly disappointed. I thought it could've been better."

Ted Carroll, soon to voluntarily bow out of Lizzy's affairs, recounts his last significant moves with – and on behalf of – Thin Lizzy, machinations that were put in motion far before the realization of the *Nightlife* album.

"Right, so there we were, March '73, on the back of a hit, just putting out 'Randolph's Tango' to try and get another hit, and of course we were getting ready to start recording *Vagabonds*, and we were worried about the fact that we didn't think that Decca... because they were coming to the end of the contract, that Decca would put much resources behind that album. So we did a deal. Chris and myself went in and saw Decca, had some meetings with them and we agreed to give them an extension, a six-month extension of the deal. So instead of the deal finishing in September '73, the deal went through to March of '74, and that gave them a chance, because we could see that the *Vagabonds* album was going to come out in September of '73. So that gave them time to release the album and get behind it and see how it did, and then, you know, be in a position to know how serious they were about the band. And they also advanced us £10,000 at that stage. It was just our money, and it was in the pipeline from the hit, but it was obviously very handy for us at that point in time."

"So that was the deal that was done, and so we agreed on a budget for promotion and everything. At the same time, there was a young promotion guy who was working, who had come to work with Decca. I don't remember his name now but he was very good, and he was very keen on the band. He worked very hard with the band and did a good job, and so things had improved a bit as far as our perspective on Decca's efforts. We had pretty good budgets, which we were able to allocate for like full-page ads in the *Melody Maker* and papers like that, posters, all the various things. So we were pretty happy with the campaign for the *Vagabonds* album."

Do you remember how Vagabonds had sold?

"I have no idea (laughs). At this stage, I mean, obviously, it sold better than the others, but again, it didn't go mad. It didn't go into the charts or anything like that. It probably did, at the time, three, four, 5000 copies for us, over the first few months. And we were negotiating with Decca to re-sign with them, but we couldn't agree on a deal, because, well, we didn't really want to re-sign with them. So we were negotiating with them at the same time we were talking to other companies, but nobody was interested. So we were keeping Decca as a sort of safety, linchpin, if you like, so if all else failed, at least we'd have the Decca deal to fall back on. So we were trying to screw as much money as we could out of them."

"So these negotiations were probably going on seriously January and February and March of '74, and just as we had kind of been turned down... I mean, I remember Geoff Hannington at RCA was interested in signing the band, but he didn't want to give us an advance, and we needed an advance. Phonogram, PolyGram turned the band down, CBS turned the band down. Island were very interested. Richard Williams who had been editor of *Melody Maker* was now working as head of A&R there. He was very keen to sign the band, but some of the other people at Island weren't so keen. They didn't think Thin Lizzy was right for Island, and we were very up and hoping for a deal with Island, and then it didn't happen. So it looked like we were going to have to go back to Decca, not exactly cap in hand, but it wasn't the result we wanted."

"And then one day a registered letter arrives – this was toward the end of March. A registered letter arrived at the office from Decca saying that they were no longer interested in signing the band for another period. And so that kind of pulled the rug out from beneath us. I remember Chris Morrison looking like he had seen a ghost (laughs), when he opened that letter. So that happened, literally, on a Tuesday or a Wednesday, and on the Saturday, at this time, in addition to managing the band, I was running my Rock On record stall, part-time, and I just had one outlet. It was a little stall in the back of a flea market off of Portobello Road, and Nigel Grainge from Phonogram was one of my customers. He used to come in most weeks, and he came in and said he had been involved with reissuing stuff at Phonogram, you know, reissuing stuff from the Sun label and Chess and Modern, and he said, 'I've moved over to A&R.' I said good, and he said, 'If you know any bands, or come across anything interesting, let me know' and I said okay."

"The penny didn't drop for a moment," continues Ted with a chuckle. "Because we kind of thought that Phonogram or PolyGram were more or less the same company. We didn't realize that they were two totally separate companies, because they were both sort of out of Holland and Germany, which was the link between them. We thought because we had been turned down by Wayne Bickerton at PolyGram, that Phonogram wouldn't be interested. So anyway, I said, just as Nigel is leaving the shop, 'There is actually...' I just suddenly realized; I said, 'You know I'm involved in managing Thin Lizzy, but I'm actually in the process of bailing out. I'm quitting to concentrate on doing this, but Thin Lizzy are looking for a deal.' He said, 'I thought they were signed with Decca?' And I said, 'Well, Decca are trying to re-sign the band. We're talking with them about re-signing, but we're not that keen, because we don't feel they've done a great job for us.' So his ears were flapping, and he said, 'Oh, yes, that would be great. That would be really... I'd really be interested.'"

"So I gave him my office number and he said he would call me Monday. I went to the office Monday and told Chris that this guy from Phonogram is interested, and I don't know what will happen. So we sat there waiting for the phone call (laughs), and there was no phone call. And morning turned to noon and Chris wanted to call, and I said, 'No, wait, don't call; you'll look too eager.' And about quarter to three in the afternoon on a Monday, the phone rang and it was Nigel and he said, 'Yeah, we're definitely interested; can you come in and talk?' So that was it, you know, and actually I didn't get involved in negotiations, because I'm just waiting to leave. As soon as we had a deal and we were able to pay off all the bills, straighten financial things out, I was out of there, and so it was Chris Morrison and Chris O'Donnell, who was working at the time for us as an agent. He was Thin Lizzy's agent and with a few other bands, and because we had an agency in the office and he was the agent, he was going to take over, step into my shoes, managing Thin Lizzy, in partnership with Chris Morrison. And so the two Chris's went to get the deal with Phonogram."

It is of note that Chris Morrison hadn't yet been told by Ted that he was leaving. "Correct. I'd told Chris O'Donnell who worked for Carroll/Morrison Agency as our sole booker, or Arfur Booker, as we sometimes called him, that I had decided to leave as soon as we had gotten the band's finances sorted out with a new record deal. I had not intended to tell Chris Morrison straight away, as he was almost suicidal having just copped the Decca letter confirming that they did not wish to continue negotiations to re-sign the band. However O'Donnell persuaded me to tell Morry and I did, choosing a suitable moment."

It's also curious that Carroll doesn't mention Vertigo once. This begins to make sense when you begin to realize that the Phonogram imprint was still an afterthought, a formality in 1974, nothing worth mentioning. For one, Vertigo was no longer the youthful, risk-taking label it once was, nor did it have the esteemed reputation it would enjoy beginning a few years hence, growing more robust through the decades. In the context of the times, its identity and its wild reputation had been lost. And strangely, in this listless year for music, one dominated in the UK by an embarrassing glam phase, Vertigo and Thin Lizzy would be in the same boat, namely searching for a direction.

"Well, you have to put it in perspective," explains Carroll. "At that moment in time, Vertigo hadn't really taken on that reputation. Put it like this: Island had a fantastic reputation as a very cutting edge rock label, but Vertigo didn't. And of course, in the late '60s, early '70s, most of the majors tried it; Decca did it with Deram, and Phonogram did it with Vertigo. They created these sort of boutique labels that were aimed specifically at the rock market. I suppose it was a marketing ploy to perhaps put them on a slightly more even footing with Island, which was perceived to be super-hip. But at that time, we're looking at early '74, even though they had several very successful bands like Black Sabbath and that on Vertigo, it hadn't really taken on that cachet. That didn't come until about three or four years later. And a lot of the albums that they put out, various progressive acts, had basically sank without a trace. And what happened was around '76, that's when people started collecting Vertigo as a label. Then of course these albums that had come out on Vertigo and sold very tiny amounts, started to become hugely collectible, and that's where the focus on Vertigo as a collectible rock label started to build."

Nigel Grainge, penner of Thin Lizzy to the Vertigo camp, paints a similar picture of a label not quite getting the plot.

"It was funny, because at the time, when I first got my job at Philips, before it was called Phonogram, I actually had to go in as a credit control clerk. They had asked if I wanted that gig and I said, 'Well, I just want to be in the record business.' And I didn't realize it had nothing to do with the record business. And I was lucky that when I went back to personnel and said, 'This is not what I want to do,' it just happened that there was a job, an opening, in the sales department assisting the sales manager. So I got that gig, which was amazing, because I was helping the sales guys preparing their monthly sales folder that they would go out with, collating all the new artwork and hit points, all the various information I was collecting from the managers and various people who look after the bands and the labels we distributed, pulling it all together for the sales guys."

"Which is great experience. And I did that for about two years, before I became display manager, but in that time, because of my nature and my enthusiasm, I would try to make my presence felt with opinions. I would go into the A&R department and I would ask them if I could hear something. And it was really funny, because I remember, I think it was Rod Stewart when he put out *Every Picture Tells A Story*, and I made a suggestion about what I thought they should put out as a single, and as I walked out of the room, I remember someone, I don't think it was Olav Wyper, but somebody who worked for Olav, who said, 'That's the trouble in here. Everybody thinks they're a fucking A&R man.'"

"And it was very funny, because the company, despite their personalities, weren't having any hits. They hadn't broken anybody. They had a hit with Black Sabbath, but they hadn't really had too much else going. And all those guys left. They all went to RCA, to start a label called Neon there. And it was at that time that I... when they all left, obviously the company was short executive people, and the guy who'd been looking after the American labels had done a complete shambles. He was basically the nephew of the chairman, and he was a public school idiot who knew nothing about records. So he got fired and I took over, and straightaway we started having hits with all these American acts. Because we had the rights to a lot of them, and it was basically selecting the right ones and pushing the right buttons on the right tracks. I was able to do that because of my knowledge, and so I was very successful in that. But Rod Stewart, the first single came out, and it was 'Reason To Believe', and on the b-side it was 'Maggie May', and of course they were having trouble at radio with 'Reason To Believe', so I came in and said, 'We should flip this and go with the other one, the b-side.' And of course that was his career taking off, so I got a gold ribbon for that."

The philosophy and even cult of the Vertigo label as it exists today... Grainge, like Carroll, cautions against romanticizing it. "Well, it was kind of abused. That was weird about the Vertigo label. When it started, it had some really cool stuff, and then all of a sudden, there were hundreds of things getting signed, like Ben and Mike Absalom and Gravy Train and Clear Blue Sky. You know, these things were selling in their tens, never mind about 100s! Ramases and stuff like this (laughs). I don't know if you know too much about the history of Vertigo. I mean, the most interesting thing about it was their covers. But most of those records, if you play them, they're absolute shit. And the funny thing is, they've become so collectible, as a label. A lot of the really, really terrible records, like Mike Absalom and Ben, which were unlistenable. They go for like three, £4000 now, just for completists who want everything on the Vertigo label. Oh yeah, terrible bands. I mean, these bands did nothing. Cressida actually had two albums out! There were one or two that were good. May Blitz were fantastic and the Uriah Heep *Very 'Eavy, Very 'Umble* record was fantastic. But that's really when the label was happening."

Enter Thin Lizzy… "Right, because I was collecting records in my spare time, I went to this record shop in London. It was only open on a Saturday, and you know, I'm just talking to the guy who owns the store, and I said, 'Well what are you doing the rest of the week?' He said, 'I'm managing a band.' And he told me it was Thin Lizzy. I said, 'Wow, I love Thin Lizzy. Why the fuck are you with Decca?' I said, 'They're crap.' He says, 'I know they are. We're trying… we're getting off them at the moment.' I said, 'Why don't you come with us?' And he said, 'Make me an offer.' So I went, blimey, I don't even know what an offer is. I was looking after the American labels. I wasn't in A&R; there wasn't actually an A&R department at that time. Olav had gone, and so the guy who was looking after the company at the time and I had this meeting with the two managers, Chris O'Donnell and Chris Morrison."

As discussed, Ted Carroll was at this point transitioning himself out into what would become a lifelong love of records. Carroll would take £500 for his 15% share in Pippin The Friendly Ranger, the band's publishing company, moving on to devote time to his Rock On record retail business as well as Chiswick Records (where he signed Motorhead in 1977) and Ace Records. Curiously, it is also said that one of Ted's rationales for the move was his inclination toward thinking Phil would always be ensconced in one drama or another concerning his guitarist or guitarists. It was Phil's band, Phil was the songwriter, Phil had an ego, and yet his musicianship wasn't up to the standards of the guitarists he would necessarily have to accompany. Plus, guitarists usually come with egos as well, not to mention, unsurprisingly, songwriting aspirations.

"I've been lucky enough to be able to work in music for most of my life," says Ted, outlining his motivations for his shift away from managing flesh and blood into throwing around boxes of black vinyl. "I mean, I traded a model aircraft engine for a guitar when I was about 15, started learning to play the guitar, played in a few garage bands. The first band I was in really became quite successful in Ireland. And so I've always been involved in the music business, and initially as a musician. I wasn't a great musician by any means, but I was good enough to work in a band that was extremely good. And then I did management and promotion and so on, right up until I quit managing Thin Lizzy."

"I started, actually, dealing in records, in 1969, with a little bit of mail order, and then in '71 I opened this flea market stall for weekends. I was dealing basically in '50s rock 'n' roll, doo-wop, blues, soul, and I was also selling a lot of '60s kind of garage punk stuff like Question Mark & The Mysterians, The Standells and that stuff, which of course was only six, seven, eight years old. That music wasn't that old when we started to resurrect it, and found that there was a market for it."

Ironically, it was through Ted's work with Thin Lizzy, that the seed would be planted for him to eventually leave the band.

"I suppose so. I mean, when I was managing Thin Lizzy... basically this is the first year; this is '71, the first year they were in England. The band weren't making any money. I mean, they were basically getting by. Brian, my partner, was bankrolling them, but they were living as cheaply as you can possibly live. And they basically would come back to Ireland every six months or so and do a tour in Ireland where they could earn maybe £150, £200 a night, as compared to five, ten, £25 in England. And that money would help to sort of pump up the coffers and pay off the debt that they were building up. So I wasn't in a position for me to be making any money out of the band."

"So I had to kind of support myself, and I did it with a bit of wheeling and dealing, and so I decided that I would get a little record store going to make some money that way. So I found the premises. It was a shop off Portobello Road that was being converted into a small flea market, with about a dozen or 15 stalls. I said okay, I'll basically rent one of those. It was about a month before it opened, and I said I won't actually be here the weekend you opened, because I'll be away in Ireland, because I think Thin Lizzy were on tour in Ireland, in August of '71. But I'll be back the following week. So I'm in Ireland with Thin Lizzy and I discovered that our Irish distributor that distributes for Decca Records in London had this room upstairs of their premises, which was full of old records under the London America label, fantastic records, doo-wop, rock 'n' roll, rockabilly, everything you can think of. So I bought almost about 2000 45s at three-and-a-half pence a throw and brought them back. Prior to getting that, I just had a bunch of second-hand stuff that I built up over a few years. I had some stuff that I bought in America when I was there with Skid Row. And so this batch of London Records is what got the business off the ground. After that, they were lined up to get into the place."

"Yes, Ted had been more active," notes Grainge, picking up the tale, "but he wanted to expand his record store, and decided to spend less time. So he passed over the management to Chris and Chris. Ted was very involved at that stage, but once we were negotiating the deal, the negotiation wasn't with Ted at all. So there must have been some kind of deal that was done to give Ted either an override for some kind of payoff. And so it was very interesting, because the negotiation was ridiculous. None of us knew what we were doing. I didn't know what a negotiation was. Chris and Chris were pretty green as well, and so we worked out this ridiculous deal with the band, like £15,000 or something."

Chris Morrison confirms the above cited number, only that it was in fact a rare two-record deal, for £30,000 total. Yet given the £20,000 in accumulated debts, the money was soon gone, allocated to put Thin Lizzy back in black, pick up a new van and to make their first Vertigo record on the cheap.

Lizzy would enter the studio with a good base of road-tested songs, but the foundation on which *Nightlife* would be built upon would be undermined by the tentative hiring and subsequent actualisation of not one but two new members of the band, to boot, in the all-important guitar slot(s), namely Brian Robertson and Scott Gorham, the first a Scotsman, the latter an American. No one knew it yet, nor would they for another couple of years, but Philip and Brian Downey had planted within the band the seed of a swell sound that would take Lizzy admirably far, both commercially and critically.

Brian "Robbo" David Robertson, from East Renfrewshire, just south of Glasgow, would arrive into the Thin Lizzy fold in June '74 a mere teenager, with no experience to speak of, other than a formative foundation in cello, piano, drums and guitar, a music bedrock aided by the fact that Brian's father was a jazz performer who had played with Art Blakey. Robertson's first band was Rue Morgue back in '69 with his brother Glen. Brian then working his way through bit acts such as Heidi and Dream Police, the latter later morphing into the Average White Band.

"Oh boy, I came down from Glasgow when I was 17, 18 just to do auditions, basically," explains Robertson. 'My best friend Charlie McLennan was actually a roadie for Thin Lizzy at the time, so it was his idea really for me to go to the audition. Basically I just went up there and played and got it – end of story really. There had been a few guys before me. I think it'd gotten to a stage where they wanted to chuck it in basically. Charlie, my friend said, 'No, you've got to listen to Rob before you chuck it in,' so he did, and we continued on from there."

"By that time I was into John Mayall, Fleetwood Mac, all of those sorts of British blues acts at the time," continues Brian, laying bare his musical stripes. "I was listening to them more than pop or anything like that. I mean, one of my favourite guitar players was Peter Green. Hard rock stems from blues I suppose in the end. There are only so many chords you can play, you know what I mean? Downey was a blues man as well, as was Phil. He was a big Fleetwood Mac fan too. Scott, I don't really know what his influences were; more west coast sort of stuff I would have thought. He was not really into heavy rock. My heavy rock comes from Hendrix and Zeppelin, I suppose. Zeppelin just did it their own way, really; I mean, there was nothing like them around and there still isn't."

Being Scottish, one would have thought that Nazareth, in operation since '69, might have been an inspiration on Brian. "Not a lot really. I know they were very big in Canada and still are. We sort of became friends and whatnot, but musically they didn't have much to do with influence on me, no. My earliest concerts… Wishbone Ash was one of them. Elton John… they had the Average White Band supporting them and I loved them. Didn't really see an awful lot actually. I wasn't really into going to a lot of live gigs. I was being brought up on classical and blues, so I would be listening to more left field stuff like Little Feat. That would be more of what I listened to. But really, I was more into going out and playing gigs myself with my own band."

And pre-Lizzy for Brian, this would mean… "You'd have to do your show band stuff; you'd have to play the Top 10 sort of thing, but you could also slip in some of The Who or whatever. So you were just playing clubs, working men's clubs and whatnot."

Asked whether Phil might have seen in Brian the possibility of a multi-instrumentalist, Robertson figures, "No, I was hired for my guitar playing, but even at that stage, when I auditioned for Lizzy, I came down to London and I had a set of drum sticks and a guitar with me. So the first audition I did, I did as a drummer, for the band Slack Alice. I got that audition, and a week later, I got the job as guitar player with Thin Lizzy, so I had to go and tell them, 'Sorry, I can't play drums for you, because I'm playing guitar for them.' They sort of got a bit weird about it, and funnily enough, they ended up supporting us on a British tour as well. Kind of weird."

Also weird is that this was not the first time the Lizzy guys had met Robbo. Downey recalls that during a Lizzy stop in Glasgow during the Gary Moore era, Robertson had dropped by his hotel room along with his guitar and his girlfriend, then proceeding to play a few Lizzy tunes, much to Brian's amusement.

"They were staying at a hotel that was down the road from my house in Scotland," recalls Robertson, "and it was my local hotel, my local bar. I had been out doing a gig. I walked in with my guitar case to have a drink, and I saw Phil and the boys at the end of the bar, so I went up and said hello, because at that point, they were one of my favourite bands. Downey and I ended up in his hotel room upstairs. He had his drum sticks out, playing on the bed, and I was playing my electric guitar with no amplifier and we had a bit of a jam and that was it. Then I went off, walked back home, and a little while later I ended up in the band. Downey remembered me when I showed up at the audition and he said, 'I've seen you before!'"

And you actually knew some Thin Lizzy songs? "I knew all of them. Apart from 'Whisky In The Jar', which I hated."

Onto London, Brian says he arrived with his guitar, a pair of drumsticks and £25 to his name, at which time he had to cool his heels for three weeks while Phil ruminated over continuing with Thin Lizzy at all. At Brian's audition, held at African drummer Ginger Johnson's Iroquo Country Club in Haverstock Hill, Brian played a bit of 'Vagabonds' plus some blues and wound up with the job. "It was a local country club, in Haverstock Hill, which is up West Hampstead way," recalls Robbo. "It was a ramshackle place. A load of African guys were there, who had bags of weed all the time – basically just a drug dealing joint, that people rehearsed in. It was a very strange place for a young Scotsman to walk into. It kind of freaked me a little bit, but not too much."

William Scott Gorham, born March 17, 1951 in Glendale, California would soon join Brian in this whole reconstituted Thin Lizzy. Back in California, Scott had worked his way through bands such as The Jesters, Mudd, The Catchy, Hands Across and The Ilford Subway before uprooting to London. Gorham recalls working at a record distribution business to scrape up enough dough to cover his plane ticket, resorting to stealing records for covert resale to speed the process along.

Stealing records ain't the half of it though. "I should have been dead a long time ago because of all the shit I used to do with my brother-in-law Bobby," said Scott back in '76, in conversation with the NME. "Strung out on fucking downers, going into the heroin thing. I've been busted eight times, actually in jail at times. My old man and my lawyer had to come down each time and go to court. I was strung out on downers for about four years. It's a heavy physical thing coming off them, but it's an even heavier thing mentally: incredible depression. I was crying all the time. In California it's really easy to get lazy – sitting there catching the rays. You smoke a joint and it's so hot outside you don't feel like doing anything. 'Ah well, I'll just stay in bed.' (laughs)."

"Great hair," laughs Robertson, when asked what he thought when he first heard Scott Gorham play guitar. "No, he just turned up, you know? Phil kind of wanted to do a three-piece but everybody thought let's do it as a four-piece. So we started looking for another player again. Once we tried a couple then Scott turned up, and he had great hair so he got the gig (laughs). Initially he had come over to audition for Supertramp as lead guitar player 'cause his brother-in-law was Bobby Siebenberg, the drummer. But then when he got here they had already got the sax player, John Helliwell, so they didn't need a lead guitar player. So he was stuck in London with no gig. I guess he was just sort of hanging about London at that time, just looking for something to do."

Curiously, Siebenberg was considered the back-up plan for Thin Lizzy's percussion perch had Downey chosen to make a fast exit. Further on the Supertramp situation, Gorham is said not to have gotten the call because Roger Hodgson, having deliberated over playing keyboards or guitar in the band, decided upon both. After not winding up in Supertramp, Scott had in fact formed a band called Fast Buck and got to gigging, mostly in London's East End. At one of their shows, saxophonist Ruan O'Lochlaun from the band Bees Make Honey tipped Scott off that Lizzy had been looking for a second guitarist. Gorham then duly showed up at the same country club in Hampstead where Robertson had first played with Philip and Brian.

"For the first time in my life, I went out and hustled for myself instead of other people hustling for me," recalls Scott, also in the '76 NME piece. "I was like a one-man hustling show. Getting the band together, getting the rehearsal room together, going out to the pubs, hustling the band on to pubs. It was great therapy to actually get out there and push myself, because I'd always been a shy person who was never convinced that I was any good at playing guitar. And after a while, I was making 12 quid a week and my bills came to 15 quid a week."

As for his fateful rehearsal with Lizzy... "I went down to the club were they were rehearsing, and Phil looked like a real moody bastard sitting on the amp. This big heavy-looking spade guy. And Brian Robertson, the punk who wouldn't give you a look-in, and Brian Downey just wouldn't say anything to anybody. I thought it was kind of a weird outfit. 'What have I walked into?' I'm trying to be all, 'How yuh doin'?' and they just didn't want to know."

"At the end of the day, they were all huddled together and I thought, 'That's that,' and I started to walk out of the club thinking, 'At least I gave it a try.' I asked Phil, 'Can I get your phone number?' and he pulls out this tiny piece of paper and writes it really small. I thought it was a definite no. I said, 'okay, I'll see you later' and walked out. Phil called out, 'Hey, listen, why don't you come back tomorrow?' Then he called me up that night and asked me to join the band. He really was a moody bastard, though, when I first met him. Tried to be real heavy, really aloof. 'Don't get too close because you might not be around too long.' He seemed like the kind of guy who can be very standoff-ish but as soon as the barriers were broken down, he could be the nicest guy in the whole world. But he could be heavy."

So Scott, somewhat like Gary in the early days, indeed lacked confidence when it came to his playing abilities. "Well, I can't blame him," says Robbo, "because I was a right little shit in those days. It must've been pretty daunting for him to walk in to me, Brian and Phil, standing there. And he only had a little Les Paul copy with him, right? I think he was a bit embarrassed about that. But we auditioned a few people that day. Phil and I went back to Phil's place. We taped everything on a reel-to-reel tape, and we went through all the tapes, and listened to Scott's, and it was his rhythm playing that first struck home. Very good rhythm player, and we went, 'Well, that will do, plus he's got good hair' (laughs). So the image was good, and the rhythm thing was good, so we took it from there, really."

Scott confirmed in other interviews how mentally daunting that first meeting was, showing up in the pouring rain, the band quite sullen lurking in the dark amongst the African iconography adorning the room, obviously worn down by listening to all these guitarists who they had no hope of liking. Furthermore, he winces at the impression he must have made, especially carting around his Japanese Les Paul copy. The band worked their way through assorted numbers including 'The Rocker', with Phil disappearing to a backroom between jams, as it turns out, to check on the recordings the guys were making of each prospective employee. Once offered the gig, Scott figured he'd take it, first based on the fact that his pay would be going up from £12 a week to £30.

New line-up in place but not exactly brimming with chemistry, sessions for *Nightlife* would be tentative, especially given the strong presence of a producer in one Ron Nevison, possibly not the best choice for a band just formed. First however, the band would get some gigs in, playing their first show in front of a half dozen onlookers in Wolverhampton, June '74, following up with an Irish jaunt through the summer, culminating at a Reading stop on August 24th.

Frank Murray, who was in Dublin during the recording of *Nightlife* recalls Phil sending him cassettes of the songs in progress. Considering the hiring in of Nevison, Murray says, "You think you're going a step up the ladder; you're working with someone who worked with the Stones, and you almost felt like, this is the way up. We're not going down and working with apprentice engineers or whatever. But that was a difficult time, because I remember they went around on two or three band tours. I think there was a band called City Boy and someone else, and it was almost like, they had done that before with the Eric Bell line-up. They had done that with a rival and somebody else, a three-band tour, and you're the middle band or the starting band. So those times were pretty lean, you know, dragging your ass around Britain – again."

"Ron Nevison pretty much looked at us and didn't give a shit about who we were or what we had done," remembers Gorham, recalling the September sessions for the album. "Because at this point we hadn't done anything. His next project was probably going to be Eric Clapton or Jeff Beck or something, so we were kind of this interim band. And as we were recording this thing, he was kind of rushing each of us through parts. 'Come on, let's go, it's not going to get any better than that. Come on, next,' that kind of thing. So we got pretty pissed off with that."

"Ron was a bit of a nightmare in the end," concurs Downey, "because he kind of had lots of opinions which weren't suitable for us. He'd worked for Rod Stewart and people like that previously, but I think he came in with preconditions. He didn't really realize what the band was about, and it translated into this album. I think he put his stamp on, which we didn't like. It wasn't hard-edged enough for us."

"Ron was more, 'This is the way you're supposed to do it, so do it' sort of thing," adds Brian Robertson. "Which was fine at the time, because I didn't know any better. I didn't know mixing desks and whatever. I did know about amplifiers, but he got involved with the amps as well, which pissed me off. But we made friends later, in fact, at a UFO session up in Air Studios. He was doing one of their albums, and Jimmy Bain and me went up to visit and we sort of buried the hatchet there (laughs). But yeah, he was sort of authoritative, and didn't really take advice too well (laughs). Let's put it that way. It's like, 'Look, I'm the goddamn producer; do as you're told,' sort of thing. Which is alright in certain respects, but if you have ideas of your own, and after all, they are your songs. And you want them to be coming out the way you envisage them. I mean, that sort of producer's great if you don't know what you're doing. And he can put some insight into what you're trying to do, then that works. But if you already have something in your head as to how you want the song to turn out, or the album to turn out, or you want the drums to sound, you know what I mean? Then it becomes a bit of a stumbling block, really. And I guess maybe certain people, including myself, I guess, towards the end of the first album, I was learning so much more. You get certain people that he's worked with, they would find that a bit grating. But that's not to take anything away from what he does. Because he is a very good producer. Otherwise these people wouldn't work with him. It's a clash of personalities and all that sort of thing."

Nevison, about to embark on a huge catalogue of hits that would stretch decades, concurs with this idea that the making of the *Nightlife* record was not a satisfying experience, nor was the result. "Of all the UK stuff… the first half of the '70s, obviously, I did the *Tommy* album and the Tommy film for The Who. I did *Physical Graffiti*, I did the first three Bad Company albums that were very successful. Right there are five enormous albums as an engineer I worked on. And I mixed all of those, except for *Physical Graffiti*, and I did not mix the last, the third Bad Company album, *Run With The Pack* - Eddie Kramer did that. But otherwise I recorded and mixed all of those records. And I remember the Thin Lizzy record. Out of all the records, that was one record I wasn't happy with the mix on. I'd mixed at a place I'd never mix before, at Trident Studios off Wardour Street, and just listening back, sometimes I think, 'Oh man, that's fantastic,' and other times, 'What was I thinking?' And that was one of them where I thought I must have fell asleep at the wheel a little bit. But I loved working with Phil Lynott and Scott and the other guitar player; it was all a great experience. It was a fun experience. I love working with two guitar players, and I've done plenty of that."

Nevison was in fact hired by Phil due to his history of big guitar sounds, but Robbo soon found out that Nevison wasn't going to let him play through his Marshalls, prodding him toward a Fender twin-reverb and tiny Pignose practice amp.

"But yes, mostly I remember not being happy working at Trident Studios," continues Ron. "It was weird; the control room was on another floor from the studio. You couldn't see down, who you were recording. It was kind of weird, the whole situation. I am surprised when I listen to *Nightlife*, how bad it is. Not how bad it is, but how bad a job I did. Sometimes I listen to stuff and go, 'Shit, that album rules!' and sometimes I go, 'Was I there?' (laughs). The vocals aren't loud enough, and I don't know what happened. That album could've rocked better. It's one of the albums that I hope that interviewers don't ask me about."

On the subject of working with two guitarists, both of which were new to the band, Ron surmises that, "I probably didn't even know they were new! I just met them, 'Oh, the guys in the band.' That's the first that it was new to me. There's one track with Gary Moore, and he was a legend, but yes, Brian and Scott Gorham, the LA boy, they were both really solid. I just remember two things: I remember not being happy using that studio, and I remember that working with Phil was a joy, as far as vocals and everything, because obviously as the bass player in the group, he was finished once you'd done the basic tracks."

"I knew about Ron's history, but I didn't have any meetings with him," recalls Grainge. "They met him and they decided they liked him. So I kind of went along with it. Because of my kind of greenness, I didn't have any involvement in the recording process of that record at all. Basically, they ran out of money in no time. So that they had to kind of renegotiate, which was refused, at the time. It was frustration all-around, but the relationship was good, with us. It was mutual. The way that first album had gone. It was like, how did that happen? How did that happen, that we weren't in control of it? How did that happen that it just wasn't good enough? We can't let that happen again."

Nightlife as a record indeed lacks the bite of its lively predecessor, even if it's obvious the band had taken a huge leap forward in meticulousness, detail, class. Weirdly though, there are only two heavy rockers on the record, both 'It's Only Money' and 'Sha La La' forming a set, with the non-LP 'Black Boys On The Corner', as these sort of complicated rhythmic takes on the newly forming genre of heavy metal.

Says Brian Robertson of 'It's Only Money', "I always felt the riff was really strong, but we were very, very rushed at that point, to do that album, as you can tell. The album is quite disjointed. We didn't have a lot of time to work with it. I didn't really understand a lot about arrangements and all the rest of it. But having said that, over the years, I think I've played it quite a lot with a lot of different bands. *Nightlife* is kind of mellow because we didn't have an awful lot of material. We were using stuff that Phil had demoed. 'It's Only Money', he demoed with Gary Moore. And that was a really cool version as well, but the version that we put out there was, as you say, laid-back. I don't know, I think it was just the timing as well. In 1974 we weren't really sort of as heavy then as we were later on. And a lot of the songs were kind of stuff that Phil had lying about, really. Like I say, we only had a few months to do the album, so there wasn't a lot of time to start thinking about production and everything else, so I don't think the production was particularly great either."

No less than 'Showdown', 'Dear Heart', 'Still In Love With You', opener 'She Knows' and the bluesy title track – half the album – portray the band as surprise possessors of black music chops, each down a different historical path but made comprehensive through R&B. Further perplexing, normally a rock band starts a record with a bit of a high energy track and that is emphatically not the case with the studio muso skills of 'She Knows'. As well, it is rare that a title track is one of the most laid-back song on a record, and 'Night Life', with its country picking guitar solo and shameless elaborate string arrangements... well it's enough to cause a punter revolt. In any event, both those slots are generally receptacles of showcasing and Thin Lizzy abdicates.

Brian Robertson disagrees that *Nightlife* was substantially an exploration of black musics. "No, not at all. To be honest, *Nightlife* was a transitional period between Thin Lizzy and a new band, although we called the new band Thin Lizzy. It was a stopgap. I mean, okay, we did 'Dear Heart', which was kind of a Barry White-type thing. Phil was a big Barry White fan; he really was. He used to play that in the car all the time, and I used to think, what the fuck are you playing? Barry White!? It made no sense to me. But I can listen to Barry White now and think, gee, the guy was a genius, to be honest. I love his music, but at the time I was into rock 'n' roll and I'm a youngster and thinking, what the hell is this Barry White shit, you know? I don't think there's anything else, sort of black-orientated on that album. There's 'Showdown', but that's more rock, to me."

Nor does he think that components of the *Nightlife* canon might have been intended for a Phil Lynott solo album, as has been bandied about. That theory however somewhat holds up, given the very real possibility that Thin Lizzy might not have continued at all.

"I don't think so, not at that point. Unless he was considering just not going ahead with the band, which possibly he was at that point, because we definitely hadn't proved ourselves as a band. Like I say, we weren't even going to call it Thin Lizzy at that point. The only reason it was called Lizzy was because the management insisted. You know, Phil wanted to start a brand-new band. So with that in mind, I wouldn't have said he was thinking particularly of solo album-type stuff. In any case, you listen to his solo stuff, it has nothing whatsoever to do with what we were about at the time anyway."

"I don't think anybody gave a shit about Phil Lynott solo albums, to be perfectly honest," scoffs Brian, having, it seems, lived the experience of hearing about Phil as a solo artist for much of his run with the band. "Because you hear some of his ideas for it, and you just think, it's nothing to do with us, really. It's nowhere close to what Lizzy are. So who cares? And then get on with it. And it certainly wasn't up my street, any of the stuff he was recording. I just didn't like it. I thought it was sort of anal, really, and not really very strong songs, going into the reggae and all this, and back to his roots. As far as I'm concerned, his roots were in Dublin! Not bloody Jamaica, right? It was all, well, Phil was black, and it's like, no he wasn't, he was Irish! (laughs). That's the only way I ever looked at Phil. He was Irish! And he was Irish through and through. And this sort of back to my roots, going to Jamaica and all that sort of nonsense, it was, as I say, nonsense, as far as I'm concerned, right? I mean, I'm Scottish (laughs). He's Irish, and that is all I see in Phil, is a strong Irishman. I don't see any of these roots-type things, which... and I think it reflects very much on when he tried to sort of embrace the black music scene. It was rubbish! It was crap. The reggae was crap, you know what I mean? There was no connection there, and bloody hell, for some reason he wouldn't give up on that. He just always wanted to go back to that. And with his solo stuff, I don't think the record company was too impressed with it either. Certainly the record buying public weren't (laughs)."

"Well, he's not left-handed, is he?" cracks Robbo, asked about Phil's disappointment – one of his great life disappointments, actually – at not realizing his dream of playing Jimi Hendrix on film. "I mean, you know, this was sort of bandied about as a sort of possibility. Phil didn't really talk too much about it. It was more just sort of rumours going around the office. And we were all thinking – well, I know I was; I don't know what the boys were thinking – but I just thought it was ridiculous. Because number one, he's right-handed, number two, he can't play lead guitar anyway, so how's he going to get rid of that? You know, knowing what I know now, they probably could've got away with it, but what are you going to do with the Irish accent? Come on! It's ridiculous (laughs). And Jimi was quite a short guy, probably the same size as me; he wasn't a big tall geezer, and Phil is like six-two. I mean, I don't think it was ever going to float, to be honest. I think it was more a question of it was good publicity for the time, because it was in the gossip columns quite a lot. So it was more sort of like, keep the profile of Phil Lynott up rather than anything serious. Who could possibly be serious about him doing that? It was ridiculous. It's like, that show CSI, the black guy, Warrick (Brown; played by Gary Dourdan). Now he's been offered, apparently, from what we hear on the net, the role to play Phil Lynott. And I thought, well that makes a bit more sense, than him playing Hendrix, you know what I mean? I think that might be quite good. But then what would he have to do with the accent? Then again he's a professional actor! Phil had his own TV series over a year, trying to introduce live bands, and he was dreadful at it! He was so embarrassing in front of the camera. On stage, he owned that, but in front of the camera, he just froze. So really, if you think about it, there was no way on earth that he could have possibly done the Hendrix thing. That was just PR nonsense."

Back to the record at hand... supporting *Nightlife's* Irish side, Phil offers 'Philomena' – in affected Irish accent no less – on which Scott and Brian craft some of their best inaugural twin leads, pronounced of characteristic due to the Irish melody of it all. 'Philomena', recorded on Phil's 25th birthday, was of course a composition in dedication to the mother who had supported Phil and his decision to be an entertainer.

Discussing with Harry Doherty his attempts at singing in an Irish accent – at least some tura lura's – on the *Vagabonds* album, Phil explains that, "Shortly after that I did 'Philomena', where I took it a stage further and tried singing lyrics in an Irish accent. But I got slammed to fucking death. And where did I get slammed to death the most? In fucking Ireland. I got taken apart. But the producer at the time, Ron Nevison, had no inkling of what I was trying to do. He'd just come from working on the Bad Company album, and it was Brian's and Scott's first time in the studio, so he had no idea what I was trying to do with Irish songs. The song sounded really empty. I just wanted to put one song down where I sang as I spoke."

Elsewhere, 'Banshee', all 1:27 of it, is an ethnic masterpiece, maybe the album's highlight, given its gorgeous evocation of both Phil's Irish heritage and his romanticism of the cowboy life. Frankie Carroll (a nod to manager Ted Carroll and road dog Frank Murray) does much the same, only now with piano, strings and close, intimate vocal.

The blustery 'Sha La La' and the bluesy 'Still In Love With You' are the only tracks that would lead a full life within Lizzy's live repertoire, 'Sha La La' for its Brian Downey workout, 'Still In Love With You' for a soft respite, bonus being its bed for history-steeped soloing, on the record, played by exiting guitarist Gary Moore, given that Robbo insisted Gary's "perfect" take be kept.

Explains Nigel, "The funny thing was that during that transition, the demo that I was played, when Chris and Chris came in, was 'Still In Love With You', and they told me that the line-up had changed, that this was a demo that I was listening to. Legend has it that while I was raving about the guitar solo, and I was saying, 'Is this the new guy?' they told me it was. That they were kicking each other under the table not to say anything. But it was actually Gary playing on 'Still In Love With You'. And they didn't tell me. They lied, and of course when I went to see them, the new guys were in the line-up, Scott and Brian, and they played it exactly. I mean, they were brilliant guitarists anyway. They played 'Still In Love With You' with Gary's solo note for note, and they did it brilliantly. So no, I never knew until only a few years ago, that it was actually Gary playing the guitar on that demo, which was actually used for the album."

For Brian Robertson, 'Sha La La' revealed as much about Scott as it did the band's drummer. "Our approaches were totally different," began Brian, in conversation with *Melody Maker's* Harry Doherty, circa 1976. "Mine is probably a lot looser. I suppose I'm orthodox to an extent, only because I had classical training on piano, but a lot of my playing is still unorthodox. So my basic ideas are fairly orthodox, but that's as far as it goes, because if you play too orthodox, then you're just going to sound like everybody else. But Scott is all unorthodox. He plays a solo on 'Sha La La' that was completely ridiculous as far as I'm concerned. The whole song was in minor and he played the solo in major and, at the time, he was having real trouble because he couldn't take solos in minor. That's very unorthodox!"

"That was just Scott, wasn't it?" reflects Brian, asked about the track 35 years on. "When I got in the band, as far as I was concerned, we were looking for a rhythm player, not another lead player. Phil wanted, you know, both of us playing, I guess to be politically correct. 'Scott, you take this solo,' and he did it and I went, oh my God, this is in the wrong key, what is he doing?! But you know, as we all were, we were all sort of fresh at everything, and he thought it was great. But me being classically trained and whatever, I knew it was out of key. But then again, there's the weird side I like. Like Jeff Beck – he plays stuff that you just never think of doing; you just wouldn't think about it. And so there's the odd solo, like you say. 'Sha La La', he plays completely in major, but the whole song is in minor, but to me it worked. I just thought yeah, okay, it's weird, I don't know if anybody will like it, but I like it. Just one of those things."

Added Gorham in his defence, "I guess I tend to play more what's in my head than what is exactly right. I'll go for strange notes or weird notes and really like them and everybody will say, 'No, man, that's not right; do it again.' That's what pissed me off, because to me it sounded great. After a while it got to be a real hassle, and then I got down to it and sat down and started learning the minors and the majors and what you can do and what you can't do. And for a while, it was restricting the shit out of me because before I didn't really care what was right and what was wrong as long as it sounded good to me. It's more orthodox now than it was. Definitely, I'm more into hitting the exact note and being spot-on and all that, but listening to the old solos on tapes and hearing some of the really weird things I was doing, I thought they were kinda neat."

"Oh, that's a nasty question, isn't it," laughs Brian, addressing in 2009, the difference between himself and Scott. "We're two totally different players. I'm classically trained on several instruments, and I approach things totally differently, and of course I was into the blues from a very young age, as my father was a jazz musician. So I grew up with Glenn Miller and Mugsy Spaniel's jazz and Benny Goodman, that sort of stuff. I don't honestly think that's what Californians grew up with at that time (laughs). So I mean, my favourite artists were like Fleetwood Mac – Peter Green was my favourite guitar player."

But Lizzy was not a blues band... "No, Lizzy was Lizzy. It was what it was – there were influences from all over. I mean you only have to listen to the first three Lizzy albums with Eric Bell and then listen to what we were doing when we had the four-piece together. It was a totally different band. As I say, Phil didn't even want to call it Thin Lizzy when we got together. He wanted to call it a different name, and the management said no, you've got to keep the name. So it was still called Thin Lizzy."

"There were a lot of teething problems on *Nightlife*," continued Brian, somewhat coming around on the record. "The only gigs we'd done beforehand were on a four-day Irish tour. It was pretty hairy. We'd never been in a studio before to actually record an album that would be released and be with me for the rest of my life. But I think it's a good album, the one album we've recorded that I can listen to over and over again. There's a lot of variety on it. The teething troubles were just generally getting into each other's playing."

" 'Sha La La' was probably the first harmony thing that we ever did," remarks Scott, touching upon a characteristic of the band that would mean so much. "It was Phil's song and he already had that basic line written out. He showed Brian and me the line and we just got into doing it. It became a little bit blunt because the original riff was so simple that you could kinda do it in your sleep, so we worked on it and that started it. But I don't think the dual lead harmony stuff really came until the second album. We just got more and more into it instead of just playing the lead here and there. It was more fun to come up with harmony lines and it filled the songs out a lot. Really, we just fell into it, not with any purpose in mind."

"But sure, I remember that I was lacking confidence at the time," reiterates Gorham. "When I joined Lizzy, I'd just been playing guitar for about two-and-a-half years and I'd never really taken it seriously. I never regarded it as a viable moneymaking prospect because I never really thought I was any good. But I learned a lot from that album, about what I was doing wrong, which was good for me."

For all the bad vibes around the making of *Nightlife*, one wonders if Nevison is too hard on himself with respect to the sound of the album. In fact, there's very little to complain about there. *Nightlife* was the band's best-produced album to date, all frequencies captured, if perhaps a touch twee at the bass end. Nay, if there are complaints to be fired off, they should be levelled at the songs, and even then, only because so many don't fit the Lizzy mandate established previously or the radically different one again to be established after.

If there's another complaint, it would be of the type one would expect to come from Grainge or any man in his position, the idea that there were no clear hits on it, hit, on the positive, being code for really, solid, memorable songs. I'd venture to say there are a couple or three high quality compositions on here, namely 'Banshee', 'Frankie Carroll' and 'Sha La La', but none of those, each for their own reasons, have any of the boxes ticked that a hit single must have. One could posit that 'She Knows', with its deft Steely Dan energy, is the closest thing to a single on the album, but single choices actually went to 'Philomena' in the UK, 'It's Only Money' in Germany and 'Showdown' in the US.

Said one reviewer of advance single 'Philomena', " *When all the singles sound either like impressions of The Glitter Band or processed Philly cheese, something as moderately entertaining as this can find itself elevated to Single Of The Week by reason of its simple honesty. The playing is rumbustious, the guitar riff lodges firm in the memory, and there are words about wild rovers and the wind in the trees that somehow recall John Leyton. I imagine they might even have enjoyed making this record.*"

Speaking of 'She Knows', this first Scott Gorham credit ever was the cause of one of the more memorable of many rows the band's two guitarists would have with Nevison. Having been scheduled to perform some backing vocals on the track, the guys went for a drink down the pub instead, returning to the studio well lubricated.

"I've made up with Ron since that album, okay?" laughs Robbo, asked to divulge the tale. "In my opinion he made a complete mess of the album. But there were drug issues at the time with him. I've met him since and we've straightened that out - that he wasn't really on the same planet as us at the time. He was driving around in the middle of the summer in a Rolls-Royce with a silver fox fur coat on (laughs), and it just didn't make any sense to me. You know, he's bitching about like, you're trying to put an acoustic guitar down, and he'd go, 'No, we need to do that again.' I'd say, 'Why's that, then?' He said, 'Well, the strings are squeaking.' I'm going, 'Yeah, but Ron, they're brand-new strings, and you're going to hear if you go up the fretboard – on any guitar!' Nope, can't have that. I'm thinking oh, for fuck's sake, something wrong here. It was pretty hard work with Ron, and plus we were on a very, very tight schedule for that first album. As far as 'She Knows' is concerned, yeah, he kept saying that Scott and me were singing out of key, and of course we weren't. And so I turned around to him and said, 'Right, you think you can fucking sing it, fuck off in there and sing it yourself, you asshole!' I really had a big bust-up with him about it. So he ran into the studio in Olympic, and sang, 'She knooowwws' and he was out of tune. And when we mixed it I was standing behind Ron, and without him knowing… I mean, this is very petty, I know it was, but I was a youngster at the time, but just to get my own back, I moved the fader on his vocal up a shade, so his vocal, which was out of tune, was louder, and he didn't even notice it. That's how coked-out out he was! It was the '70s; everybody was a bit out of it. I hadn't actually got to that point at the time, so my ears were pretty fresh. But he was obviously having a bit of a hard time with the '70s and the cocaine sort of culture, and of course, we all know that cocaine destroys your ears. I didn't realize until a few years later, that that's what was occurring."

"But yeah, I mean, I think you'll find that he would admit that himself," continues a Robbo, softened by 35 years of growing up. "And then I met him later on with Michael Schenker Group; I went up to the studio, Air Studios and met him, and he was sort of saying, 'Well, sorry about that; that's just the way it was.' And he was entirely correct. We all go through these things. He's actually a very lovely man, and still a great producer. It just didn't happen with us. It was one of those things."

Nice story, but a close listen to the track reveals no significant sharpening or flatness in the backing harmony at any point, and certainly not to distraction, even if Robbo says listening to the song cracks him up every time.

"Oh yes, the album is definitely lighter," says Brian Downey, concurring with band, producer, label guy and fan opinion that *Nightlife* had turned out underwhelming. "I think it's because of the fact that when we had the auditions and got Scott and Brian, we had maybe a month of auditions, lots, and most of the auditions relied on laid-back songs. We weren't really rocking out too hard because of the fact that there were so many people coming and going. But having said that, there were a couple of instances where we did rock out quite heavily, but most of the time we were just sort of finding our feet, and finding exactly what these guys could do, to be versatile enough to be able to play in the band."

"And I think another reason that that particular album became kind of soft rock was because of the fact that the guys were new in the band, they didn't have that much experience, and everybody was still sort of finding their feet. With the result that it was a little bit apprehensive playing-wise. Phil's writing is a little laid back because, as I say, we had a lot of auditions under our belt and he was writing as well as playing in that period. So his writing wasn't up to scratch, as far as I could see. But having said that, there are some good rock songs on there, like 'Sha La La' is a pretty good one, and there were another couple of tunes that I can't remember offhand. But I do remember saying to myself, it is soft, and it's not what I expected."

"Phil's writing was just not quite there after the Decca period," continues Downey. "We were still finding our feet. But there are some good songs on there, and the guys just weren't too long in the band when we recorded that album, and we changed labels as well. That was the first album for Phonogram. But that whole change, that period - that was a complete change in the band. Instead of having a three-piece, the focus was so different and the whole psychological thing was playing on our consciousness. And I think that rubbed off on the whole recording experience in the studio, with Ron Nevison as well. Because Ron was the kind of guy who didn't really listen to too many ideas. He was a fairly independent guy and he wanted to make this album... well, he wanted to put his stamp on it, which, I know Brian Robertson found a bit disconcerting because of the fact that he didn't get much input when he suggested a few things in the studio. Ron told them to calm down fairly drastically in some of the ideas – it was a very strange experience for Brian, and I think Scott was in the same boat."

"And so the whole experience of the *Nightlife* album, was pretty strange, to say the least. And with us not being too conversant with each other, not long together, as I say, it just so happened that the band wasn't on top form when we went into the studio, as far as I can see. Although there are a couple of nice numbers on there, generally we could've done better."

"Well, only on a professional basis," was Phil's qualification upon his liking of the album, in conversation back in 1977. "I like the album, but because we were only three months together and hadn't done any tours, there was no aggression in it, and a lot of tracks were for a solo album that I was preparing at the time. It was subdued, you know, because a lot of the stuff was romantic. So as far as an album representing the band as a live act, it wasn't really a very good debut album. By *Fighting*, we were back on the trail again of what we wanted to do."

Although *Nightlife* isn't rife with twin leads, the guys couldn't help but realize there was at least a germination of an idea that Scott and Brian might one day create something special. Brian Downey certain saw it. "Oh well, I mean, that idea came about in the actual rehearsal studios when we were rehearsing for the *Nightlife* album. We had a fleeting idea of what twin guitars were about because of the fact that there were certain bands around – Wishbone Ash was one of them, that comes to mind immediately – and we were very influenced, not influenced, but we liked their sound and style, and they were more bluesy in what they were doing around at that time, and that appealed to us as well. But the conscious decision to make it a dual guitar thing, wasn't so much conscious as we just so happened to be experimenting with this stuff, and it just happened that Phil was writing these really melodic tunes, which lent itself to some nice dual guitar harmonies, which we wanted to try as well, and that came about literally from the time that they came into the band. From the first auditions, maybe, when we were trying to get them to play in a dual way, and harmonize with themselves. So that was fairly conscious, but there again, we left it kind of loose as well. It wasn't cautious to the extent that every song had to have a dual guitar, harmony guitar piece in it. We left it open, and lucky enough, because of the melodic aspect of the songs - this dual guitar harmony stuff really seemed to fit in well with it. That was fantastic and that was great, but we had also, don't forget, a little bit of harmony guitar on the earlier albums. Even though we were a three-piece band, we used to do some overdubs. Eric Bell was a very good exponent of that. He used to obviously harmonize with himself on some of the overdubs, so it came in back there as well. So subconsciously it was always there. We wanted to try it, and then obviously when the two guys came in, we had the opportunity to physically get down and do it, and that's what happened."

Perhaps one's surprise at the soft and soulful direction of *Nightlife's* music becomes increasingly pronounced by the fact that the album was wrapped in such a flashy rock 'n' roll album cover, Jim Fitzpatrick once again called upon to perform his magic.

"That's a composite from a number of different photographs," begins Jim, addressing first the skyline of the piece. "I was very influenced by an artist called Jim Steranko, who was a friend of mine at the time, and it's kind of based on one of his images. I was also influenced by Jack Kirby who did these montages in Marvel Comics, so there's an element of that to it as well: The black panther... I can talk about it now but I couldn't talk about it then, but I was a great admirer of the Black Panthers. A lot of people will disagree with me on that, but I lived in New Haven and met some of them, I lived outside New Haven in a place called Madison, Connecticut, and these, to me, weren't terrorists, they were people who had a political agenda that I agreed with. So before I ever got near Madison, Connecticut, or New Haven, where their headquarters were, I knew the writings of Huey Newton and Bobby Seale, and I talked to Philip a great deal about them. But we sort of put the panther in without saying it was a Black Panther, or any reference to the movement. So it was kind of political, to be honest. Philip was a very patriotic Irish man. He never saw himself as a black, black man. And I suppose I was trying to point him in that direction. But that was a very political album. Martin Luther King, I did work for his widow, actually, and Malcolm X – those were two of my heroes. The whole civil rights movement was forced on America by Kennedy, and I remember reading a story about Jack Kennedy, when he was standing for election; it was a very fine-run thing, and he only won by a hundred thousand votes or something. For a vast country like America, that was very close. When Martin Luther King was arrested by the FBI, before the election, Jack Kennedy picked up the phone, to Coretta King, to say how outraged he was. That could have cost him the election. When Bobby Kennedy marched in the funeral for Martin Luther King, that was a seminal moment. And our civil rights struggle, which actually became a war over here, and in Northern Ireland, was actually based on the black civil rights movement."

Did Phil face any prejudice for being either Irish or black?

"No, he said to me a couple of times, when I asked him what it was like being black in Ireland. Because there weren't many blacks; I knew all two of them, you know (laughs). Dave Murphy was the other one. But not to be facetious, there were about half a dozen, but no more. So Phil was very noticeable. But just like having cauliflower ears, people look at you, but they didn't say anything. I did experience... he did get racism when I was walking down the street with him one day in Grafton Street. Someone shouted out the N-word, and he was lucky to escape with his life, because they ran after him."

"We met at the Bailey, and I hit it off with them immediately," says Jim, about meeting Brian and Scott for the first time. "Phil liked them both. Scott is a real laid-back kind of California gentlemen, you know? And Brian was a crazy Scot, and still is. They were brilliant but total opposites. I love their playing; I loved Brian's playing and I loved Scott's playing. But very, very different. Scott is the more studied and meticulous, where Brian just wings it, but both are extraordinary players. But Brian was crazy. There were two guys, Gary Moore and Brian Robertson, in and out of the band. And I liked them both. Brian I liked immensely; Gary I was wary of. They were geniuses, but they also lived life, you know, to the full, and occasionally went off the rails. And Brian went off the rails more than once. It is said that he cost them the American tour, that one time, when they were breaking with 'The Boys Are Back In Town' on the charts, and I was actually living in America, coming round the turnpike, and listening to 'The Boys Are Back In Town' thinking this was really cool. But they were both... I don't want to say they were both trouble. They were geniuses, you know? Well, Brian still is. But Gary was a very troubled person. Brian, on the other hand, is a typical Scotsman. He loves to drink and he loved a bit of a scrap, you know? But also very funny."

"Gary, I felt he was always so down on himself," continues Jim. "He was always borderline violent. He was always unpredictable. You never knew what the hell he was going to do or what he was going to get us all into. I mean I always acknowledged him and got on with him, but I always stayed away from him (laughs). If they were all going out and Gary was there, I was thinking, hmm, might leave that until tomorrow night."

"The painting is about 16 inches," recalls Jim, back to *Nightlife*. "They were usually about 16 inches square. Worked somewhere between 14 and 16 inches square. And that one again, that was a complete composite. Again I photographed what I call the negative artwork; it's a paste-up. You can see clearly the places where I pasted skyscrapers on top of one of the other to give it that feeling of depth. And I printed that, in my own darkroom, on film, painted that artwork. By the way, I would like to get some of this artwork back! Because that artwork was never returned to me. Nobody seems to know where it is. I tried many years ago to get it back. You see, the way it worked was, whoever got it in those days put it into a file, and it stayed there. It's only much later I got into the habit of photographing and transparencies and all that kind of thing."

Nightlife emerged November 8th 1974, accompanied by the first UK single, 'Philomena', two weeks previous along with the small-scale publication of Phil's first poetry book, *Songs For While I'm Away*. The title of the slim volume seems to be directed toward the tumultuous love of Phil's life, Gail, who had finally had enough of Phil's constantly checking up on her from various tour stops, resulting in Gail departing from his life by the end of the year.

6

FIGHTING

"They didn't say anything, and they left"

Fighting my way back, indeed, and, arguably, from a position on the ropes, once again. The cool blues of *Nightlife*, unsurprisingly, failed to ignite imaginations and Phil and the boys were looking for a way out – and up. The album that would result, *Fighting*, would find the band turning up, recapturing the fire of *Vagabonds Of The Western World*, and, in tandem, discovering the magic that would become their trademark, the duellng and duo guitars of Scott Gorham and Brian Robertson.

Downey addresses the thorny-for-Thin Lizzy subject of hard rock, each and all members of the band perennially somewhat wrinkling their noses at the term, especially when it's supplanted by an even more adversarial one, heavy metal.

"When we were signed to Deram, before Scott and Brian came in, we were doing sort of hard rock on those albums. I mean, if you listen to *Vagabonds Of The Western World*, you can hear hard rock songs like 'The Rocker' and a couple of others on there. So we had the idea from the very start that we weren't going to be the soft rocker ballad group people thought Thin Lizzy was, because we recorded 'Whisky In The Jar'. We had, since the early days before the band even formed, a great idea of what we wanted to do with regard to our songs, because I came from a band playing in the blues tradition and Phil was in a band called Skid Row. They were playing kind of East Coast rock songs, and so we knew when we got to *Fighting*, that the way to go was getting obviously into hard rock more so than not. Because, I mean, we had a varied style anyway. We could do rock, we could do folk, we could do Phil's ballads, and we had an idea where we wanted to go. We didn't want to confine ourselves to any particular style."

"There were a lot of breakthrough moments on *Fighting*, in terms of the songwriting and the arrangements," figures Robertson. "*Nightlife* was rushed and we basically had to get it done and get it out. *Fighting* wasn't so rushed. We recorded at Olympic Studios which was famous for all sorts of bands from Zeppelin to the Stones. So we recorded that one there and it was a lot more intense, and we had a lot more time to work things out. Hence it was a better album. Writing-wise, basically Phil would come up with a basic thing and we'd all go and have a look at it. Again it's not something you can just sort of put into compartments and just say, well right, we did this or we did that. The roles depend on who came up with the ideas for whatever song, and then we tried new ideas for each song."

"It just so happens on the *Fighting* album that all the songs seemed to come together," continues Brian. "Phil was writing fairly hard songs, with the result that we had a whole album of rock songs. Previous to that, we had, as I said, Vagabonds on the Decca label, before the lads came in, and we had some great rock songs on there. But as regards the whole album being a rock album, *Fighting* was definitely a change in direction. You're right in that respect. But again, it wasn't really a conscious decision. It just sort of happened and evolved into that rather than consciously making an attempt to become a hard rock band. We were going in that direction anyway."

"I don't think we even thought about it that way," agrees Scott, on positioning Lizzy as a hard rock band. "We pretty much thought of ourselves as a band out there on our own. I don't think we ever wanted to be compared to any other bands or slotted in with this category of bands. I'm pretty sure that we never even thought in those kinds of ways at all. And if anybody actually called us heavy metal, we would actually jump all over them and the correction would start there. You know, we considered ourselves an absolute hard rock band, but definitely not a metal band. Now, the difference, between the two genres, to be a metal band, it all depends on the riff. You know, the drum groove and the guitar riff. Whereas with hard rock, it's all about the groove and the lyrics and the melody of the song. And that's why we went out of our way to explain that we are not heavy metal, we are a rock band."

Still, Gorham doesn't deny that *Fighting* (which found the band once again recording at Olympic, but with engineer Keith Harwood presiding) possessed more wattage than *Nightlife*. "It was essentially Phil who produced the *Fighting* album, and he wanted to introduce what we were actually playing on stage, rather than just this kind of sterile studio sound that we were getting. But basically, on *Fighting* we still didn't get it. We still didn't get the sound we were looking for. But yeah, essentially that's probably going to be the difference right there, the switch from Ron Nevison to Phil. Plus Robbo and I now had one album under our belts."

"Keith Harwood was a gem, absolute gem," notes Robbo. "Sadly missed, I have to say. I loved the guy to death. He was just a real gentleman, and he had all the ideas. Phil hadn't produced an album in his life before. You know, when it says, 'Produced by Phil Lynott,' no it wasn't. It was really produced by Keith Harwood, with a few ideas from Phil. That's all it was."

Okay, not metal says Scott, but right there in '74, '75, with Sweet, Slade and even Mud capturing eyeballs, had anybody ever pressured Lizzy to jump on the glam bandwagon? "No," laughs Gorham. "Nobody pressured us into doing anything. In fact, the record companies couldn't tell us what to do. Pretty much management couldn't tell us what to do. If we didn't feel comfortable with any aspect of anything, we just didn't do it. So, you know, that whole... I guess we all kind of looked at the glam thing as a joke anyway. And with the makeup and the really sparkly clothes, it just didn't gel with us at all."

"That's one thing we didn't get into," agrees Robbo. "I mean, there was a certain amount of stagecraft that you put on, but as far as the glitter... I mean we all had platform boots and stuff like that but we weren't paedophiles (laughs). Sweet was the only sort of rock band we liked as far as the glittery stuff was concerned. But again, they were pretty good musicians."

Glam for the most part avoided, Vertigo exec Nigel Grainge turned out to be instrumental on moving the band forward, feeling that the guys were due to start delivering a hit or two.

"Yes, well, they went into the album that became *Fighting*, and this was when I really started to exercise some A&R chops, and actually told them it wasn't good enough, and that they had to record more tracks. It was basically learning A&R without any training. As I said, I kind of went into the A&R department, and I was pretty much the only person there, and I had to learn how to be an A&R man without anyone showing me. I didn't work under anybody, so things like negotiations and how to talk to artists... it was total naïveté, where I really had no control at all. It was my reputation now on the line because I signed this band. We'd gotten to a second album and I couldn't just let them do their thing if I was unhappy with it. Because I was going to have to take the rap if nothing happens."

"So they came in with the album, and the whole band were in my office, and it wasn't a big office, so it was cramped. And we played the whole album, and they were looking at me and said, 'What do you think?' And I said, 'Well I've only heard it once, but I'm disappointed.' You know, 'It sounds good. I mean, it's a lot more aggressive than the first album,' which was very kind of laid-back. But there was nothing like a single. And I said, 'You've reached this stage in your career now where you've had your Top Five single with 'Whisky In The Jar', you had your previous incarnation, you've gone through that, you had three albums on Decca, and now a second album on Vertigo, so you really need to take a big forward step, and this isn't taking a big forward step.' And of course, they'd run out of money, and they said, 'Well, what do you want us to do?' And I said, 'I want you to go and write the best four tracks on the album.' And so it kind of worked, because, they didn't say anything, and they left. And really, the best thing that happened was they came in with four of the best tracks on the album."

"One was definitely 'King's Vengeance', but I can't remember the others," continues Nigel, who is said to have rejected one track called 'Christmas', and in general, songs that were "forced" and leaned "mindlessly hard" even while only soft tracks can be found! "I mean, 'Rosalie' was a kind of add-on. That was a Bob Seger song that they decided to do because they wanted 'the' single. It came out as a single, although I didn't really like it very much; I didn't think it was a great version. But I know that 'King's Vengeance' became so big in their live set that it kind of did the job. It kind of gave them a real song for the new format of rock radio that was exploding in America."

"I know we came back with 'Rosalie'," confirms Robbo, wary of much of Nigel's memory of the situation. "Obviously Nigel didn't think anything was on there for a single, so that was the first single that went out from that album. So obviously that's the one we took back to him. I don't think he told us to go away and write a single or whatever. Again, in those days, everybody wanted a single, everybody wanted to be on Top Of The Pops, but we were basically a rock band. Certainly from my point of view, at that time, being a young rocker, I wasn't really interested in Top Of The Pops. I hated it, but obviously Phil and the management had a little bit more suss than I did, and realized that that's going to sell records. I wasn't really thinking about that. I'm just thinking about playing in the band. But we came back with 'Rosalie', and they accepted that as the single."

One fully-fledged '75 track that didn't show up on the album was the R&B-ish 'Try A Little Harder'. "I remember that one very well," notes Robertson, "because I ripped that off from the M*A*S*H song, the TV comedy show about the Korean War, 'Suicide Is Painless'. It was just the opening chords of that, an A minor seventh; I took a bit of that and a little bit of 'Still In Love With You' and stuck it together, and that's how that came about. I guess there were too many different songs floating about, and you've also got to remember, Phil was Phil, you know, and the management were obviously much more into Phil than they were anybody else, so he was the main songwriter as far as anybody was concerned. And I don't think Phil tried a little harder, on 'Try A Little

Harder'. He wanted to do lyrics, so I said yeah, okay, so I stopped working on them. I don't think he worked too hard on it, because he wanted his own songs on there. Because that's where the money is. Simple as that."

Makes sense. "It did to him! It didn't make any sense to us, and I didn't know any better, so there you go."

"I always thought the cover was shit as well," continues Nigel, referring to *Fighting's* UK sleeve, essentially a shot of the band in all their blue-jeaned glory, looking like a street gang. "The North American one was slightly better; it was them in a building site. I think both of them were pretty deadly. But the English one, with them all with their arms folded looking as if they were fighting, it was pathetic."

How did that happen? "It happened because our art department was shit, basically. You know, they were just very old school. It was very hard to actually convey what you were trying to do with an act. It was very disappointing." Famed Vertigo conceptualist Keef by this point was no longer in the building... "Yeah, his work had kind of finished roundabout the time the new art department took over, led by a guy named Jack Wood, 'round about '74."

"*Fighting*, I don't know what happened there," muses Jim Fitzpatrick, asked why after two covers for the band, he was shut out this time. "That was the first time the new Thin Lizzy logo was used on the front of a cover. *Nightlife*, they only used it on the back. You see, record companies, people are changing constantly, and the new guy wants to put his imprint on everything, and I think *Fighting* is one of the most disastrous covers I've ever seen, to be honest, for any band. The guys are standing there with iron bars looking like a bunch of thugs. I fucking hated it. I said to Philip, 'Philip, you've got style. That cover has no style.' But they used the logo for the very first time, anyway, because on *Nightlife* I used that very Roger Dean-ish logo on the front. Because I loved Roger Dean's work – I still do."

"You see, the problem was that a lot of people did Thin Lizzy artwork, but a lot of them were variations of my work," continues Jim. "But like any art department, they want to do their own thing. If you look at all the ads... put it this way, I worked in advertising, and I learned, when you created an image, you applied it right across the board without variation, right? In other words, you gave the subject an image and stuck with it. Thin Lizzy and record companies, they just kept changing all the time. The logo, I created the most beautiful logo of all time, a mirrored version, a metallic version of the logo – it never even got bloody used. So I got very discouraged. The record company would commission this work, and they would never fucking pay, because I never had a written order. Now, I never had a written order in my life. All this kind of crap.

That's why Philip tried to make it up for me by getting me some sort of private work, like doing him and the kids in the garden. Fatalistic Attitude, same story; the record company wouldn't hear of it because it was too serious. You've got people who are being driven by different motives to your own. What they want is an image of the band. They don't want artwork anymore. It's what I call the end of the vinyl period. It was being replaced by photography because photography is much cheaper. But I was getting paid a fortune. Philip used to screw the arse off them to get me money."

Robertson will always remember the photo chosen for the North American version as particularly odd given that it was one of the rare times he had been talked into shaving off his beard. "Yeah, yeah," laughs Brian, as to why he clung vociferously to his beard. "I guess I wanted to look slightly older, because everybody else in the band was slightly older. I basically had bum fluff, really. There were two album covers for that album. The first one, I refused to shave my beard off, and then we did the photo shoot anyway, and the idea was to have all these weapons, which I guess, looking back, was a really stupid idea. It wasn't the only idea. There were some shots taken in the studio where we had a film makeup artist come in and make us look like we'd all been beaten up, but the record company thought it was too gory (laughs). I thought it was brilliant, actually. I didn't have a beard on that session. But you know, Scott had a busted head and I had a bloody nose and a split lip; everybody had something done, but the record company wouldn't go for that one. So the next idea was with the weapons, so to speak, which we had shot in Kensington, as I remember, which is kind of a posh area of London. In the middle of the shoot, because we had a shotgun... as you know, Phil was holding a shotgun up, and somebody phoned the police, and they turned up and tried to arrest us. But the thing was, the shotgun was a prop; it was actually welded shut so you couldn't put cartridges in it. They eventually let us continue with the photo shoot. But it was a bit scary, to be honest."

The title *Fighting* even caused controversy. Noted Phil to *Scene's* Cliff Michalski, "I was amazed how many people came up to us and said, 'You're inciting the kids to fight.' I wasn't. I was just trying to show the young kids feeling powerful, getting strong. It's not unnatural to feel that way for a teenager."

Past the slapdash package and into the music, *Fighting*, issued September 12, 1975, opens with the aforementioned cover of Bob Seger's 'Rosalie'. Previous to the recording of the album, Thin Lizzy embarked upon their first tour of America, playing with the likes of Bachman-Turner Overdrive, ZZ Top, Styx and Detroit's nice guy, Seger himself. Phil was knocked out by the new frontier, Texas in particular fuelling his cowboy convictions, New York and LA intensifying his love of the night life.

Asked where he got the idea to cover 'Rosalie', Phil said that, "Bob Seger, Nils Lofgren and Bob Dylan to me are three artists who all do great versions of their own material, but you can always do a version equally as good. Like the Byrds or the Band always did equally as good versions of Dylan, and the same with Nils Lofgren. Bob Seger strikes me like that. I got his album from a chick I went out with who was from Detroit."

"Like I say, 'Rosalie' was the only commercial – in inverted commas – track, but I didn't think it was good enough," notes Grainge. "And you know, consequently I think the pressure was on them, really, for the third album to deliver." 'Tis true, that although the roots rock of 'Rosalie' supported nicely, maybe even richly, Phil's American side – Seger, of course, but also Springsteen with perhaps a bit of Francine courtesy of ZZ Top – it was a bit old hat, like something from *Vagabonds* or a tarted-up piece of Stonesy crumpet from a past-due glam band, say, perhaps, Mott The Hoople. In any event, one comes to Thin Lizzy, in part, to bask in Phil's songwriting and he didn't write that one.

In fact, 'Rosalie' had been issued as a single (b/w the non-LP 'Halfcaste') a full three months before the launch of the album, just after UK and European tour dates with BTO, a galvanizing time for the band, says Grainge.

"Yes, well, they were kind of consolidating their live show. In fact, one of the things I'd done before I went into A&R and before I signed Lizzy, was BTO. Because I'd gone on the road with Randy Bachman. What happened was, the first album came out, and 'Blue Collar' was becoming a hit in America. I was in America just at the time Randy was about to embark on a radio tour, and I remember going for a full day of radio promo with the Detroit promotion man, spent the whole day with Randy, and we just got on like a house on fire. I came back and made it my mission to break BTO in England. When you had 'You Ain't Seen Nothing Yet' come out, we had a No.1 record with that. When BTO came over to tour, with a hit album, *Not Fragile*, Thin Lizzy were the support act, and they absolutely blew BTO away. Because they had the look and they already had an audience. You know, at least half the audience were coming to see them anyway. Obviously BTO went down well, but they obviously ain't a great-looking band, and Thin Lizzy had all the style and content and attitude and everything. So it was a great tour for them. They really broke the UK on that Bachman-Turner Overdrive tour."

"Phil didn't have to say anything to get us fired up," laughs Robbo, asked about the rumoured drill sergeant tendencies of the boss that had helped turn Lizzy into such a fierce fighting force live. "We were already fired up. We were fired up against anybody, whoever it was that we were supporting. Sort of the premise of the whole thing was, 'Right, let's get on and kick their asses.' That's the way to do it on the road and we spent a lot of time doing exactly that. That kind of made the band more than hit singles or anything. Because, well, we had a couple of hit singles, but not a lot. There wasn't a plethora of No.1s or any of that. It was basically an album band, and live, which of course, doesn't really happen these days (laughs)."

"What I do remember about Philip was, if there was a problem, you were going to solve it," notes road dog Frank Murray (pictured at right), about life on the road with Lizzy. "If you were only partially solving it or you couldn't solve it, if you went in, if you started a sentence with, 'Philip, I can't...' he would stop you in his tracks and say, 'okay, there's no such words as I can't.' He would say that and he'd look at you and you would go, 'Are you serious, man?' He would go, 'Frank, I'm telling you, there's no such...' so you became very good and very skilled at exhausting every avenue of solving a problem, okay? I must say that served me well over the years."

Past 'Rosalie', the initial track on the *Fighting* album, 'For Those Who Love To Live' is possibly the first Thin Lizzy song full up with the chemistry exemplified by these four guys, the classic Thin Lizzy line-up, as it were.

"'For Those Who Love To Live' was kind of a joint effort for the band," recalls Downey, who shares credit on the track with Phil – it is the drummer's only credit on the album. "I think I came up with the suggestion toward the shuffle end of it, the shuffle beat. There were all sorts of tempos being thrown around. I was kind of insistent that we try different tempos, and I think at the end of the day, there were a couple of different takes of that at different tempos. I think at the end of the day I got my way (laughs), so yeah, I think 'For Those Who Love To Live' was basically down to my tempos."

Confirms Robertson, "There was an awful lot of work done by Brian and myself on that because as people probably know, the image of Phil being the big songwriter is actually not true. He would bring the bones of a song to the band, but it was the input from everybody else, and the chemistry from everybody else, that would bring the song to life. Which is why a few of us are a little bit bitter about not being included in the writing credits. And Downey is entirely correct on that. Brian is – was, and is – a very honest man, and he wouldn't say stuff like that unless it was true; I can assure you of that. It wasn't so much the tempo thing – he did an awful lot with the arrangement of the thing. And these days, now, if you arrange a song, you get your publishing. In those days you didn't. So he's entirely correct in that."

All told, the track is a taut jazz rocker, restrained and dark, graced with tasty rhythm playing as well as twin leads, not to mention sweet tom and snare fills from Downey.

"'For Those Who Love To Live' was inspired by the life and times of George Best," explained Phil, back in January of '77, referring to the Northern Ireland football great. "When I met Georgie, I really liked him. There he was, he was going through a bad stage in his career. He'd just gone through that Marjorie Wallace thing. I met him at ma's place and he was really nice. I'd been up and was going down as well, right, and United, the football team – I know it sounds silly, but they were going through bad times too. There was Bestie and he had such dignity, even though he was going down and people were ready to put the boot in. Georgie was still a great man. He was a real boy, and really gave me that vibe that you catch on something like 'The Boys Are Back In Town' – Georgie being a real boy. Being a Jack The Lad. That's the best English term I can catch for it. I always had that character that Georgie Best seemed to give me, you know, 'Fuck it, there you go, Phil. That's football.' It was great. It was just what I needed. I really needed to meet somebody like that then. Stan Bowles is exactly the same. Great character. I know like in their private moments, which I've never seen, they must go through very happy and sad head trips and think about it all, but when on show, in public, they have this great face for everybody. I thought, for those who love to live, why put down somebody just because he enjoyed going out and saying, 'Come on, take the ball off me,' and growing his hair and being a bit cocky and all the time threatening the system. That's the good side I see in Brian Robertson. Well, Bestie really had that down to an art. There were all these chicks running after him, especially in Manchester, and he could handle it really well. It was Georgie's Irish spirit coming through."

But it's the twin leads that propel the track forward, giving it a flash sense of drama. "That's when they both came forward as really great guitarists," agrees Grainge, looking at the *Fighting* experience in general. "Whereas Nevison really didn't capture that at all; they were tentative, because they were both young, especially Brian – they were very timid on that first album. It wasn't until, you know, a good year on the road, a lot of drink, a lot of drugs, a lot of partying, and a lot of attitude and great reviews... it meant that all of a sudden they were expressing themselves. They became a lot flashier, and the difference in guitar style, from the first album to the second album is really quite amazing."

Back to *Fighting's* sequence of events, 'Suicide' is next, and it's a shuffle as well, only now within a decisive heavy rock context. Scott and Brian step it up with the twin leads, turning in their most complete and well-reasoned performance to date, weaving solos that are memorable, lengthy and cogently quasi-Irish. It's track three and the third track in a row featuring proper names, Phil expanding his cast of cagey characters, while borrowing one of Bob Seger's along the way.

Guitarist Andy Gee figures that 'Suicide' is the only Thin Lizzy track on which he perhaps should have received a writing credit. "Yes, I only had input into 'Suicide'," begins Gee. "Because we were in a hotel in Lüneburger Heide and Phil comes in with his bass and says, 'Look, I've just written a song. Can you put a sort of chorus, solo, middle eight to it?' He played me the riff and everything, and we got it straight away. John wasn't even in the room. It was only Phil, Brian and me, in my hotel room, and I listened to what he played and I said, 'Well, how about this?' It was a five-minute thing. He said, 'That's great! Thank you very much.' You know, they went back to their own rooms. We never played it live. We never sort of rehearsed it or anything."

"And then, (laughs), years later, I see 'Suicide' on one of the album covers, and I listened to it. I hear Brian Robertson and Scott playing every note of my solo (laughs), and I'm thinking, oh, listen, you owe me for this one. I remember I was at a gig. I can't remember who was playing, and there weren't that many people in the hall, and it was before the band that started. Suddenly Phil comes in with this whole entourage, like doing the conga kind of thing, like a snake – he was at the front and everybody else had to follow. He must've had 50 hangers-on, sort of coming in, and he spotted me in the corner, and he made a bee-line for me and said, 'Look, I owe you for Suicide,' because he never put my name on it or anything. He said, 'Look, why don't come up to my house, and I'll spot you some recording time. You just have to pay the engineer.' I went to Kew Gardens where his place was, and I'd arranged Nick South, who played with Ellis and Vinegar Joe, Robert Palmer. I arranged him to play bass, and I had Peter Bardens come in the next day to put some keyboards on; I met Caroline, she was really nice. I didn't even see Phil. I had to bring my son along because I just sort of… it must've been around '83 or '84. I'd just got custody of my son. He was keeping himself busy on the lawn and playing with Phil's cricket bats and stuff, keeps himself happy. Caroline asked him in the house as well. She was making us cups of tea. And my singer was sort of in the house just getting a cup of tea, and there was a knock at the door. He opened the door and Phil's there with a couple of his minders on each side (laughs). I didn't get to see him. He didn't even come by and say hello or anything. Danny, my son, told me he saw him, and Chris said he really looked ill, even at that time. He was very bloated and jaundiced and really didn't look well at all. But he wasn't in the house very long, so I don't think things were too good with the marital home.

I was just so under pressure regarding time. I mean, I had to scrape 150 quid together. I managed to do that. I was then offered the master tape and the one-inch tape to buy, and that was another 150 quid, and I had to say, 'I'm sorry guys; I just don't have the money.' I just walked away with a cassette tape of the tracks. It never did get released. I still have the cassette."

"I was so under time pressure, I only went into the kitchen, to be honest," continues Andy, asked how Phil had been living. "I didn't see the rest of the house. But my son said there was a room with a pinball machine, and lots of machines on the walls and stuff where you had to stick an old penny in and it fell through and you got sweets out of it. Ancient sort of games, old machines and stuff on the walls. I also remember... and I got quite upset about this, but he took Phil's cricket bat, and he used it to sort of knock the stumps into the ground and I think he put a few dents in it. I didn't see it because I was in the studio and my son was all quiet and happy outside. Then Caroline asked him in and I didn't see him for an hour. Everything was cool, but when I saw the bat, I felt a bit bad about that. I couldn't really tell him off, because he was only eight or nine (laughs)."

Back to *Fighting* and following 'Suicide', there's yet another Thin Lizzy classic of taste, restraint, desperado rock and twin leads. 'Wild One' adds to Phil's pile of adventure sagas, set to balladic acoustic strumming that evokes images of the Texas outback, perhaps circa ZZ Top's languid *Tejas* album of the following year. Mournful leads of various lengths are placed along the road and Downey gets to make his point as well. 'Wild One' would follow 'Rosalie' as the album's second single, issued a month after the launch of the album, with 'For Those Who Love To Live' as its b-side.

Phil's 'Wild One' lyric draws at least a small measure of influence from The Flight Of The Wild Geese, a phenomena in history whereby Irish soldiers left to fight for continental European armies, through the 16th, 17th and 18th centuries. "The tale of The Wild Geese was a very strong influence on me," explains Phil. "The whole thing was 'Wild Geese, come back, we need you in Ireland. We need your creativity.' You know the way you get, especially living in Ireland sometimes. You think if everybody would only come back, we could do it. We could really get something going, and I was just feeling that. I was just thinking generally about people who had left the country. Anybody that was hip. Like there's an awful lot of really clever Irish people in London, right? The amount of Irish guys there are, hustling on the King's Road is great. They're all deluxe hustlers. Only the cream go away and survive in London. I just thought in the song that it was a terrible waste of talent. The song is really very simple. The lyrics are very simple. 'You go your way and I'll try to follow, and if you change your mind, I'll be waiting here tomorrow.' All the time, 'I' is supposed to represent Ireland. The call of Ireland to its wild ones to come back. That was the idea, but I put it in such a way that it came across as if it was a love song."

As with 'Wild One', Brian Downey is also a big part of hard-rocking side one-closer 'Fighting My Way Back', ersatz title track to the album and yet another character sketch of a wild one, of a hard man. During the explosive punctuations of the chorus, Downey's deft feel is on impressive display, an aspect of his playing that evokes admiring comparisons with Ian Paice as well as Sweet's Mick Tucker. Still, it's a song somewhat nose-wrinkled by a sweet and sour melody, a track cited by those who figure the band hadn't quite found the plot yet, that they were still grasping at creative straws.

"I guess you're right. Ian Paice is a light drummer who packs a punch, and it's kind of the same way with Brian," reflects Scott. "You know, Brian is not like a really heavy stick guy, but there's a ton of dexterity there. He doesn't really need to pound away like a lot of the drummers do. Ian is the same thing. They both have a really good rock feel to them, a lot of finesse. So that's a good point. I hadn't thought of that either. I can see the correlation between the two guys."

"I think he's a secret weapon for anybody," adds Robbo. "He's a very strange drummer. He's jazz-taught, so the way he plays, he's very powerful although he doesn't look it, because he kind of plays from the wrist rather than the arms or the shoulders. As opposed to like Simon Kirke, who I've worked with a lot, from Bad Company. He plays more from the shoulder. But he's very deceptive as well, and both fantastic drummers. But Downey is a one-off, I think, in rock. It just all jelled with us. I mean, even on the early albums before I joined the band, his drumming is completely impressive."

Over to side two and the boys respond with 'King's Vengeance', a spirited and lyrically enigmatic rocker combining acoustics and power chords like the best from the hit album to come the following year. Incidentally, also along the lines of 'Jailbreak' is 'Freedom Song', which bears no little resemblance to 'The Boys Are Back In Town', through singing across chords, through lyric, through placement and style of twin leads. Commented Phil on Freedom Song, "Subconsciously, I'm sure the black or the Irish in me was saying, 'Freedom! Right on, brother.' It could either have been for a man being hung because he was a nigger or a man being hung because he had the wrong faith when all his neighbours had the other one."

"Scott came up with the sort of chords at the beginning of it," recalls Robbo, asked about the track, "you know (sings it), that stuff, and then I put the riff over the top of it. The band changed so much over the period from *Nightlife* to *Fighting*, and then by the time we got to *Jailbreak*, we'd sorted out how we were writing and which direction we were going. It was still a transitional period as far as *Fighting* was concerned. But it was a seminal point where we decided to go in a certain direction, and there were shades of what was to come in *Fighting*, whereas with *Nightlife*, it was just everybody trying to just feel each other out, really."

Elsewhere on side two, there's brooding ballad 'Spirit Slips Away' and Little Feat-styled blues rocker 'Silver Dollar' on which Phil becomes the proverbial pot calling the kettle black! Then there's album closer 'Ballad Of A Hard Man' which is arguably Thin Lizzy's heaviest moment to date, even if it's turned out to be a difficult obscurity. Lyrically speaking, this claustrophobic noisemaker houses a short, shocked portrait of a hard case battling all demonic comers, including heroin.

Sum it up grimly, and like each Thin Lizzy album past, *Fighting* painted quite the dark worldview. And yet, somehow, one always gets the impression the outsider inside of Phil's stories will prevail in the end, or, if physically or psychologically scarred, emerge with a lesson that at minimum builds character.

"Sad things appeal to me much more than happy things," mused Phil. "The main reason I write is to share. Somebody like John Lennon preaches at you and it's great because it forces you into an opinion. Too many people listen to the stereo and think it's God speaking to you. Once it's recorded on wax, they think it's the law, the way it should be. And I like Lennon because he says things you can disagree with. I disagree with him an awful lot, but when he gets it right I go, 'Brilliant.' The only time I'll preach is when I know I'm right; say on ecology or man's injustice to man or a racial thing or Ireland."

"I write mainly to share," continues Phil. "The romantic songs are mostly about being hurt and the hard ones, the rock ones… I write a lot of gang lyrics like 'Showdown' and 'The Rocker' and 'Jailbreak'. When I write fight songs, they're basically because when you're about 14 you get a lot of strength that you don't know what to do with. You're stronger than girls all of a sudden and you've got all this energy. I try to channel it into songs, to show kids that it happens to everybody, that you get these feelings that you want to kick down doors. But I like being melancholy. I like that tinge of the lonely guy. Like Marvel comic heroes, they're admired, and yet behind it all they're a bit sad."

Despite *Fighting* doubling up on the sales of *Nightlife*, this still amounted to a paltry and frankly embarrassing 20,000 units shifted in the band's UK home territory, although an additional bright spot comes with the album being the first for the band to chart, at No.60 in the UK and No.49 in Sweden.

Label, management, the band, heck, the crew... everybody in the Lizzy cabal desperately needed the band to deliver another hit song, a hit album, something to juice the modestly positive trajectory of the band's career. Fortunately for all, Phil would soon unlock a sort of songwriter's Pandora's Box, bestowing upon a ready and eager fan base a tidy number of gleaming anthems – 'The Boys Are Back In Town' at the fore – coalescing upon a flash stash of an album we like to call *Jailbreak*.

7

JAILBREAK

"The guillotine was just hanging over the neck"

The general consensus on Thin Lizzy as 1976 rolled around was that the flash new twin guitar line-up had finally gelled as a live act but still hadn't captured the general public's imagination on record. Fair enough – *Fighting* was a cynical, intimate, dark album. Not exaggeratingly so in any of those directions, but sip in the wee hours without hope a little of all three, and what comes out the other end is a vague downer.

A change of environment was in order, the lads finding themselves at The Who's Ramport Studios in Battersea, South London with John Alcock as producer. Alcock was part of the Who camp but mainly as producer for John Entwistle as a solo act, and not much of note after Lizzy save for maybe The Runaways. Amidst the album's recording sessions, on February 12th, Phil's father Cecil had made arrangements to meet his son for the first time. The conversation did not go well and Phil rarely discussed the relationship throughout the rest of his life.

In conversation with American entertainment weekly *Scene*, Phil provided a survey of the band's production woes leading up to the hiring of John Alcock. "When we did *Nightlife*, it was the first time in the studio for Scott and Brian. I co-produced it with Ron Nevison, and he wound up being very heavy on the two lads; they both said no way for the next one. We tried to get Roy Thomas Baker; he knows how to get a good guitar sound. But we couldn't get him, so I said I'd do it myself. But with writing songs, singing, playing bass and producing, it all got to be too much. In the end, I let my vocal slip; I saved them until last and I was rushing them. So *Fighting* suffered a bit; it was too much for one person to do in a month. So on this one we figured we'd go for a co-producer, but when it came to doing the sleeve notes, John Alcock's name was the only one listed, even though it was a partnership."

"Probably panic," laughs Scott Gorham, recalling the mood

surrounding the January and February '76 sessions that would result in the *Jailbreak* album. "Oh god yeah, we were desperate for a hit! You know, we knew it was make-or-break time, there's no doubt about that. Back then it was, you got three albums and on the third one you were supposed to do it. The first one is kind of a, 'okay everybody, this is who we are,' the second one is the album where you're supposed to learn your craft and how to record an album, write songs and all that, and the third one, you've got all that under your belts, now you've got to produce the goods. And obviously today it's totally different. You've got to get out there on your first one and have a hit straight off the bat. But we're on our third album, and management comes in, 'This is it; we need a hit off of this.' Record company's saying the same thing. At this point, you know, I wouldn't call it panic, but we knew that the guillotine was just hanging over the neck."

"So what we did is we rented this little, kind of a farm situation. I wouldn't call it a studio, but it had a big room in the back so we could take our eight-track Teac machine with us, and just put up one microphone, with everybody, and just... we stayed there for about two or three weeks, just writing and recording these things, and writing and recording, rehearsing. And so after three weeks, I think we came up with 15 songs. At this point, you know, you can only put ten tracks on an album, just because of time and quality-wise. You can only get so many minutes per side on an LP, so we whittled it down to ten that we thought were the ones that we were going to record. But that's when Chris O'Donnell drove down; he was the manager, right? One of them, one half of the management, and he was the one who said let me have a listen to what you guys are doing here. He listened to all 15, and read the tracks that we'd picked out, and he said, 'You know this song you've got here...' I don't think it even had a title at that point. Or it wasn't cast in stone. And he says, 'Let's just call it The Boys,' right? 'This song, The Boys, you have here – how come you don't have this on the list?' And we just kind of go, 'Well, you know, it just... we don't know. I mean, do you like it?' 'Yeah, I'd actually like to see you record this one instead of this one here that you picked.' And that's sort of how 'The Boys Are Back In Town' made it onto the album."

"Not a lot," laughs Scott, responding to the question of John Alcock and his contribution to the process. "You know, I hate to... he didn't impress me at all, with the production. And I don't think he impressed the rest of us either. John was brought in because he was a big guy, six-foot-four, a big imposing figure, and you know, management thought they needed somebody in there as an imposing figure to keep us down. Because we would get in the studio and just do all sorts of crazy-ass shit, and I think they just figured that if they get this guy in, he's just going to stand up and everybody's going to cower back and do whatever this guy demanded. And right from the first day, Phil put his foot down and said, 'That shit ain't gonna happen.' And this guy just sat back down and we just went on and kept doing what we were doing. Sound-wise, I listen to the album, and I just don't think it's of quality at all."

"We went away and did some writing for *Jailbreak* rather than just did it in the studio," confirms Robbo, giving his general view on the record. "So we did some pre-rehearsals or whatever. It was probably the first album we did sort of demos and such for. It probably shows a bit more on that album that it was considered more before it was taken into the studio."

On the subject of the album's brighter production butted up against the antiquity browns of *Fighting*, Brian figures, "Well, Phil produced *Fighting* along with Keith Harwood, who was the engineer. And then *Jailbreak* we had John Alcock; it was different years, different studios; we were using The Who's studio which is a different pool of fish. John, he just basically had fresh ears and got it recorded right. That was the main thing. You know, at that point I wasn't really into the production side as I obviously was later on. I was really in there as a musician. And in fact, John Alcock didn't hardly touch the mixing desk (laughs). He just sat there and told Will Dick, the engineer, what he wanted, which I found kind of strange, to be honest. Not at the time, but I do now, because I'm very hands on. I like to get my hands on the desk, play with the microphones, focus the microphones and whatever. John didn't do a lot of that, so he was using the technical abilities of Will Reid Dick. Phil wasn't touching desks either (laughs). But I mean, obviously, you don't have to be on top of the desk to produce somebody. If you've got an engineer there that you trust, and can translate what you're saying to them, there's no reason you should be all over the place."

'Tis true that *Jailbreak* is not a monster, sonically speaking. If *Nightlife* was a bit small, and *Fighting* a bit too round and old school, *Jailbreak* tends to lack in bottom end, a slight flaw exacerbated by the extremely tight playing, a single-minded performance that is to the point of constriction.

"Once again, it was a case of all of us throwing our opinions in," says Scott, asked who really was doing the heavy lifting on the production end of things. "I think probably Phil more than any of us, because Phil was a lot more opinionated at the time. He thought he knew more of what he wanted and what he wanted to hear. You know, John also; he was definitely the producer on those two albums, but there were a lot of suggestions from the back bench too, about how we wanted things to go."

"I think there was more confidence with all of us," adds Scott, on the band's maturity level at this juncture. "All of us were contributing at that point. We had been on the road for, I guess about two years. After you've been together for two years and you've played on the road for that long, your sort of interaction with each other is a lot easier. With the first two albums, everybody was still kind of eyeballing each other, trying to find their place within that little space there. I think by the time *Jailbreak* came around, your space was pretty well defined. So it made things a lot easier; things came easier. People were more apt to take suggestions a lot easier."

If one might surmise that the production as well as the level of performances on *Jailbreak* is sharper, more in focus, shinier, than the sum total of *Fighting*, one could also apply this sentiment to the literary and visual aspects of the record. Neither *Fighting* nor *Jailbreak* are concept albums about rogues per se, yet both are loosely in that place, *Jailbreak*, slightly more tightly.

"It's funny you say that," says Scott, "because in the beginning, the very beginning, it was probably in Phil's mind going to be a concept kind of an album, right? You can see with the artwork that Jim Fitzpatrick did, the alien thing, and Phil had written a song 'Jailbreak', to kind of fit in with all that. And there were all the liner notes on the back. But that's as far as the concept got (laughs). It's kind of a one song concept."

Yet the album is full of characters, many of them designated by name... "Well, that's how Phil liked to write. He liked to keep everything extremely colourful. You just can't say that Phil was a dull guy. You could even see it in his lyric writing. His head was kind of constantly spinning, coming up with these different ideas, different characters, different situations."

"No, no, absolutely none," is Brian Robertson's take on whether the album housed a concept. "I mean, the album cover was the album cover. I guess you could say it looks like that sort of album, but it certainly was not written and recorded as a concept album, no."

Illustrator Jim Fitzpatrick leans further than both Scott and Brian into the idea of *Jailbreak* being conceived as a concept album. "It was, yes, and it was around the time of concept albums, which were coming to the fore. There was a great concept album that disappeared beyond trace called *White Mansions* that we liked. Don't forget, toward the end of that conceptual album movement, after *Jailbreak*, was *War Of The Worlds*, which has endured; an extraordinary concept album. But *Jailbreak*, he had these great ideas, and he wanted to tie in the whole text. Black Rose was a concept album too. We were doing all these allegorical references to Cuchulain and stuff. But *Jailbreak* was more pronounced. I wrote a lot of text for the back of it, as I did for the sleeve notes for Black Rose. But it was my job to sort of wield that thing into a cohesive whole. The idea of the cut-out on the front cover was something Philip fought tooth and nail for. In America it was simply a flat album, but in Europe it was a gatefold. And being an artist, I loved gatefolds (laughs). When people asked me to design a CD cover I think, oh yeah, right. They'll ask me to do a postage stamp next. But vinyl covers… to be alive and to see your work in shop windows en masse – I've got photographs of them – it was the biggest thrill of all. Much bigger thrill than being in the Louvre or something. This was on every corner you turned; there was your album in the window."

"The concept of *Jailbreak* was this sort of time lord," continues Jim. "I suppose it was influenced by Dr. Who, a time lord overseeing all of our… he was a bit like God, overseeing all our foibles. We were both reading *War Of The Worlds* at the time, and there was a comic also, by Marvel, based on *War Of The Worlds*. I think was called Killraven, going on memory. And that had a huge influence on us. We used to hang out in his flat smoking dope and reading comics, and I would say, 'Geez, this Killraven is really well drawn,' and he'd be saying, 'Oh, I don't like that guy's work; I like this guy's work.' 'I like the way those tripod Martians are drawn.' That came out of those conversations. He was into an HG Wells kind of album, is a better explanation. Of course Dr. Who was on television, and he was a time lord, so there was all that stuff coming in; there was a quasi-religious aspect to it as well."

Apply that art and that storyline to the explosive proto-metal opener of the record at hand and you've got a loud world that sticks to the memory circuits. *Jailbreak* finds the band's many subtle talents draped over the frame of a riff that is the band's 'Smoke On The Water', 'Whole Lotta Love' and 'Iron Man'. There's also an exciting break that is literally a break, a cinematic portrayal in sound of the cads and rascals – conceivably those all over the *Fighting* album and/or those from this album's smash hit – smashing their way out of jail. Just for good measure, Brian whacks a little wah-wah into it, but it is the cascading melody of the chorus (and interestingly not so much twin leads) that threatens to overpower the riff for control of the memory banks.

"I think somewhere, along the line, he found his niche on that one," muses Brian Robertson solo album co-producer Søren Lindberg, asked about the guitarist's preoccupation with wah-wah. "Yet he doesn't play the same as a lot of other players do. A lot of people just stamp on the thing and it goes 'wah-wah' whereas Robbo is more… he's got his foot on the wah-wah all the time, and uses it for various different sounds and not just the wah-wah. It could be a slow one, a quick one, a long one, a short one. I think he's kind of refined the technique very much over the years. I know that Scott was using a wah-wah at a certain point, so I can't really tell you exactly whether it's all Robbo throughout the catalogue, but from '74 to '78, I would say that at least 95% is Robbo."

Asked to distinguish further between Robertson and Gorham as guitarists, Lindberg ventures that, "They are totally different guitar players with totally different backgrounds. You have the obvious: one is American and one of them is from the UK. So Robbo had grown up on British blues, John Mayall And The Bluesbreakers, Jimmy Page and all that. Scott grew up on American bands and an American style of playing. If you're talking about the years '74 to '78 when the boys played together, Rob had an edgier yet still bluesier style than Scott, at the time. Even though I think Scott developed, maybe, more than Robbo. Robbo was already there in '74 while Scott was still learning. So toward the end of their stint together, I think it started to sound pretty cool, as you hear on *Live And Dangerous*, where Scott has matured, and like I say, Robbo already had it. But to compare the two, I would say that Robbo is much more a product of classical training, and he's got the blues, whereas Scott is very much so a self-learned guitar player – he can do some weird things, because he doesn't really know the rules (laughs)."

Yet over at the equipment side of things, both guitarists were essentially faithful to the Gibson Les Paul. "If you would ask Robbo, he could tell you exactly what he was using on this album and that album, but for the majority of us, you can't really hear the differences there," notes Søren. "But yes, Robbo's always been a Les Paul man, and always will be, even though some things that were actually done in the studio were recorded on a Fender Stratocaster, which I suppose a lot of people don't know. One of his most famous solos, on 'Don't Believe A Word', is actually a Fender Stratocaster, which everybody actually thinks is typical Les Paul, but it wasn't. As for Scott, you know the story. When he turned up to audition for the band, he had a horrible, horrible Japanese Les Paul copy. So obviously they realized straightaway, if he's going to be part of the band, we're going to have to get him a proper guitar. Scott stayed with the same guitar all the way through with Lizzy. Obviously, if we're talking about the era after Robbo was in the band, he used some other guitars as well, recording-wise. But never on stage though. It's that very classic Les Paul guitar that you see in all the pictures of Thin Lizzy. Funny story though, which I heard years later, when Scott actually had that guitar repaired recently, like five or ten years ago or something, the guy who repaired it actually told me that wow, this isn't really what Scott thinks it is. Because it had been doctored, obviously before he bought it back in 1974. There's a big piece of wood in there that shouldn't be there. So basically it's been fixed, probably from some accident or something. The actual wood has been tampered with."

Back to *Jailbreak* tracks, 'Angel From The Coast', somewhat relegated to obscurity, nonetheless demonstrates the band's deft rhythm section skills, along with chemistry, sophistication and versatility in the twin lead department. 'Running Back' adds an extra level of charm to the band's growing canon, evoking the melodies of Van Morrison or more so Bruce Springsteen.

"He loved Elvis," notes Scott, "but Van Morrison he really loved, probably a little more. He'd like Van Morrison way more than he liked Elvis, just because Van was Irish, and when Van would get in to write a song, he would really write a story. He was also a storyteller, so I imagine, now that you're talking about it, the Bruce Springsteen thing, he liked Bruce Springsteen because he was a storyteller also. I know later on, he did like Bruce."

'Angel From The Coast' would show up as the b-side to 'Cowboy Song', launched as a single in Canada and the US. 'Running Back' would be the b-side to the UK launch of 'Jailbreak' as a single. As regards the title track, its slow seep into the consciousness of North American classic rock would be accelerated by it in turn being used as the b-side to smash single 'The Boys Are Back In Town', subconsciously causing the two songs to be linked together as a sort of mini concept suite, over and above any linkage either of them had with 'Cowboy Song'.

On the subject of the growing inventiveness of his and Scott's twin leads, Robertson figures, "That just sort of happened gradually and it was a total accident. It just happened that one song had a bit on it and the next song we had a bit more. It went album by album. I think it really started to happen on *Fighting*, which was the second one we did."

Mention Allman Brothers and Wishbone Ash, and Brian says, "Yeah, yeah. I mean, I listened to the albums and Wishbone, I even had some of their albums. I definitely listened to them but if that was a subliminal thing that I took on with me, I don't know. I don't think it was actually; I think it was just more of a case of a patent. I know that some people wish that there was this great big story behind it but there isn't. It's something that develops organically. There was twin lead around before Lizzy, but probably not quite as melodic, and as you say, the Allman Brothers Band were doing it a long ways before Thin Lizzy was doing it (laughs). I don't think there is a seminal moment that can explain it. But if you listen back to the first album we did, *Nightlife*, there wasn't a lot of twin lead on that. It really progressed on the *Fighting* album; that's where it came to fruition a bit more."

The crafting of 'Running Back' was one of the early but larger points of contention in Robertson's relationship with the band – although mainly with Phil – that would give the lads pause that he was just too much of a handful to last as part of the fold. Says Robbo, "I didn't actually play on 'Running Back' on *Jailbreak*, because I had an argument with Phil about how it should be done. I wanted to do blues, and I was in the studio playing boogie piano and whatnot. And he just pressed the button and said, 'No, no, we're not doing it that way.' So I said, right, then you're not even giving me a chance. So fuck you, basically (laughs). And I walked out of the studio and him and Scott got the track down, and of course it's very much a pop song, the way they did it. I love the song, but I didn't like the way they did it. That's Scott's guitar, and it sounds like a banjo, you're right (laughs)."

Robbo mentions piano there, and that was also a point of contention, namely, that he was never really allowed to play any keyboards with Lizzy, even though he could. "Well, he could just kind of get by," counters Gorham. "But I was always pretty amazed that he could play keyboards anyway in the first place. In fact, the first time I saw him do it, I thought holy crap, this cat plays really good guitar and the fucker can play keyboards?! (laughs). But he wasn't an amazing, accomplished keyboard player, but if you asked him to do something, sort of medium simple, he could provide it; he could do it. But if there was something, say a keyboard thing we needed on the album that was a little more complicated, we would actually rent in somebody to do the gig. On the new deluxe edition of *Jailbreak*, there's a song that I wrote called 'Song For Jesse' (a.k.a. Scott's Tune) and Brian is actually playing the piano on that, and I think he did a really good job on it."

"I did a few bits and pieces," says Robbo. "But generally Phil didn't like me playing keyboards, because, I don't know, he probably just wanted me to concentrate on guitar. So you generally had people come in and do the keyboards, which kind of annoyed me sometimes. I thought well, why are we paying this guy shitloads of money when I could do it? I don't have that problem now; I can do what I want (laughs)."

But it was more so the blues approach to 'Running Back' that was important to Robbo (although 'Running Back' did include a guest keyboard player, one Tim Hinkley). "Well, yeah, I've always grown up with jazz and blues, Peter Green being my hero guitar player, in Fleetwood Mac. I did try to get the blues in there quite a lot. So yeah, I did a blues version of 'Running Back' on my solo album. We played with ZZ Top quite a lot; well, not quite a lot, but a fair few gigs with them. I'm a big ZZ fan anyway, from the early stuff, *La Grange* and whatnot. I first heard that when I was touring in Texas, I think, which wasn't with ZZ. I heard it at a truck stop and thought, 'Wow, that's great, I like that.' But I didn't consciously put that into my playing."

As for Scott's take on the 'Running Back' row, "You know, at that point, I don't think he actually wanted to do it a different way – I think he didn't have a different way of doing it at all at that point. He just didn't want to play on it. I mean, now, thinking back, it was probably that song that spelled the end for Brian, or at least it sowed the seeds. You just can't refuse to play on a song. I mean, if you don't like it, go ahead and voice your opinion, but he actually refused to play on it, and that just really doesn't work. But I've heard the version that he's done lately – it's actually pretty good."

Next up on the album was another track doomed to become no more than a deep album track. 'Romeo And The Lonely Girl' was sprightly and light like 'Angel From The Coast' and Phil got some stick for his playful rhyming. But again, there was storytelling and there were characters, Thin Lizzy's incubator of outsiders growing by the tune.

Side one of *Jailbreak* finds the band churning up the dust of another heavy classic, 'Warriors' also lyrically feeding a conceptual view of the album. Scott Gorham gets co-credit for songwriting with Phil, the trend being built that we would be seeing much more Gorham in the mix than Robertson.

"Well, it's the same thing," says Scott on the process, not taking too much credit onto himself. "You have a lot of guitar bits, riffs, choruses, verses, all that, and when we got together, everybody just started to include these things together. 'Well, I've got a bit for that one over there; let's try this over here.' You know, that's basically how the album came about. I don't think there was any really one particular song where the whole song was completely written."

As to why he is listed more often than Robbo, Scott figures, "Well, Phil and I would always be up at his place, and grab acoustic guitars and sit there and just batter ideas back and forth. We worked a lot of the albums like that, without the band being around the whole thing, the whole kafuffle of drums and trying to get guitar sounds and all that. He and I would just sit around his living room, in London, and just grab acoustics and start batting ideas back and forth with each other."

So perhaps Scott's ideas had an advantage because Phil was usually there for the germination of the idea, feeling some sense of ownership... "Yeah, I guess so. I mean, that sounds kind of sinister (laughs). Well, the thing was, with any of our songs, even if you wrote it, it was a given that you had to collaborate with Phil because he was the lyricist. Nobody got a look in on writing the lyrics, except for Phil. You know, that was fine with me, because I just felt he was an amazing lyricist anyways, and who was I to try and top anything that he could come up with? So I was perfectly okay with that. Now with Brian Robertson, I don't know, maybe he wasn't okay with that. I never really asked him that question. But even though you don't get sort of writing credits, we were all in there throwing the bits in, throwing harmony guitar things in. Everybody was throwing this suggestion and that suggestion. So really, it spans the whole thing. Even though Phil would write and say, 'Listen, I've got this song,' it would be this real skeletal kind of thing. That's when everybody would jump in and just fill the whole thing out and pretty much finish the song off."

"Well I think that's fairly well documented for me," notes Robertson, meaning his dissatisfaction with the amount of credits he chalks up within the Lizzy canon. "I think it was a bit of a travesty, the whole thing, as far as publishing and writing is concerned. Because you reckon a song wasn't just coming up with... in those days, if you wrote three chords and the lyrics, that was it. Nowadays it's different. If you do an arrangement, you get a third of the track, right? And also, I was so young - all I liked to do was play guitar. So I didn't know you were making money from publishing, not just from royalties and whatever. So I'm a bit bitter about that, but hey, it's water under the bridge. I don't do that anymore (laughs). I think Phil knew quite well what he was up to. I mean, how can't you, when you've got a million pound house while the boys are all renting flats? (laughs). No, he knew. Basically the situation was that there wouldn't be any band without him, so the management kind of kept him sweet. All the time. Hey, I can understand that. I don't particularly feel too bitter about it. You live and learn, and you learn the hard way, but there you go."

Side two opener 'The Boys Are Back In Town' would be the world-beating hit single that would take the *Jailbreak* album to all-important gold status in the US (for sales of 500,000 copies), the first and last time Thin Lizzy would ever reach that plateau.

"'The Boys Are Back In Town' was just a pretty basic verse chord pattern that Phil had," explains Scott, "and that's when myself and Robbo just kind of jumped on it and started putting in all the extra guitar bits and all that. Downey put a shuffle kind of groove on there which threw us into another direction. That was going on, where you would have a chord pattern or line or something and suddenly someone else would start to play on it and they would throw you in a completely different direction, using the same chord pattern.""

The song indeed lives and breathes by its yearning chord structure and not built on riffing so much, although the hooky twin leads are so insistent and defined, one must consider them riffs. The melody and the vibe and the story... very much a Springsteen thing there, and truth be told, the song benefited from the chatter of such comparisons. There's also the call and response of the chorus, Phil and then a gang vocal both calling out the title, plain and simple.

Interestingly though, Robertson, also a bit of a singer himself, says that, "the backing vocals I did with Lizzy, were mainly done live. Not so much in the studio. Because Phil usually covered all that. His voice is pretty distinctive and so it was a lot tighter. He knew what he wanted, and he had quite a strange way of going for the harmonies. He just didn't sing straight harmonies. He sang some pretty strange stuff; it was pretty cool. And then Scott and I would take those parts over live."

On press comparisons to Springsteen, Phil mused that, "It happened for a while... until they saw me. No way could they compare an Irish man with some guy from New Jersey. I mean, what can I say? I really dig Bruce Springsteen, we work in the same area, he does a street thing and I do an urban city thing. It's just man songs – as opposed to writing songs for girls, it's for the lads. That's the only similarity I can think of. In America, stories get syndicated, so obviously people read about it and reporters kept asking me about it and from then on I was defending myself. I didn't mean it; I took it as a compliment. If somebody thought I was actually ripping the geezer, I give them a dig in the mouth. I used to get interviewers who would say, 'Were you influenced by him?' I'd say no. Then they'd say, 'Were you subconsciously influenced by him?' How the fuck can I answer that question? I mean, if somebody asked me about 'Running Back' off the *Jailbreak* album, the chorus lines are all derived from the years I spent listening to Van Morrison; nobody asked me about that. I mean, 'The Boys Are Back In Town', I wasn't even thinking about Springsteen. It was an angle; the guy had been through so much, maybe he needed the publicity. No seriously, it didn't bug me, but it became the most boring question I was asked and the question I was asked the most."

Robbo intimates that, like Phil, around this time he had also been toying with solo album plans. "Yeah, I had a different idea at that time. I basically wanted to do a whole album of me just playing all the instruments. It's just something that was stuck in my head at the time. But obviously, with Lizzy you didn't get time to do that. Because the minute you finished recording you were straight back out on the road. So there was no time to get into all that. It would be a lot easier for me to do now and do all the instruments, because you've got your computers and everything. So you can make sure that everything is in time and whatnot."

"I wasn't real single-orientated in those days," continues Robertson, exempting himself from the debate over whether 'The Boys Are Back In Town' should have prevailed over the lighter and less choppy 'Running Back' as *Jailbreak's* first single. "I just wanted to play lead solos everywhere (laughs), which you can't do on singles, you know what I mean? All of those decisions were left to management or the record company and Phil. We obviously passed comment, but it's pretty obvious that 'The Boys Are Back In Town' has the hardest hook. And for the time, that stuck out as the one to do. But yes, production-wise, in hindsight, yes, you're right, saying the album is a little too midrange. It lacked a bit of bottom end to it. But I guess that's why they brought in John Alcock, because he does have that sort of ear where it was more for radio than anything. That's why it's all mid, really. Because in those days you only had mono radio, so you had to do mono mixes for the radio as well. So I think I agree with you on that. When we got to Johnny The Fox, it wasn't quite as midrange as *Jailbreak*; *Jailbreak* was more of a commercial album, and I think that reflected in the mix. Because, like I say, in those days, you've got to do everything for radio (laughs), so I think that probably had some sort of influence on the production. And that's probably why I like Johnny better; it probably wasn't as commercial, but it gave us a lot more scope."

"John was on the short list of producers for the *Jailbreak* album," adds Downey, on the producer who would be with the band for two albums in a row, "and we picked him because of his pedigree. He had a bit of experience under his belt and we knew that, and he also knew the studio, which is Ramport Studios in Battersea. He knew the studio, he knew the guys who owned it, he knew some of the guys from The Who, and he also knew the engineer, which was a really handy way to approach it. So we asked him to do it and he accepted. We knew his pedigree, we had a good rapport with him, and we went in and absolutely no problems. We had a great sense of, 'Let's get this done fairly quickly,' because John seemed to know the ropes from the word go. He got a great drum sound there for me. I was very pleased with it, no real problems. The guitar sounds came fairly easy, and don't forget, it was a really good studio, a well-equipped studio for that time. The Who owned it, and we were under no illusions. We knew we had to get in there and play ourselves, but what happened was, we knew the studio was equally as good as us, and once that happens, that's half the battle. We knew that we had to honestly get in there and do the takes to the best of our abilities, but John encouraged us to do that, along with ourselves. We were well up for it. We were well versed on that album, and we knew what we had to do. John encouraged us to get the best possible sound that he could for us in the studio, and he was just there all the time as a rock. He was very helpful, no problems, never had an argument or anything like that. There weren't any problems in that respect. So I found that album kind of easy to play. Because as I say, we were well versed and there were no problems in the studio. It went really smoothly."

Back to the track that would break the boys on radio, Phil McNeill, reviewing 'The Boys Are Back In Town' in the NME, called it, "*a lilting Phil Lynott song, radiating warmth and hooliganism sung by the man who is heir to Van Morrison's Irish soul, cascading words over a tricky eight-bar line, each one a different picture.*"

Addressing this fortuitous choice of single, Downey recalls that, " 'The Boys Are Back In Town' was one of a few. *Jailbreak* was another contender to be a single. But ultimately, it came down to one of the record company people that was hanging around the studio. They always liked the sound of 'The Boys Are Back In Town'. There wasn't anything wrong with the rest of our judgments either. We liked it, but we weren't exactly sure which one to actually pick for a single. 'Running Back' was another one that was knocked around as a candidate for a single. But at the end, one of the record company people who happened to come down to listen, he came back with the idea that maybe that should be the single. It just happened to be that when we went to the meeting, I think they considered 'Boys Are Back In Town' was more commercial than the rest of the songs that we had in contention. I mean, I thought personally 'Jailbreak' at one stage could've been the single. It's one of those songs that sounded more commercial than 'The Boys Are Back In Town' (laughs). But how wrong can you be? (laughs). But I think 'The Boys Are Back In Town', having listened to it over the years, with the shuffle beat and the quick-fire lyrics, it just escaped us at the time, but there again, the record company were seriously very impressed with it, and we went and abided with their judgments."

"Of course, when 'The Boys Are Back In Town' came in, it was like, what the fuck's this?!" remembers Nigel Grainge. "It was amazing. So they really delivered on that third album. I mean, there was never really any disagreement that that was going to be a single. I can't remember if it was the first single off the album. I can't imagine that it wouldn't have been. But I was getting busy at the time. I had signed 10CC, I had signed Steve Miller, so we were having a lot of success. The company was really happening. We were also having a lot of American success, with R&B things, that I was sort of in the middle of too. So my day wasn't 100% concerned with Thin Lizzy. I was really tied up with the acts I was working on. But when this came in, obviously we were thrilled, and it really exploded."

"The big millstone we had all the way through was Mercury," continues Grainge, referring to the label that was issuing Thin Lizzy product in the US and Canada. "They were appalling. It was just like dealing with the town hall – just clueless. Funnily enough, very good people worked there, in terms of the promotion people, marketing people; not so much the marketing people, but certainly the press people and the promotion guys, were fantastic. But they were overruled by heads of the company who just fixed their priorities and were clueless. Mercury was 100% wholly-owned, bought by Philips, and it was owned by Phonogram. So basically it was a company that ran out of Chicago that was owned by Philips. Basically we were the rest-of-world distributor for their records. We automatically had the right, and in turn, they had the right of first refusal for anything that we put out. Which is why they automatically got off of Thin Lizzy. They released *Fighting*, but Chris and Chris had had the same kind of complications of personality and belief that I had had, and we just felt they didn't have a clue how to promote them properly. And this is a recurring problem I've had with virtually any act I signed. Certainly had it with Graham Parker, where they didn't have a clue, and also had another problem later with Boomtown Rats, with Mercury. Where they would not listen to us, with our ideas, of how to promote them. They had nothing like any kind of new wave or punk acts to work with. They were just stuck in this kind of American bland FM format of working things."

"As I said, it was a question of relating," continues Grainge, asked specifically what was wrong with the way the band was marketed stateside. "We just felt that the marketing was just badly handled. Copy lines of the adverts were pathetic. It was very old-fashioned thinking, very normal, very staid. There was nothing modern about the way it was being presented, and it was just being… you knew the things they were pressing the buttons on and it certainly wasn't Thin Lizzy."

Yet still, 'The Boys Are Back In Town' was a hit, as was the record's title track, as was second to last track on side two 'Cowboy Song', another middle volume yet spirited rocker with a sing-song twin lead. One trivia note, the deluxe reissue of *Jailbreak* includes an early version of 'Cowboy Song', provisionally (spontaneously?) entitled 'Derby Blues', said work-in-progress containing some alternate lyrics.

Elsewhere on the second side of *Jailbreak* there's bluesy ballad 'Fight Or Fall' – again, the deluxe edition includes an alternate version, this one extended studio, and with extra guitar licks and R&B-ish ad-libs from Phil. All told, it's a somewhat mournful ballad, very much a *Fighting*-style track, another lighter *Jailbreak* moment politely put aside, allowing for the flashier and more electric material to shine – and shine the light on a purpose for Thin Lizzy right to the end.

Closing the album is the masterful 'Emerald', a triumphant concoction mixing heavy rock with Irish folk, somewhat a precursor to Black Rose and, as NME's Phil McNeill called it, "*a pulverizingly violent piece that crescendos into a positive military assault by a battery of guitars and drums.*" Explains Downey, " 'Emerald' came about because we were into Irish traditional music. There's a certain instrument called the bodhran here in Ireland, an acoustic instrument that people play, folk musicians, traditional musicians. It has a sort of raw, ethnic feel to it. It sounds like a tom-tom that can be tuned as you play it. So lots of guys play it with the 6/8 feel, because most traditional songs are played in a good 6/8 or 3/4 format. So I tried to get the 6/8 feel on 'Emerald', even though it's in 4/4 (laughs). I knew I had to do it, because we wanted to get a Celtic – and especially a Gaelic Celtic – feel to it, which was obviously an Irish feel.

"The whole idea behind the 'Emerald' song was this mythological thing that Phil was going through at the time. We remember our lessons from school, Cuchulain, and all the mythological heroes that were around in Irish mythology in school, and Phil came up with this great lyric that had connotations of some of the stuff we were learning in school from way back, and he wanted to put this into a song. So yeah, I remembered this traditional beat that was happening, but I wanted to put my own inflection on it, which became the tom-tom part in 'Emerald', where it goes from one part of the song into this instrumental part, with the dual guitars as well, which take over. The drums obviously laid in with this fairly ethnic-sounding beat. So that was the whole idea behind that, and that's what my contribution to that song was. I came up with the idea of maybe putting a bodhran feel to it, and that's what happened."

"Philip was totally into the whole Irish thing," adds artist Jim Fitzpatrick. "Philip was a very, very strongly patriotic Irishman. I used to have arguments with him because I'm a pacifist and I felt that the whole Provo… you know the Provisional IRA Campaign was a disaster, but he was a great admirer of the people involved, Bobby Sands, the people who died in the hunger strikes and all that, and we would have slight arguments about it. Because I would take the piss out of him a bit. Not about Bobby Sands, but about his attitude towards him. I thought there was another way forward, but he was very, very into being Irish, and very proud of it too. It was only later that he began to really look at his black roots and realized that there was a whole avenue there. Because I was a fanatic. When we would go over to Vertigo, I remember, we would go down to the basement; I had a special carrier bag, leather, that was square, the you can shove full with albums (laughs), and we used to go down and loot the place. But I would be taking Little Walker and Howlin' Wolf and all that sort of Mississippi blues shit. This was manna from heaven for me. You didn't get stuff like that in Dublin. Philip would say, 'What are you getting that stuff for?' I would say, 'These are the real black artists. These are the men that rock 'n' roll came from.' Rock 'n' roll was a white phenomenon – Bill Haley And The Comets and Elvis Presley – but it came from black roots. It has to be taken back there. I was blacker than Philip. I mean, the whole black movement… in America now, in America, there's equality. There's Oprah, we have things happening like Obama that we could never have imagined in our lifetime. But like the year I left school, that was the year that you had the riots in Little Rock. Where they had to send in the American army.

So black students could go to white schools. And we identified with them, because we had the same problem with being Irish and you know, our history here of 800 years of oppression."

Noted Phil, in conversation with Harry Doherty, "On 'Emerald', I wanted the war raging in Ireland, the violence. I was just thinking of a generalization. It was just to show that violence has been going on for years. You could almost relate it to any period of time. There's a part in the song where you hear the nice side of the Emerald Isle, the nice melody, then it's back into the battle of the guitars. It's really a very simple concept."

Touring for the *Jailbreak* album would first find the band traversing the UK, supported by Graham Parker and the Rumour, an act with which Thin Lizzy signer Nigel Grainge would soon be involved. Post-UK, the band hit the US for the second time, April through June '76, playing with the likes of Rush, Be Bop Deluxe, Golden Earring, Aerosmith, Slade, The Tubes, Pavlov's Dog, Charlie Daniels Band, Journey, Nazareth and the Ian Gillan Band.

"They were really good mates of ours, actually, and still are," recalls Robbo of Rush. "Really good times with the band. They liked to party a lot. I mean, obviously not as much now; they've all grown up and whatnot. As I say, I haven't really, but there you go (laughs). But we had some good partying times together. There was one occasion where we were trying to get out of Chicago to get to the gig in a blizzard, I think the worst they had in 50 years. We crashed the car, and Chris O'Donnell, our manager who was driving it, in fact, he got arrested. It was only 25 miles, to get out of Kenosha. We ended up in the police station. But we get all the way to the gig, and of course we were late. Kiss were headlining, and they were like, 'Oh, you guys got to go on,' to Rush. They said, 'No, we're going to wait. We'll cut our set down, to wait to see if we get there.' So they actually cut their set to give us time to get there. Really sweet guys. As it happened, we were about five minutes late, but I thought it was really sweet of the guys, you know? Any time they play in London I usually go to see them and have a chat backstage, talk about the old times, the mischief we got up to."

Rush was known amongst bands they toured with for their comedy sketches, Lizzy being the beneficiary as well. "Yeah, they came in with the smoking jacket and the pipe, and Geddy had this nightdress on (laughs). And we're all sitting there. I think it was either Phil's room or my room, having a wee puff or whatever and a few drinks. Alex then came in. We hadn't seen Leave It To Beaver at that point, and we're just thinking, what are these guys up to? They went into this whole sketch thing, and we're just looking at each other going, 'What the fuck?!' It was funny, but not because we understood the humour. It's because we knew the lads, and we were thinking, what are these guys up to? You know a bottle of Chivas Regal in hand, right? Doing all that stuff, and we're going, 'Fuckin' 'ell. These guys are mental!' But it was fun (laughs)."

"But Bachman-Turner were a bit difficult, to be honest," continues Brian, panning back to the previous year's Canucks du jour. "We played a couple of pranks on them and they took it badly and cut the lights and cut the PA (laughs). We did one show with ZZ Top where we weren't even allowed into the sound check. Plus they all drove up, three of them, in like three Cadillacs, one in each, right? We had to be parked further away from them. They went in and did their sound check, we went in and got about three minutes. But yeah, Rush were brilliant. They were great to tour with. You know, there are a few that were a bit difficult, a bit full of themselves. Styx, where they actually got thrown off the tour. So Rush moved us up the bill (laughs). Styx were always fighting in the dressing room and throwing chairs at each other, so the boys said, 'Oh, we've had enough of this,' kicked them off the tour, right? 'You're off,' from the boys."

"But yeah, BTO… it was funny in a lot of ways, and it was nightmare in other ways. Funnily enough, I've actually worked with somebody recently who worked with Randy Bachman, and he was extolling how such a great guy this guy was, and I said, 'Well, he wasn't when I was on tour with them.' He's a Mormon, you know? Or as Brian Downey called him, a moron. Fred Turner was just a great big bear and a lovely geezer, and the guitar player, Blair, he had a moustache and a mullet. He was a nice chap; he was not in to the Mormon thing. But obviously Randy's brother, who was the drummer, I guess at the time, and very young at the time, same as I was, I felt he was kind of forced into this, 'no drink, no drugs, no women, no nothing, no rock 'n' roll.' It was a bit of a hard tour with us. It was easier when we brought them over to Europe, because we kicked their ass. That was cool."

Which is somewhat a confirmation of how Nigel saw the '75 *Fighting* campaign as well. "True, but that was a conscious decision," continues Brian, "because they actually asked, in England and Europe, if we could double headline, where one night they would go on headlining and one night we would headline. But Phil was very astute, and he realized that that was a load of bollocks, because we already had our fan base in England and Europe and they didn't. They had 'You Ain't Seen Nothing Yet', one hit single, and that was it, and we had been touring for quite some time and had a pretty strong fan base, and Phil said, 'No way. We are going to support all the way.' Because he knows – and we used this through our whole career, really – if you're a good live band, which we knew we were, and probably a lot better than Bachman… I don't know, but certainly we were pretty strong; better or not is a matter of opinion, I suppose. But I think we had better songs, and I think we were probably better players, actually. It was a better position for us to be in, as the underdog, so to speak, and then kick ass. Because that's always a good position to be in. That's where you get the press, and people go, 'Wow, well, the support been were brilliant.'

So Phil'd make sure that when we were headlining, we never had a support band that was every very good (laughs)."

"They supported us on a British tour," continues Robbo with respect to another partner in crime, Graham Parker, jumping back to the current year. "They were on the same record label as us, and it was during that period where there was the sort of British singer/songwriter-type thing happening, kind of like the Bruce Springsteen thing in America. He was a lovely chap and his whole band are lovely people. They were all really nice guys and all very good musicians as well. I remember playing with The Tubes as well, in Philadelphia. I just thought they were really weird. Fee Waybill was playing Captain Quaalude at the time, with the wig on and 'White Punks On Dope' and all that. I thought they were rubbish. I just thought they were crap, because there wasn't any air time, so to speak. Of course, later on, they became one of my favourite bands. *The Completion Backward Principle* is one of my favourite ever albums, and I kind of realized what brilliant musicians they were. But I didn't see it, when we were playing with them. I remember they had the stage all covered in TVs, as opposed to lights, and all the way around, where you would see amps, well, you saw these TVs and they would flick stuff on and off, and I thought that was quite impressive. The show was impressive, but I didn't really get off on the music at all. But having said that, as I say, later on I started to listen to them very carefully, and realized that Prairie, wow, what a drummer, and just the musicianship of all of them, and the lyrics, one of my favourite all-time bands, The Tubes."

"Actually, I was a friend of Phil's for a while," recalls that band's Fee Waybill. "We would talk on the phone, and he introduced me to this radio guy from WMMS in Philadelphia, and we did a bunch of East Coast dates with them. And I thought they were great; I love that band. Thought they were really cool. Played the Tower Theatre in Philadelphia; I remember that really well. It was sad to see him go. But I didn't know him that well. He seemed to be a great guy; really fun to play with, a really cool guy. I didn't really know him all that well, just on the stage, and that kind of superficial, 'Let's hang out; let's get drunk.' But I didn't know any secrets or his private life."

Toward the end of the three month jaunt, with 'The Boys Are Back In Town' steaming up the charts and Lizzy all set to join in on a power-packed bill with Rainbow, Phil's drinking and drug taking ways caught up with him, marking what many believed to be a permanent, if gradual, decline in the thin man's physical well-being, specifically, with Phil's liver function having been diminished.

"I don't think we did any shows with Rainbow, as far as I remember," says Robertson. "I think we were going to start that tour the night that he got sick. Jimmy was playing bass for them at the time and we were looking forward to doing that, but we didn't get to do it, because of that." Adds Scott, "We never played a single note on that tour because Phil was suffering from hepatitis weeks before we even got to Ohio where the tour was to begin. The day we got to Ohio, Phil more or less nearly collapsed with exhaustion and was taken to the hospital where he was told that he had contracted hepatitis and was to immediately fly back to London. Back in London he was put in the intensive care unit for a couple of weeks. It's a shame because it would have been a great tour for Lizzy."

Officially called a virus infection but in actuality hepatitis, Phil's illness hit hard in Omaha, Nebraska, resulting in the cancellation of the band's last handful of dates, including the Beacon Theater in New York City. "When the doctors in America diagnosed the virus, they said that Phil should be admitted to the hospital as soon as possible," stated Chris O'Donnell in the press, with Scott adding that, "We were really worried about Phil but he's not too bad now. This virus has completely put him out of action. We were disappointed about having to cancel the American shows but it looks as if he'll be okay for Hammersmith, which is a relief."

After a stay in a Manchester hospital and months of not being well, Phil remarked that he was still, "very tired. But I've been very good. I haven't been with any women, or touched a drop of alcohol! I was stopped from drinking for six months before, but I gave in and drank after three months. Then I fell ill again, so I went back to the doctor and now he's stopped me for another six!"

"There's a different kind of strain out there," added Phil. "Over here, you can plan your tour so you don't have too far to travel at once, but in America, you're going thousands of miles, and it's always changing. One day you can be in some laid-back Southern state, and the next in New York, where it's all incredibly fast moving. So it all adds up to a very different kind of pressure."

"He got some form of hepatitis, the mild form of hepatitis, and he came back and he was in hospital for a while," confirms Frank Murray. "I guess we started to tour Europe, and he wasn't too bad about it. He was just told to lay off drink, but after awhile some doctor made the mistake of saying, well, maybe he could drink a little bit of white wine or champagne (laughs). All of a sudden he was demanding champagne because he couldn't drink anything else, and it was almost like, 'I'm under doctor's orders here!'"

"I don't really want to get into a discussion about drugs," sighs Robertson. "Because in those days, everybody was at it. You can't really put it down as something only we were doing. It was more just like smoking some weed or whatever, a bit of coke, and that was it. But it wasn't out of control by any manner or means. It was few and far between. But it's the same as any band. When you start getting bigger, then you get hangers-on hanging about and giving you shit, and you are more famous so people want to be around you, and it doesn't cost them anything to give you a bit of this or a bit of that, and I guess it just got out of control near the end. I mean, we all have our vices, but some of them will kill you."

So... add the band's increasing indulgences and show cancellations (while the going was good) to the fact that Mercury weren't doing that hot a job with the band on the record end of things, and you can't help but think Thin Lizzy was faltering. Not exactly blowing it, but nonetheless making mistakes.

"Everything was right in America," Phil told Pete Makowski from *Sounds*, "because we had made an impression when we did a support with BTO. All the promoters were saying, 'Yes, they were good band; we'll have them back.' The album was bubbling, the single was bubbling, we were tighter, because we knew what we were going into this time. We had an English tour behind us, so we were really tight. The reason I think I got so fucked up, was because I was just going mad, doing it to death. You know what we are like on the road; we go berserk – wine, women and song. 'Course I was doing more than my fair share of all and I got run down and that may be susceptible to hepatitis. So I went to the doctor; I thought I had the dose! That was the symptom – my piss was going dark; I was feeling very listless. And I always look after my old man – print that for the girls – my old man is always looked after; I'm always very clean, girls (laughs). So I went to the doctor, and he took samples of my blood and piss, came back two hours later and said, 'you've got hepatitis.' It really added to my image; everybody thinks I'm a junkie. All these people kept coming up to me and saying, 'I know.'"

Enter 1977, and there's additional scotching (pun intended – but that's a story for later) of US dates, due to Brian Robertson slicing up his hand in a bar fight in the early morning hours before what should have been conquering times for the boys in rock 'n' roll's promised land.

To be sure, the *Jailbreak* album and its attendant trio of hard-charging hit anthems would stick stateside. Yet at gold and no further, this wasn't the robust triumph that band and management would have hoped for. Little did they know that despite a suite of records to come that would be among some of the most well-regarded among discerning fans of vintage hard rock, Thin Lizzy would never again reach any kind of official certification in the US, compartmentalized forevermore, very much like UFO, as a middle-tier band struggling to overcome its rife internal vices.

"I'm looking at him right now, actually," continues Robbo in closing, asked about Phil and his desire to be a rock star, with all the trimmings. "I've got a big photograph from Chalkie Davis on the wall, which is sort of a limited edition thing. And he's got the shades on and whatnot, and he's only playing in his front room, right? (laughs). No, he loved the whole thing. He lived for it and he died for it as well. That's the problem.

8

JOHNNY THE FOX

"More of a muso album"

As Thin Lizzy moved like a shark through 1976, the band had grown impressively to embody the swagger that was always part and parcel of its flash leader, one Philip Lynott. There was always something to complain about within the band's long line of commercial loser albums. But not so with *Jailbreak*. 'Cowboy Song', 'Warrior', 'Emerald', 'Jailbreak', 'The Boys Are Back In Town'… the record was studded with hits at radio and hits as lasting deep album cuts for the eons, and it was time for the band to strike while the iron was hot, and hope, through exhaustion, stress and dirty temptation, that the rock 'n' roll muse was sympathetic to the band's plight and starry status in sight.

Jailbreak was the third record to be crafted by what is considered the classic Thin Lizzy line-up, namely Brian Robertson and Scott Gorham on twin rhythms and even more twin leads, the long-suffering Brian Downey on deft drums and Phil Lynott on bass, vocals and charming interviews.

Having toured the states for the second time, Phil celebrated the event by contracting hepatitis and landing himself in the hospital, first on the June 19 and then again on July 17, after getting out against doctor's orders to perform a "thank you" show at the Hammersmith, old mates Graham Parker & The Rumour supporting.

"Phil was diagnosed with hepatitis C," recalls California kid Scott Gorham. "You see, that's the deadly one. And it was like the last show of the seven-week period in the US. Phil walked into the dressing room and he just laid down on the floor and couldn't get up. And that was it. I remember standing over him going, 'Holy shit, man, you look bad.' His skin colour was gone; the eyes were gone. So the manager came in and he says, 'Right, well, we've got a flight to Ohio tonight; we'll fly into Ohio and we'll get Phil a doctor in the morning.' Which we did, and the doctor was actually pissed off after he saw Phil. He's said, 'Man, you should not be out here, you should not be walking around, you should not have contact with anybody, your tour is over. We're going to have to fly you back to England and put you in an emergency hospital.' And that was it – tour over. And we were all crushed. This was the tour where we thought we were going to show everybody that this band was more than just 'The Boys Are Back In Town', or the *Jailbreak* album. We were convinced this tour was going to put us on the map, and we didn't get to prove anything (laughs)."

In England and returning to his convalescence, this time Phil decides to make hay while the sun shines and try write some songs, songs that would show up on the band's second album of the year, *Johnny The Fox*, perennially to be considered timid cousin to its steely and confident predecessor. Meanwhile, end of the month, *Jailbreak* coughs up its proto-metal title track (b/w 'Running Back' as its second single, with US radio already well apprised of the song's ability to stand tall against white-hot records from Kiss, Rush, Aerosmith and Ted Nugent.

"*Johnny The Fox* was written quite quickly by Phil," recalls Downey. "Phil was obviously doing the bulk of the songwriting on *Johnny The Fox*, but the problem was, just before we recorded the album, Phil came down with hepatitis which meant that most of those songs were actually written in his hospital bed, believe it or not. We had to cancel half of our tour and come back to England, because Phil was pretty sick. I mean, I went up to visit him once or twice and he had an acoustic guitar and there and he was playing me these songs while he was recovering from hepatitis, saying, 'Check out some of this stuff.' So that's maybe four songs written in his hospital bed, and it was quite weird, because he had a guitar in there, and he was playing the guitar, and started singing along to some of the songs (laughs). I'm thinking hang on, Phil, you should be resting up here; you've got to get better. But he was adamant he was okay and he wanted to demonstrate some of these songs for me."

"He wasn't going to let a little thing like hepatitis stop him from working," laughs Scott. "That's what he would do. You're sitting in bed, you're pretty ill, but what are you going to do? At that point there's nothing on TV. So he just sat down got a pencil and pad out and paper and start writing lyrics. You know, I think it was a case of he already had sort of a sketchy idea on a couple of songs, but you know, probably the illness forced him into laying down or sitting down and here's a great way of being able to concentrate on just the lyrics alone. Because he can't do anything else."

"He might have done some lyrics and stuff," adds Brian Robertson, dismissively, "changed lyrics around, but I don't think he was in any fit state to be actually writing. I think that's probably PR that you're getting.

I didn't visit him. You couldn't do that. It was hepatitis! You weren't even allowed to have contact. It was way too contagious for that. In any case, I don't like hospitals (laughs). They'll end up keeping me or something."

"When Phil got out a week or two later, he had very little time to recuperate at home," continues Downey. "We just went straight into the studio and started rehearsing these songs in the studio, and I was recording some of them. When we got into the rehearsal studio, we obviously had a good rehearsal, but I think it was rushed to the extent that the time factor between Phil getting out of hospital and the actual album being recorded, wasn't that long, maybe a couple of weeks. So he was still recuperating from his hepatitis, and I think that threw him a little bit. He wasn't 100%. But then again, listening back to *Johnny The Fox*, I mean, it sounds pretty good to me. There's nothing radically wrong with it. It might sound slightly off-kilter compared to, say, *Jailbreak*, but there is nothing wrong with it. I thought the songwriting was really coming into its own, from *Jailbreak*, that point, maybe up to say *Renegade* – that period of Phil's songwriting was excellent. And I think generally, it's one of my favourite albums, in fact, *Johnny The Fox*. There are some great tunes on there. And some lovely feels, some funky kind of tunes as well."

"But yeah, there's a huge contrast," figures Downey, asked to compare the new record to its surprise hit predecessor. "It's completely different from *Jailbreak*. Because *Jailbreak* was completely rehearsed outside the recording studio. We had a demo studio to rehearse it. But with *Johnny The Fox*, it was more of a complete studio situation where you'd go in to rehearse and play and record, and at the same time, and so it's a little bit more experimental than *Jailbreak*. I think because of that, obviously the sound was slightly different than *Jailbreak*. Actually, quite odd; I love the sound on Johnny The Fox. But for some reason, and I don't really know why, it never really took off commercially. It didn't have the same impact, obviously, and I have really no idea why. The quality of the songwriting is superb, and the sound of it was good, and we were in top form as well. But maybe it's just because of that little dip of having to cancel the tours; we weren't as active mainly around that, as we should have been, tour-wise. Maybe that had an impact on the commercial aspect of that album."

Another bad omen might have been the band's aborted attempt to record the album at Musicland in Munich, with the brunt of the work taking place at The Who's Ramport Studios in south London, once again John Alcock producing. But at Musicland, Alcock, although not a technical engineer-styled producer by any means took an instant dislike to the equipment, matters being complicated by clashes with Robbo. Adding to the frustration at not being able to get sounds in Munich,

Robertson wound up cutting his hand with a bread knife, requiring five stitches, diminishing both his mood as well as his playing abilities. What's more, the plane the band was travelling on to Germany had to make an emergency landing when its landing gear failed to engage.

In any event, having crossed the sea on August 9th to give Musicland a try, the band left the Arabella Hotel and its even more storied basement studio after two weeks and retreated to familiar surroundings to complete the sessions late August into September. Indeed what tapes the crew had pulled out of Musicland had inexplicably been shedding their oxide, making them unusable. Meanwhile, back briefly in Dublin, on September 15, Eric Bell gets in a casual gig with the boys, accompanying Phil, Brian Downey, Jimmy Faulkner (a potential Lizzy guitarist) and Ditch Cassidy (part of the story of Lizzy's signing) on a loose set list of blues covers and Lizzy originals. During this time as well, 'Cowboy Song' is launched stateside as a single, backed with 'Angel From The Coast', giving *Jailbreak* and by extension, the band, further legs in America.

"Fuck all, in a word. In two words, actually," laughs, Robertson, asked what indeed the band had accomplished at Musicland. "I don't know why that was, because it wouldn't have been that way with me now, not today. Because I know so much more about the business and how to record and studios and all the rest of it. We were there to get out of London and so everybody is in the same place at the same time. Bowie was there recording stuff, and so many other bands had recorded there. But you know, three days to get a snare sound. I'm sorry, that's just total shit. Whereas if I was in there today with Brian Downey, I would have a snare sound in half an hour. So I really don't know what went on there. I know that because Bowie was in at the same time, our drums were moved quite a lot, because he had to get his drummer in and whatever. But that still doesn't make up for the fact that the drums are completely gone. I don't like that for one second. I know Brian wasn't happy with it. But I think it was more down to the engineer at the studio, and whether he was doing double duty, in fact, working with us all day and working with Bowie all night."

"And again, there was the drug thing going on," continues Robbo. "Not with Brian, don't get me wrong, because he was never that way inclined. But with other people there certainly was, and I think that probably has a lot to do with it. Because Bowie was such a big act, they would've put so much into him, and as I say, maybe the engineers were doing double shifts, I don't know. But certainly when you would go back in, the snare would be ringing. I know how to produce now and I can get rid of the ring on a snare drum in two seconds; it's no big problem. You've got Neumann microphones and fucking compressors and limiters, but at that point you don't know what's occurring. You're leaving it to the engineer, the house engineer or whatever, the producer, and you know, it wasn't happening. It was a waste of time, to be honest."

A much better vibe occurred back at Ramport. "Well, all the crew, all The Who's boys, were big fans, and we were fans of them. I've become very close friends with some of them. It was fun, you know, but again you're talking the '70s, so there was a bit of misbehaving going on. Well, actually quite a lot (laughs). Which probably got in the way of a lot of work, but I always enjoyed my time at Ramport, and the boys from The Who and ML and all the companies associated, were just really, really kind to us. You know, really helped us."

"It was just crazy in Munich," said Phil. "We'd recorded there before and it went okay, but this time around, something didn't work right for us. So we spent the whole of August in the Ramport Studios over here getting the album done. We had a schedule to meet for the new album and we met it."

"It was in the basement of a huge hotel," begins road manager Frank Murray, on his recollection of events. "Deep Purple had recorded there, and I believe Rory Gallagher, and anyway, it's supposed to be a great studio, Musicland. But after a while John Alcock didn't like the sound. But the funny thing was, we went there for tax reasons, to record outside of Britain. Management had set up some kind of tax scheme where you weren't supposed to be recording in Britain. The masters had to be made abroad. So off we went, and normally when you've done that, you always make sure it was in the newspapers that you were away (laughs). So the tax man, if he was reading it, he could see that Thin Lizzy were in Germany. We used to finish there around midnight, and David Bowie used to come in with Iggy Pop. David was producing an Iggy Pop record there at the time, and we would often meet with him on the way out. Sometimes we would be taking a little longer, and they're maybe getting frustrated outside, waiting for us to get out so they could get in. But after about ten days or so, John decided that he wasn't liking it, and we were going to go back to Ramport."

Ships in the night, is how Frank sums up any interaction with David and/or Iggy. "They would record through the night and they weren't for hanging around during the day. We were recording during the day. But records tended to take a while. Sometimes it would take a couple of days to get a drum sound. I don't know why, because the reason seem to be that somebody had a great sound on a record that you might be listening to, and then somebody else would say, 'Yeah, the secret of that is that it took them two days to get the drums played in.'. So you kind of felt obliged to actually do the same thing (laughs). You respected the amount of work that went in on it, so we would take that. I remember doing a lot of that stuff, taking forever to get a Brian Downey drum sound. Phil was a perfectionist as well. He liked to experiment a lot in the studio on his own sound. It was never a problem to say to Phil, 'Would you like to give that another shot?' It was always, 'Sure!' He would keep trying until he got it exactly right. It wouldn't be like, two takes, that's great. He took as many takes as it took (laughs)."

"Another thing about Phil I remember, is that Philip always had cassettes made up for the car with various people's music on them. And in some ways, that would be subliminal. It would have a subliminal effect on him, but that's why he had done it. He particularly liked Van Morrison's voice, and Rod Stewart's, with the Faces and on 'Gasoline Alley' and stuff like that."

Back to the record, a Lizzy fan's first introduction to *Johnny The Fox*, however, might have been through a meeting with its album cover, yet another rich and intriguing work at the hands of Jim Fitzpatrick, imagist for Thin Lizzy at this point for three of the last four records. "I think it's a very subtle cover whereas *Jailbreak* is sort of in your face isn't it?" notes Robertson, "It just shows that Jim can change from one album to the next, you know?"

Many a fan favourite, the gorgeously and regally appointed *Johnny The Fox* sleeve is also a favourite of the artist at hand. "There's two of them," says Jim. "*Black Rose* is the obvious one, because it's kind of iconic, but truthfully I much prefer the *Johnny The Fox* album cover. It has a lot of qualities I like in other people's work, and I applied some of that criteria to myself. I think it's the most complete of all the covers, but it doesn't match *Black Rose* in terms of iconography. If you look at my work generally, it varies between iconographic work and so crazily complex work that could never become iconographic (laughs). And that goes for some of my Celtic work."

And *Johnny The Fox* would be the most involved in this respect... "Right. That's where I did a kind of neo-Celt, manga version of Celtic art and Celtic borders. I'd done a cover for Phil... I'd actually done a huge amount of cover roughs. You have to remember, I haven't had time to publish them, and I haven't been able to find many of them, but that one, I can't remember what it was for. But there was a warrior in the centre of it. It had a border, and Philip loved the border, and he said, 'I want that; we'll use that.' And that became the border for *Johnny The Fox*. He didn't have a title yet, but we had the border, with the circle blank, literally until 24 hours before it was due to go to press, to be printed. And Philip said, 'We've got a title for you – Johnny The Fox.' And I thought, there's no Johnny The Fox in the track list. There's 'Johnny The Fox Meets Jimmy The Weed', and he said, 'Oh, just give us Johnny The Fox; nobody will notice.' So I put in the centre, the fox over the city, kind of echoing *Nightlife*. So it was a rush job. I would have much preferred something more elaborate for the centre section."

The evil character in the lacework within the three-sided border evokes comparisons with *Jailbreak's* Overmaster, however Jim says, "That was just an idea that came into my head that Philip liked. It's not a personification of anyone in particular. We just wanted something sinister-looking. Celtic borders are inevitably very humorous. It's all intertwined animals, interlinking and getting up to anything you want. But I wanted something a little more sinister, but metal-ish."

"It was actually done in two stages," continues Jim. "I did a huge amount of what I called flat photographic work, in other words, printing, developing, all that kind of stuff. Which you don't do now – it's all digital. So I did a drawing of a border, and I only did half of it, and then I flipped it over, a negative, and did a negative montage. Then I printed the whole thing out on Lyco film, which is a very clear film that lasts. It's not affected by anything, I suppose, except maybe fire. I did the artwork on that. I did a Lyco print of the border, and of the border detail, and the rest is all hand-painted. So I had a black outline and I filled it with paint. That's essentially how it worked. I used that technique an awful lot in the day for doing my work, because it gave me a fallback position that if it didn't work out, I simply printed and developed another big print. These were quite large. I used a machine called a Grant, which was a huge machine that is still up in my attic. The only reason I keep it there (laughs), is because I did that big Che Guevera image that way, and if anybody ever wants any proof (laughs), the bloody thing is up in my attic (Jim's most famous piece by far is the iconic Che Guevera poster recognized the world over). For a lot of people, it was very complex. But for me it was the simplest way of doing things. It was a technique I learned in advertising. If you wanted to do something with speed and you wanted a fallback position, if you absolutely messed up, you could simply sit down and start again. So that artwork for *Johnny The Fox*, you do need that fallback position."

Fortunately, Jim didn't have to leave Ireland and visit Phil in the hospital to bring this complicated piece to fruition. "No, I talked to him all the time. Is that when he had hepatitis? He was in the hospital a couple of times (laughs). You were never quite sure. I always had to keep my mouth shut, but now it doesn't matter. No, no, we talked all the time on the phone. It was a very easy relationship; it wasn't demanding. I didn't have to fly over there and get instructions. We would just chat away on the phone and things would evolve over conversations. Before that, he used to stay at my house when he was home. He used to arrive up... he had a little moped, and he would arrive up on the moped. Not very glamorous, you know?"

As for dealing with the band's management at this point, now, with the departure of Ted Carroll, down to Chris O'Donnell and Chris Morrison, Jim says, "Well, the two Chris's were people I liked immensely. I still have contact with them occasionally. I always enjoy seeing Chris Morrison and Chris O'Donnell; again, two easy people to deal with. Because it's a tough business. I've talked to a lot of people over the years, and a lot of them are deeply unpleasant people. I would happily not go near some of them again. But people like the two Chris's, they were brilliant. They were always on my side. I always found them supportive. Chris Morrison went on to manage Blur, and very successfully too."

Johnny The Fox would arrive in the shops on October 16 1976, a mere seven months after the release of *Jailbreak*. The album would hit No.11 on the UK charts and rise to No.56 Stateside. Opening the record was 'Johnny', a heavy rocker not as relaxed as 'The Boys Are Back In Town' but not as tightly wound as 'Jailbreak' either. Perhaps serving as microcosm for the vibe of the album as a whole, it's a cozy, likeable Thin Lizzy track, but not exactly a barnstormer of a side one track one. As well, its title, in conjunction with the LP title, and songs called 'Rocky' and 'Johnny The Fox Meets Jimmy The Weed'… it was starting to feel like we had another concept album – at least semi or quasi, like last time – on our hands.

"It did have that sort of feel to me as well," muses Downey. "I mean, Philip had a lot of time in bed (laughs), to think about it as well. He was sitting there on his own, he had no distractions, and I think he had to get his thoughts together very quickly, and it maybe did become a little bit of a concept to him. But having said that, there is a fairly diverse set of tunes on there, all the way to Johnny The Fox Meets Jimmy The Weed., which is more of a funk lesson, in musicianship and playing. It's just a great song to play, and there's also things like Johnny. on there which is completely different (laughs). There was some great songwriting, as I say, and the playing, there again, but for some reason we just didn't make it commercial enough for general tastes, and I don't know why it didn't take off. But it's a nice album to listen to and everybody loves it. I can listen to it today without any problems, you know? It hasn't really aged that much, and it has great sound. We were thinking, okay, let's just get another album out. Phil came down with hepatitis unfortunately, and maybe we were a little bit down in our expectations of what we could've done. We thought, okay, he's come down with hepatitis, this could happen again. It could have that kind of effect, but then again I don't think so. I was well up for it, we were prepared for it, but Phil was still pretty ill in the actual studio. He wasn't completely recovered from the hepatitis, you know?"

"I've always liked that track, to be honest," notes Robbo, specifically addressing 'Johnny', the power chord-appointed introduction to the record. "I didn't agree with putting brass on it, at first, but then I thought well, that's pretty quirky, I quite like that (laughs). I don't know why they used Fiachra Trench for that. I might've picked somebody a little bit harder on the brass, and made it more of the guitar riff, sort of thing. It was a bit too light for me, the brass, although I liked it. I thought it was a great idea."

"Cocky Rocky," chuckles Robbo, moving on to track two, another quite metal piece of work, this one more spirited. "Apparently, Phil wrote that about me. So what am I going to say about that? (laughs). I don't know. He's probably entirely correct, for the time." Indeed with the first two tracks of the record, what we have is quite remarkable – Phil first gives us a hard-hitting, detailed and plainspoken profile of himself (as "Johnny," a recurring character through Lizzy's past canon), followed by a similar lad-ish profile of his nemesis in the band, namely his Glaswegian whisky-swilling guitarist, all of 21 years of age and full of rage.

Still, unlike Ian Gillan with 'Smooth Dancer', this singer's quite complimentary of the firecracker in the band, his portrait set to an arrangement of erudite riffs and sinewy twin leads that point to a settling and substance to Lizzy's sound that is missing on *Jailbreak*, a sense of comfort within one's skin, of groove, indeed, Downey laying down one of his most in-the-pocket beats to date, grace notes kicked in as bonus.

'Borderline' tames the record down, Phil turning in a desperado ballad like dark Eagles or Warren Zevon, folk soaked in the blues, chord changes adding pathos and indeed power ballad elements before there was much of a blueprint in that direction.

Next up was 'Don't Believe A Word', the track that lives on as this respected record's most famed single, brief that it is. "Just talking with somebody the other night, about 'Don't Believe A Word'," notes Scott. "Now that song, we timed it when I was up at Joe Elliott's house, remixing it. We actually timed it to see how long the song was, and thinking oh, it's probably around 2:40, 2:45. It's actually two minutes and 17 seconds long (laughs). That's because for some reason, we just couldn't find the third bit – we couldn't find a third bit that felt comfortable in there or felt right. It actually turned out to be a hit song over here (Ireland). So there's got to be again this world record or something for the world's shortest record actually being a hit."

Bit of controversy on this one, due to the fact that it's credited to Phil and Phil alone. "The one song that Brian did muck around with the tempos was 'Don't Believe A Word'," notes Robbo, on a song that he believes Downey as well as himself should have been credited. "I just didn't want to record it, and I just gave up on and said, 'This is just a 12 bar blues, slow blues, it's crap.' It was Downey and I, went into the rehearsal room together, and Downey came up with the shuffle thing, and then I came up with the riff. But did we get any credit for it? No we didn't."

The dead-boring blues version of the song can be heard on various live recordings as well as on the Gary Moore album, *Back On The Streets*, issued in December '78. Yep, in that guise, it's barely there. "Well, that's what I felt at the time," agrees Robertson. "Being kind of an upfront guy, I kind of told Phil, and he got slightly pissed off and disappeared for three days. And during those three days, Brian I put the basic song together, but we didn't get anything out of it."

"It wasn't initiated by me that much," demurs Downey. "I just thought it was a bit too slow. I remember me and Robbo being in the studio one day thinking, let's beef it up a bit, let's get into a bit more of a shuffle, and as we did it, the tapes were rolling, and I remember saying to Phil, when he and the rest of the guys arrived, we played it back, and they picked up on it and liked the idea. Initially, as Robbo has said, it was a very slow blues."

Emphasizing Robertson's very real contribution is Søren Lindberg, Lizzy expert and co-producer of Brian's solo work. "As Brian says, Phil brought in the slow version, and the boys didn't like it, and Phil got angry and ran off (laughs). Basically Brian Downey started a shuffle, and Robbo did actually write that riff, which is on the fast version. So if you hear the slow version, that riff isn't there at all. So that's something that I think is quite obvious. Otherwise, when you talk about credits, in all fairness, I think there's a lot of compositions with Thin Lizzy credited as a band. They should've been credited, all four of them, on a lot of tracks. But again, Phil Lynott was a much smarter businessman than the rest of the boys in those days. He realized where the cash was."

"You had to fight for your position a lot of times," says Scott, concerning the songwriting process. "You know, a lot of times you would come up with a bit and it would be obvious, that's a great bit; that is staying in there. But if two guys had a bit for the same song, and only one bit was going to fit in there, you have to get in there and fight your corner. You know, this is why my bit should be in there. This is why this sounds better. It got heated at points. I mean, I'm not talking about coming to blows. We never punched each other out or anything. But voices would get raised, and things would get really tense in there, because you always wanted your music in there. You always wanted your bit. Phil was a really strong personality. So if you didn't have your arguing chops together, you probably weren't going to win those arguments. But, yeah, 'Don't Believe A Word' actually started out as more of a blues ballad, kind of thing. With Robbo, we just naturally stepped it up. We thought, we don't want another ballad here, but this is a pretty cool vehicle for more of a rock song."

Bonus to the experience of this taut, quick rocker is a suitable succinct guitar solo that Brian figures might be his favourite of the entire catalogue ("weird," "strange," in his words), the licks bubbling out barely contained into a masterful display of phrasing and pacing. Also quite the feature is the starkly confessional lyric from Phil, in which he so much as admits he's a dog not to be trusted.

"You go through the process of chatting up the chicks," Phil told Roy Carr from the NME, "and playing the game, giving 'em the old line, and I reckon most fellas will say just about anything to get a girl into bed. So that's how I came to write 'Don't Believe A Word'. It's just to say, if you believe every line a fella hands you, you'll only get hurt. I didn't wanna disguise the message. I'd much prefer to say something simple than all artsy artsy. Yer know, 'Through a wanderlust of transparent dreams we walked on a carpet of clouds,' when all you're really saying is, I fancy you... howzabout it then!"

'Don't Believe A Word' would be issued on November 26th as a single in the UK (b/w 'Old Flame'), yet the US would be given' 'Johnny The Fox Meets Jimmy The Weed'. Also in November, the album would be certified Silver in the UK with *Jailbreak* taking Gold. More importantly, *Jailbreak* would represent the band's only certification ever stateside, peaking at Gold. There were hopes for *Johnny The Fox*, predicated upon the record being shipped in quantities of around 250,000.

"This is the great thing – the big phenomenon with the record company," explained Phil, in *Trouser Press* later on in 1977, after all of the record's attempted hit singles had blown over. "Record companies are always looking for a single. I think it really shows the difference between America and England. In England, you have to take into consideration that it's got to get onto Top Of The Pops, get played on the BBC, and just be a general disco hit as well. Well, for some reason, they figured that 'Don't Believe A Word' is more in the English style of a hit record than the American. In America, they release singles to promote the album, and the album went up and down because we didn't tour to promote it. So they first released 'Rocky' in America, you know, as a track to push on the radio, and now for this tour, they're releasing 'Johnny The Fox'. I'm glad in a way, because I prefer 'Johnny The Fox' to 'Rocky'."

Side one closer 'Fools Gold' is one of those mid-intensity rockers that feels like a *Fighting* track, like hard-hitting country, a bit Bob Seger and fully storytelling, hence the lift of part of its lyric for a prominent quite on the inner sleeve, which declines to offer the full suite of Phil's musings. The 'Fools Gold' lyric however is the most deserving of a printed quote, given its multiple scenes, beginning with a tribute to the Irish potato famine but then moving on to Phil's cherished Wild West as well as the chilling and penultimate circus scenario.

"I remember using my old '53 Les Paul," recalls Robbo, "which I'm looking at right now actually; it's up on my wall. I remember using that for a bottleneck, so it was one of the first of the bottleneck things I had done. And that's the only thing that that guitar is really useful for; you can play like blues or whatever. But it had a tone to it. And 'Fight Or Fall' was another one that I used that on. I think it was the only two tracks I did use it on, to be honest. 'Fools Gold', yeah, I remember doing the rhythm part for it, where I played pretty hard, the three-note bottom end chords, where Scott was sort of playing the rhythm part. I liked it; I like the track. As with everything, though, I have my own opinions with how it maybe should've gone."

Over to side two and the band turn in 'Johnny The Fox Meets Jimmy The Weed', a funkster like a *Nightlife* track, even if there's an integration of the band's hard rock into it, and a general confidence of playing that belies Lizzy's growing professionalism.

Describing the swooping and memorable introduction to the track, *Rolling Stone's* John Milward wrote, "*A burst of machine-gun snares settles into a funky beat that is jolted by a squeal of wah-wah guitar and the cry of 'Johnny the Fox!' from bassist Phil Lynott. And then, employing an irresistible rhythm lick, the twin guitars of Brian Robertson and Scott Gorham set into motion the hard rock machine that has established Thin Lizzy as a prime manipulator of mid-Seventies hard rock. Like Cocky Rocky, this album's archetypical rock & roll star, Thin Lizzy knows all the moves.*"

Given the atmospheric arrangement of 'Johnny The Fox Meets Jimmy The Weed', it becomes effortless to discern that *Johnny The Fox* is the band's highest fidelity album yet, a bit more FM to *Jailbreak's* AM, a bit more like *Fighting* in organic philosophy but more correctly appointed.

"The funky flavour came from the idea that we were listening to a lot of The Meters, James Brown, people like that," notes Downey. "Because I had a record collection that was very eclectic and so did Phil. We were listening to The Meters one day, and we decided to try to get a groove together, thinking about The Meters all the time, in our heads, how they would approach it. And I came up with a drumbeat that Phil had kind of suggested to me, that we listened to on a James Brown record, in fact. But it was completely different from the way we finished it. It wasn't a James Brown beat at the end of the day, but the idea was in our heads. So we were listening to these songs one day; actually it was at a party, as I remember. He said, 'Have a listen to this.' He took an acoustic guitar and went 'junga junga junga' – it was kind of a James Brown funk thing, but just purely natural, and he started singing, 'Johnny the Fox!' 'That sounds pretty good.' Next of all, there's all sorts of people there, a rap sort of thing he was coming up with. This was in a side room off of where this party was going on, I remember, in London. He was coming up with all sorts of ideas, after a few drinks. So I said, 'Let's keep this in mind,' and so it built on that. You know, Lizzy, for some reason, we were picking up on all sorts of influence in those days, very unusual, but that was one song that came together basically at a party one day and we just got into it, again, going into the studio thinking about it and rehearsing it until we got it right."

As pertains the lyric, "Jimmy The Weed was a bit of a villain from Manchester, that used to come around every so often to all these clubs where we used to play. He was a guy that was known, because of the fact that he would turn up, and I think he had some input into owning some of these rock clubs. But he was a bit of a hood, quite honest. Everybody seemed to know him, anybody in the music business; they had kind of heard of Jimmy The Weed."

"Johnny The Fox and Jimmy The Weed were actually real live characters," confirms Scott. "They were in this gang, I guess you would call it (laughs). A gang of rogues, should I put it, up in Manchester. They were called the Quality Street Gang. What they would do is, they would target wealthy and rich people who lived in these fabulous houses and go burgle them. They would never feed off of somebody who they knew just couldn't afford it. That's why they called them the Quality Street Gang. And we hung out with them a fair few times; they were actually really nice guys (laughs)." Despite the Manchester roots of the story, Phil somewhat Americanises the tale, letting his fascination of New York street life add grit to it, appropriate for the authentic American music soundtrack at hand.

"Phil used to read all the time," notes Scott. "I found that out early on, that he was an avid reader. He loved the history of everything. It's like, the first time we went to Ireland, and he would grab me, and out of the hotel, and almost gave me a guided tour of whatever small city that we were in. 'The reason for this was actually blah blah blah,' and 'You see the mountain over there? Well, the battle of blah blah blah happened.' I was amazed! That he could know all this stuff. But the embarrassing thing was, when we first got to America, we landed in New York, and as soon as the wheels touched down he said, 'Right, Scott, we're in your country now. You've got to tell me what New York is all about.' I looked at him and said, 'Jesus Phil, I've never been here my life!' (laughs). So I felt like a real dummy, you know (laughs)."

"All of these songs are a case of you walk in and you just kind of had your bits," continues Gorham, who gets a credit on 'Johnny The Fox Meets Jimmy The Weed', as well as on 'Rocky', 'Massacre' and 'Sweet Marie'. "In Thin Lizzy you definitely had to fight for your bits, to get into the song, because there had to be reasons for your line or your chord pattern or your melody line, harmony line, whatever. You had to fight to get those things in. A lot of times you put something down and it would be the absolute no-brainer. That it's, perfect. Except there was a case where, 'Geez, that sounds a little bit like...' and somebody would name the band, and you have to go, 'No, no, wait! There's no way that sounds like...' and you had to get into that argument. Because the one thing with us, if it sounded anything like anybody else, it got tossed. It was probably to our detriment, really, because I think a fair few really good ideas got tossed because they sounded maybe a bit like this band or maybe a bit like that band. As soon as that got mentioned... you had to kind of dread that somebody would say that, because it would get thrown out. So you had to kind of watch that."

"They just turned out that way because they just did," muses Robbo, on song construction. "If you are just putting down a simple riff, the arrangement brain kicks in. So you're thinking about little parts to put in here and there just to bring it out, rather than just a straight riff – turn it into something a little more interesting. I kind of always worked that way myself. I've got a nice simple riff then it comes around to overdubs and whatever. I get my ideas from there and place them where I want them."

"Phil was a great motivator in the band," adds Downey, on composing with Lynott. "He really was. I mean, if you went into the studio and you were feeling a little bit down, or not 100% with it, Phil would snap you out of it very quickly, whether you liked it or not - to get you in the mood to play. But that rarely happened. Just having Phil there was enough to motivate most of the members of the band. He had a great sense of getting everybody in the frame of mind to play to the best of their ability, and that's what his forte was. He had a great sense of leadership within the band. He was the main songwriter, which gave him even more power, because having a guy explain exactly what needs to be done on a song is just great, rather than just going in there cold, not knowing what you want to do, and going to maybe 20 takes before you get the right one. It wasn't really like that with Lizzy. We had a fair idea before we went in there. Phil was a great communicator. He told you exactly what had to be done, although rarely we had a situation where there was arguments about that or about any arrangements – it wasn't really like that with Thin Lizzy. We knew that Phil needed certain things to happen within the structure of the song, and we just followed that.

Yeah, just great to work with, great motivator, great leader. Some fantastic ideas. You were just swept along with that kind of enthusiasm that he had."

"The two guitars fill the sound out much better," explained Phil to *Melody Maker's* Harry Doherty, addressing the same subject of songwriting. "They bounce off of one another's playing. They brought in ideas that wouldn't have happened otherwise. I got the attention because I was the darkie in the middle. I was the figurehead. I feel that in the band, everybody pulls their weight, when it comes to the music. I just happen to write a lot of the songs and lyrics, but what I do with Lizzy as opposed to what I'd do if I was on my own are two completely different things. That's how I know it's a band. I let Thin Lizzy interpret my songs as it wishes. I come down with a song and Brian says that he'd like such and such a beat. Then I let the band developed the song and even if I disagree, my power's only a quarter. I'm only a figurehead as far as the press is concerned, but that's the superficial thing. I mean, Brian Downey is the quietest member of the band, but if he says he doesn't want to play a number, that's it stumped."

"I only want to be successful for what we are rather than for what people want us to be," continued Phil. "We got the brand image thing – Thin Lizzy, heavy rock. That's not true. If we wanna do soft songs and hard songs on albums, we can do them. There's a lot of subtlety in what we do. We don't want to work in a vacuum. That's self-strangulation. We're taking this on our own terms, nobody else's. If the crowd didn't like what we did, I'd have to make a definite decision whether to give the crowds what they want or stick to me guns, like I've done all me life."

Back to side two of *Johnny The Fox*, 'Old Flame' is an under-rated charmer, basically a plush pop song textured sweetened with one of Scott's and Brian's most sublime twin leads come "post-chorus" time, notwithstanding the subtle twin leads of the verse. The song's series of melodies are complex and just a touch melancholy as well, fitting perfectly with the similar sentiments one almost subconsciously draws from the rest of *Johnny The Fox's* songs, from heavy to mid-stride to light.

This idea is plainly evident on the masterful 'Massacre' as well, a lethal prog-spirited track but fully fatalistic of melody during the verse, Phil anguished from an echo chamber.

" 'Massacre' was a song that Phil had in his mind for maybe or month or two before we decided to even rehearse it," recalls Downey. "I went to his house one day, and he had a bass, and kind of a demo thing going, and he had me playing on my lap. He said, 'Just play a beat' and it was very simple. I remember he said, 'I want to keep this as kind of a simplified thing.' But it became kind of difficult to play - after we had arranged it in the studio. And generally Phil said, you know, I've got this idea that's been knocking around in my head for quite awhile now, and we should get into the studio and try something. Like I say, initially it was very, very simple. Then we just built on it over that period of time, maybe a month or so. By the time we got into the studio to record it, it was well rehearsed, with the guitars as well."

"'Massacre' came about when I was in hospital," said Phil, in conversation with *Melody Maker*. "I was amazed how much violence there is on the telly. How much death and destruction. I was really taken aback. Y' know, one day you look at the television, it's no longer that friendly object that entertains you. It starts intrudin' in your home, tellin' you that somebody chopped somebody to bits. I was lying in hospital having to watch it 'cos there was fuck all else to do. It just seemed to go on and on, and at that very time a knock came on the door. In came a Reverend. I was born a Catholic and I'm not very devout, but once a Catholic, always Catholic. It always has you. It's a real frightening religion, y' know. They always have you thinkin' in the back of your head that maybe it's true. They claim you when you're young. But he came in and asked if I would like visitors – you know, the way they do the rounds in the hospital, just in case you want any spiritual counselling. He knew like, that I wasn't into it. When he left, I thought, 'nice man, doin' his gig.' But then the two things connected and I really thought and began to say: 'God, what are you doing?' I thought I'd take on God. Why not? So I'm saying: 'If God is in Heaven, how could this occur, because in His name there are religious wars and they use weapons to cause massacres. Yeah, the whole thing of massacres in Ireland. The violence. Everybody immediately thinks Irish, but the lyric content came from the questioning of God."

'Sweet Marie' is not much more than a pause for a hot dog break (echoes of Sarah from *Black Rose*), the wrong kind of strings-infected rote ballad for Lizzy, sitars notwithstanding. Then it's a crash and a bang and we're into 'Boogie Woogie Dance', a goofy name for a prog metal masterpiece of twisted car crash metal.

"'Boogie Woogie Dance' was one of those songs that I really thought could have been a monster," reflects Downey. "There was a drum thing I had in mind, but because of the time factor in the studio, we didn't develop it. It could've been one of those situations where, you know, you just go off. Because I was thinking maybe a five minute drum solo in the song (laughs). It could've been developed, but unfortunately again, because of the album situation, you can only put on so much time. But it was a great groove. We never played it live. It was hard. But it could've been a great song."

It is a great song, even if Robbo, surprisingly doesn't quite agree… "I thought it was a kind of throwaway track at the time, when I recorded it. It didn't mean that I wouldn't play it. And I knew Downey could do it in his sleep, because that's the sort of drummer he is. He remembers everything. He's so on it. But I didn't know that it would fit in with the basic set. You know, the middle bit (sings it); that was kind of like histrionics. I kind of felt that was more like... Queen should've done that."

Speaking of Queen, "I was supposed to do the tour," says Brian, referring to the early '77 North American tour, on which Gary Moore once again deputised. "But I cut my hand up the night before they left for America. Having said that, you know, Roger used to be a good mate of mine. We used to go out partying together (laughs). I've met Brian a couple of times, a very nice man. Freddie, I used to hate, and we had a sort of hate thing going on for a bit, but then when I got married to my wife, my ex-wife, I spent New Year's Eve with him in his house, and he's a very lovely man as well. So I really regret that I didn't actually get to tour with them, because I think I really would've gotten on well with them."

'Boogie Woogie Dance', despite Downey's desire to make it even more panoramic, is a percussive tour de force. Brian, with his grace and finesse, has often been compared to the likes of Sweet's Mick Tucker and Deep Purple's Ian Paice, no coincidence on the latter says Brian. "It's funny you mention Ian Paice, because yeah, Deep Purple were a big band. When we were starting off, we used to listen to them constantly. And there's lots of other bands as well. I was always interested in listening to blues drummers and soul and funk drummers as well, Bernard Purdie, people like that, Al Jackson from the Stax stable – there are lots of influences. All of these musicians I was listening to were obviously hugely influential on my style of drumming. And just the fact that Jimi Hendrix was around with Mitch Mitchell and things like that, so yes, all sorts, blues, jazz… I loved listening to Max Roach, Elvin Jones, Buddy Rich. But sure, Ian Paice, Mitch Mitchell, Ginger Baker… all those drummers who were around on the rock scene were a huge influence for me."

"Excellent, excellent drummer; I used to love Mick," states Downey, asked specifically about the Sweet great. "Well again, the only time I ever saw Mick was on Top Of The Pops playing on TV. I never went to Sweet live, unfortunately. I never had the time. We were always on tour and we never bumped into each other on the road, and I never got the opportunity to see them live. But yeah, Mick Tucker was a fantastic drummer. I used to love the idea of him bringing on the tympani on Top Of The Pops. He would be miming away there, and next moment he'd be off the drum kit and onto the tympani, just a brilliant idea, as I used to use tympani on certain Lizzy tunes as well. But you know, he was just a fantastic technical and tasty drummer. He knew his chops really well. Some of the songs are very commercial sounding, like 'Ballroom Blitz'. I bumped into the singer, Brian Connolly, who is unfortunately dead, when Slade had a party. They had a party for their film, and because we knew Slade really well as friends, and we toured with them once in the early days, and we were invited to the film premiere. Nice guy, you know, down-to-earth guy."

All told, helped by the punctuation mark that was 'Boogie Woogie Dance, *Johnny The Fox* was arguably, or by a shade, Lizzy's heaviest rocking album to date. As alluded to however, it was not received with the same excitement as *Jailbreak*. Although the quality was there, as well as the heaviness, there was an odd and abstract lack of immediacy.

Figures Scott, "A bit of a problem we all found there with *Johnny The Fox*, is that once you come off a big album, you know, you're out constantly touring. Now there's a little bit of pressure on you. You've got a big hit single that's come off of it, you've got in album that is selling worldwide, and now you're on tour constantly. So you're not really thinking a whole lot about writing material. Now that you've been elevated to playing in bigger places, I think you're more worried about the pressure of that side of your life. Then the next album kind of creeps up on you and all of a sudden you're there doing it. I think we got a little caught with not being quite as prepared for *Johnny The Fox* as we were with *Jailbreak*. But in saying that, I think there were a few good songs that came out of that album."

Having to abort and delay tours, due to Phil, due to Robbo, didn't help either. "Well, you know something, I think that had quite a lot to do with it. Because on that tour that I mentioned with Rainbow, for us, live-wise, all the stars had just lined up. As a band we were kind of peaking at a really good time. The band was playing really well, we were sounding great, we had a real aggressive attitude going for us, and we wanted to show the Americans what they were missing, if you will. Come on guys, everybody in Europe is getting us; in fact, everybody in the rest of the world is getting us, but you. All right, we're going to show you what you've been missing. We're going to show you what you've not been getting here, and we never got a chance. I think because of that, you know, the Americans totally mistrusted us. Because tickets were sold on the promise that we were going to be there, and I think people got pissed off and so, fuck these guys."

Signer of the band to Vertigo and product champion there for a couple years, Nigel Grainge was drifting away as well. "At that time, what happened was, I had moved on. Funnily enough, it was Thin Lizzy's managers Chris and Chris who introduced me to the Boomtown Rats.

When I was starting the Ensign label, they actually introduced me to Bob Geldof, and that's what happened. I left Phonogram to start my own label, distributed by Phonogram. And continued a relationship with Chris and Chris, but Phil, I wasn't actually working directly with them anymore. And we were also suffering the Mercury problem together. But hands-on things? I mean, the two Chris's were pretty good managers. The problem was, Phil's kind of private life was getting out of hand. I mean, I saw that a lot. I would go to parties, and I would see there was a lot of drugs going down. You could see things were slipping out of control. But *Jailbreak* was a great album, and I like *Johnny The Fox* too. I thought that was good. It just didn't have a 'Boys Are Back In Town' on it. But by that time, I mean, that's when they were really big. They were doing a lot of TV. And I think if Phil hadn't had gotten involved in that lifestyle, I think he could've had a much bigger career."

"It just had a certain vibe about it, a groove to it," figures Robbo, citing *Johnny The Fox* as his favourite of the five studio records he would make with the band. "It was a bit more serious than *Jailbreak*. We experimented a bit more and I do like the playing on it. I know the majority of the band thought it wasn't as good an album, possibly, as *Jailbreak*. But to me it was a step forward, not a step back. There's a lot more depth in the sound. Even though it's the same producer, we had a little more input on that one."

But why did it have less of a commercial impact? "I really don't know. Possibly because it didn't have the same sort of pop side of it that *Jailbreak* had. It was more of a muso album, I guess. A little bit darker. I think the writing was slightly different and we approached it a little more laid-back. Still, like I say, I prefer that album to *Jailbreak*. It's consistent let's put it like that. It's consistent the whole way through."

Given its experimentation, comparisons with UFO were warranted, even if perhaps a lining up with Queen, given *Sheer Heart Attack* and *A Night At The Opera*, might be an exaggeration. "Queen were great," says Robbo. "UFO, I mean, they're all mates of mine. They were more sort of heavy metal. It's funny, you say that and it sounds cheesy; it sounds like something from *Spinal Tap*. 'No, we're not heavy metal, we're rock!' I laugh every time I see that part in the movie, because we used to do that in the band. 'We're not heavy metal!' But they were a bit heavier than us. I guess we had more sort of melodic songs, rather than just riffs all the time, you know? As Queen were. They were melodic; well, they had to be for what they were. But I wouldn't have compared Lizzy to either band, really. I don't really know what to compare us to, at our height – we were kind of strange, I guess, for the time."

"We had our own thing and we stuck to it," affirms Downey, asked if the band was cognizant of the other great hard rock records coming out at the time, from Rainbow, from Zeppelin, from Judas Priest. "We weren't overly influenced by any of those bands you just mentioned. As I said earlier, we were influenced by slightly different things, from the Irish traditional to blues, to a lot of American music. We listened to a lot of Frank Zappa I remember, as well (laughs). I don't know why, but that seemed to creep in. Listened to The Fugs and things like that, but also we were listening to a lot of funk, a lot of black music that was happening in America. As I mentioned, I remember listening to a lot of The Meters, with Modelisti on drums; Phil used to have The Meters' albums which I used to get off on. But the hard rock stuff that was happening in England, we weren't all that impressed with. We listened to Led Zeppelin, but not in the way that we were copying them or anything. It was just part of the UK scene. But our influences were slightly different, as I said, from the obvious hard rock stuff. A lot of reggae as well, was creeping in. Previously we listened to Jeff Beck and Cream and Eric Clapton and all that from the late '60s, so maybe that was subliminally there as well. But we weren't listening to Judas Priest."

And what truck does Brian give to the comparisons between Thin Lizzy and UFO at this juncture? "UFO was a band that was around playing the same circuit as Thin Lizzy. Paul Chapman was a really good friend of ours. He was one of the guitar players who played with Skid Row after Gary Moore left. And Paul got the gig in UFO. I saw UFO maybe four or five times at the Roundhouse in London, and they always struck me as being a genuinely good band. They were well into it. But again, there were lots of bands like UFO around who were just part of the scene. They weren't hugely influential on me or the rest of Thin Lizzy for that matter. They were just part of this whole really good healthy rock scene was happening in London at the time. I always liked their albums, and Paul, as I say, good friend, great guitar player, no doubt, fantastic guy. I used to get on really well with Paul. But UFO, they became a staple of taste in the end, because they started off as just an ordinary band and became brilliant. They obviously should have had more success than they had, but over the years I think they achieved that success, really."

And to what extent is there a similarity between Phil Mogg and Phil Lynott? Both are storytellers, both are Springsteen fans... "You do, you have that. I don't know if they were influenced by us; and maybe in our subconscious we were, but not intentionally. Maybe we were influenced a bit by UFO, maybe they were by us, but I can't really tell. It's just that we had that little bit in common, maybe, as regards playing the same venues around the same time, basically grew up listening to the same music. Not intentionally at all. It just so happened that we knew Paul."

"Johnny The Fox *sharpens the band's identity*," wrote Harry Doherty, reviewing the album for *Melody Maker*. "*The persona of* Jailbreak *was that of a solid, power chord band, but with plenty of melody.* Johnny The Fox *retains these characteristics and adds to them. There's more subtlety, the melodies are stronger, and most importantly, the scope of the material is much wider than the hard rock associated with Lizzy. The subtleties of* Johnny The Fox *are in the little chugging riff hidden behind the main power chord on 'Johnny', the second crisp drumbeat (Brian Downey is in impeccable form throughout) and sneaky bass line on 'Rocky', the beautiful, and admirably restrained, orchestral arrangement on 'Sweet Marie' and the tango middle section that adds a touch of humour to 'Boogie Woogie Dance'. You might also like to know that* Johnny The Fox *is, I believe, a pseudonym for Lynott, being a reference to the American expression 'foxy' and there is a loose concept to the album built on recollections of incidents involving Johnny's hectic lifestyle. To conclude,* Johnny The Fox *represents a Thin Lizzy more versatile than on* Jailbreak. *It is not as immediately powerful as* Jailbreak, *but after a few listens, you realize that its power is deceptive but nevertheless real. These are the true signs of a great album.*"

"*Trust NME to always kick a man when he's up,*" wrote Phil McNeil for that important newspaper. "*In the long run, it's possible this may seem a better album than* Jailbreak, *but from where I'm sitting,* Johnny The Fox *is a disappointment. Certainly it's more consistent than the last LP, but no track as yet got to me like 'The Boys Are Back In Town' or 'Running Back'. Throughout the album, what's there is fine – well played, sung, arranged and produced – but there's a vital spark missing in the songs. Right now, Thin Lizzy are unlikely to make anything less than a good record, but I don't think Phil Lynott's commitment to most of this material is sufficient to make it anything more.*"

Rounding out the triumvirate of influential English papers, *Sounds'* Geoff Barton chimed in with something more positive. "Johnny The Fox *is brimful of maturity and excellence, equalling, if not bettering, everything past band line-ups have committed to record. No longer are Thin Lizzy a well-honed rhythm section doing its best to support a couple of workmanlike guitarists; rather, supreme confidence is the name of the game as the band peaks and then strides for new heights to conquer. Longtime Lizzy fans may not approve of the mild MOR leanings this album has (obviously, people are hoping that one if not several of the tracks will succeed as singles) but for me this makes the band so much more credible. Also, John Alcock's production leans towards the flat, undramatic side. With someone like Bob Ezrin or Jack Douglas at the helm, the LP would've been little short of phenomenal.*"

Tucked in-between the release of *Jailbreak* and *Johnny The Fox*, August of '76, was an early years compilation album called

Remembering Part 1, Decca capitalizing on the band's recent blossoming unto success. Or, as *Melody Maker* framed it, "*An album specifically designed to remind us of how much we missed during Thin Lizzy's formative and prolific years on Decca Records from 1971-74, a period which produced lots of outstanding material but meagre recognition; yet, surprisingly,* Remembering *portrays a Lizzy whose songs were more experimental and adventurous in structure and presentation then the band of '76 that has won so much acclaim, which indicates that in the past two years, they have been more determined to establish themselves.*"

Shrugged Phil, "We had a say in it though. If a product is being put out with our name on it, we want to be sure it meets with our approval before the fans get a chance to hear it."

Features of note to the *Remembering* package would include non-LP tracks like 'Randolph's Tango', 'Black Boys On The Corner' and 'Little Darling' but mainly class rocker 'Sitamoia', unavailable to this point in any form. Also of note would be the dramatic Jim Fitzpatrick illustrations, sampled again for the North American version of the album issued one year hence called *Rocker (1971-1974)*.

First tour dates for Lizzy in support of *Johnny The Fox* found the band briefly visiting Belgium, Germany and the Netherlands twinned with Robin Trower. Then it was back to the UK, October 20th to November 16th (culminating in a famous three-night Hammersmith stand, from which much of *Live And Dangerous* is culled), the lads backed by an unknown American act called Clover, whose lead singer was none other that Huey Lewis, later of Huey Lewis & The News fame.

There's a Nigel Grainge connection to this pairing, as there was with Lizzy's cavorting with Graham Parker and his band. "What happened was, obviously Graham Parker was one of my signings, and Graham was supposed to come with me to be the first act for Ensign, before the Boomtown Rats. But it was Dave Robinson's decision, not to let me take, you know, 'Why should we go through you when we could be signed directly to the company?' So I said, 'Well, you kind of need me to A&R Graham.' Because I'd done the *Heat Treatment* album which was a great record. I had a very good relationship with Dave's partner, who was Jake Riviera. Jake was managing Elvis Costello and he told me they were going to start their own label called Stiff. He'd played me Elvis, and in fact, just to go back a little bit, just before this, while he was still managing Graham, and this was before the Stiff thing, I was going to San Francisco, and Jake said to me, 'When you go to San Francisco, there's a group there called Clover, who I think are fantastic.' He said, 'If you go and check them out and you like them and sign them, then we'll manage them.' So I had the most fantastic day with the Clover boys.

I went to see a couple gigs, thought they were amazing, and brought them over to England, signed them, brought them over to England, and Jake took over the management. Their first gig was at a Phonogram convention, and they absolutely blew the place apart, because they were amazing live. Because we had this great relationship, anyway, and we went in and did the first album, Nick Lowe produced it. I don't know if you remember, going back to what I said about the problems with the art department, the cover for the first Clover album was probably one of the worst covers put out by anybody. I mean, you should have a look. It's utter shit. But anyway, Huey was obviously the singer of Clover, and they just became huge friends. I mean, musically they weren't connected, but they were big supporters of each other."

Huey would end up playing harmonica on a Thin Lizzy record later on, but at this juncture, Phil had taken the future star under is tutelage, even routinely joining the band onstage for a goofy dance called the 'Chicken Strut', Huey later in the evening getting called up to play harmonica on Lizzy's similarly naff 'Baby Drives Me Crazy'.

But this is pertinent also because, Clover, once over, were somewhat pushed into this pub rock slot, pub rock, some say, being one of the unsung predecessors to punk rock. So here you had Thin Lizzy paired both with Clover and with Graham Parker & The Rumour, two squarely pub rock possibilities. By extension, it's not hard to envision Thin Lizzy themselves, given their voiced disdain for heavy metal tags and their soul, their funk, their Springsteen comparatives, and their 'Johnny The Fox Meets Jimmy The Weed', winding up a pub rock band. Indeed, one can envision, given a selective set list pointing that way, that on any given night one wouldn't see much difference in style and tone and vibe between the headliner and its pub band supporters. This is not a knock, but rather an indication of the number of rock worlds Lizzy straddled with alacrity.

Ever perceptive, Phil picked up on the connection between punk rock and pub rock, telling Pete Makowski in '77, "I was getting all the papers sent over to me all the time. And it was getting like it had all changed insofar as for ages and ages I'd been saying there was a new generation of kids, in the way there's a whole new movement happening, and it's just going to bust open. I could feel it; at the time there was three bands: Dr. Feelgood, The Heavy Metal Kids and there was ourselves, y' know? All of them bands were quite aware that the kids wanted something different, wanted to be attacked again, wanted aggression and stuff like that. Like within that period we were away, it really got its image with the New Wave and the papers really gave it its image. Now I knew the punk thing was going on before I went away, but it really took off."

Within that quote, Phil is talking about being away in Toronto recording *Bad Reputation* and watching punk happen from afar, in the likes of *NME, Melody Maker* and *Sounds*. But what is interesting is the framing and definition of a pre-punk pedigree, using as the gang of it, a pub rock band, a pub rock/hard rock band, and a hard rock band.

In any event, Lizzy was rescued from too much pub rock association, entering 1977 as back-up to Queen for well on 40 dates through North America, as mentioned, with Gary Moore in for Brian Robertson. Rumours were flying of Robertson's imminent permanent departure from the Lizzy ranks after one row too many, both inside the gang and out.

But what caused him to miss the all-important North American tour had been an incident on November 23rd at The Speakeasy in London, upon which he was ensconced in a drunken brawl.

"The American tour was about to happen," relates Downey, "and Brian went out with Frankie Miller one night to one of the clubs in London, and got into some kind of a row, and in fact cut his hand, cut one of his tendons in his hand. And for that to happen to a guitar player is just a death knell for any kind of tour. So we just had to cancel the tour for a while, and get somebody else in to substitute for him. Gary Moore came in to finish the tour off. So that was the problem, rather than problems within the band musically."

The date was significant in that it was the night before the band were to fly to the US for three weeks of dates designed to make up for missed shows when Phil turned yellow. But filling in Downey's telling of it, back at The Speakeasy, defending fellow rocker Frankie Miller (who had stumbled up and sung badly with a reggae band called Gonzalez), Robertson had caught a broken bottle in the hand, thrust at Frankie by an offended Gonzales band member. The end result being a severed nerve and a burst artery in Robbo's left hand, blood everywhere, with the offending Frankie Miller left completely unscathed. Robbo claims he then broke his attacker's leg and his mate's collarbone, and then head-butted another guy before getting knocked out with a second bottle. In any event, the seeds were sown for Robbo's departure from ranks of Lizzy, which would take place in painful fits and starts as the lads cooked up tracks for their next album, a flash bit of work called *Bad Reputation*.

GIG LIST

The gig list was complied by Peter Nielsen. A more extensive version, with details of support and headlining acts, reviews, press ads etc can be found at his excellent website thinlizzyguide.com

1970

16th February	Swords Cloghran National School, Swords, Ireland
20th February	St. Anthony's Hall, Dublin, Ireland
28th February	Club A Go Go, Dublin, Ireland
1st March	Lawlor's Ballroom (Lawlor's Hotel), Naas, Ireland *Cancelled*
1st March	Town Hall, Newbridge, Ireland
5th March	The Countdown Club, Dublin, Ireland
7th March	Sgt. Pepper's, Dublin, Ireland
9th March	Trinity College, Dixon Hall, Dublin, Ireland
10th March	Liberty Hall, Dublin, Ireland
13th March	Franciscan Hall, Limerick, Ireland
17th March	Queen's Hotel, Ennis, Ireland *Afternoon gig*
17th March	Carlton, Kilkenny, Ireland *Evening gig*
21st March	Greystones, Ireland
25th March	Queen's Hotel, Ennis, Ireland
28th March	Astor Club, Belfast, Northern Ireland
29th March	Maher's Bar, Ireland
30th March	The Countdown Club, Dublin, Ireland
2nd April	The City Theatre, Limerick, Ireland
4th April	Reynold's Ballroom, Longford, Ireland
5th April	Carlow, Ireland
7th April	Carlisle, Ireland
10th April	Carrick on Suir, Ireland
11th April	The Countdown Club, Dublin, Ireland
12th April	Town Hall, Newbridge, Ireland
24th April	Zig Zag Discotheque The Carousel, Belfast, Northern Ireland
1st May	Franciscan Hall, Limerick, Ireland
9th May	Longford, Ireland
10th May	Queen's University McMordie Hall, Belfast, Northern Ireland
11th May	The Town and Country Club, Dublin, Ireland
15th May	Franciscan Hall, Limerick, Ireland
16th May	The Crescent Ballroom, Athlone, Ireland
19th May	The Countdown Club, Dublin, Ireland
24th May	Carlton, Kilkenny, Ireland
31st May	Student's Club, Cork, Ireland
1st June	The Town and Country Club, Dublin, Ireland
13th June	Dundalk, Ireland
14th June	Swords, Ireland
20th June	Reynold's Ballroom, Longford, Ireland
21st June	Crystal Ballroom, Dublin, Ireland *Afternoon gig*
26th June	Embassy Ballroom, Derry, Ireland
27th June	St. Vincent's School, Glasnevin, Ireland
28th June	Kilkenny, Ireland *Afternoon gig*
28th June	Student's Club, Cork, Ireland *Evening gig*
3rd July	Palmerstown, Dublin, Ireland
4th July	Terenure, Dublin, Ireland

5th July	Fairview, Dublin, Ireland
11th July	Countdown Club, Dublin, Ireland
12th July	Glasnevin Lawn Tennis Club, Glasnevin, Dublin, Ireland
18th July	Club A Go Go, Dublin, Ireland
25th July	Afton Club, Dundalk, Ireland
2nd August	Castaways Club, Clondalkin, Ireland
3rd August	The Star Club, Dublin, Ireland
4th August	Tiffany's, Dublin, Ireland
6th August	St. John's Hall CYMS, Tralee, Ireland
7th August	St. Aidan's Hall, Dublin, Ireland
8th August	Club A Go Go, Dublin, Ireland
9th August	Ballina, Ireland
13th August	Aras Phedraig, Killarney, Ireland
14th August	Revolution, Galway, Ireland
15th August	Pavillion, Galway, Ireland
16th August	The Television Club, Dublin, Ireland *Afternoon gig*
16th August	Fairview, Dublin, Ireland *Evening gig*
17th August	The Town and Country Club, Dublin, Ireland
20th August	Tiffany's, Dublin, Ireland
22nd August	Garden Fete, Grounds Vernon Avenue, Dublin, Ireland
23rd August	Garden Fete, Grounds Vernon Avenue, Dublin, Ireland
	Not sure if Lizzy played both nights
23rd August	Countdown Club, Dublin, Ireland
25th August	Marion Hall, Tipperary, Ireland
29th August	Dundalk, Ireland
3rd September	CYMS, Tralee, Ireland
4th September	Open Air Festival, Richmond Park, Dublin, Ireland
5th September	Temperance Hall, Longford, Ireland
6th September	The Star Club, Dublin, Ireland
7th September	The Television Club, Dublin, Ireland
8th September	Dundalk, Ireland
11th September	Festival of Living Music, Theatre Royal, Wexford, Ireland
12th September	Club A Go Go, Dublin, Ireland
13th September	St John of Gods, Islandbridge, Dublin, Ireland
17th September	Tiffany's, Dublin, Ireland
19th September	Hangar, Galway, Ireland
1st October	Tiffany's, Dublin, Ireland
3rd October	St.Paul's Collage, Raheny, Dublin, Ireland
4th October	Hotel Silver Swan, Sligo, Ireland
8th October	The Star Club, Dublin, Ireland
10th October	Club A Go Go, Dublin, Ireland
11th October	Glasnevin Lawn Tennis Club, Glasnevin, Dublin, Ireland
14th October	National Stadium, Dublin, Ireland *Supporting Taste*
16th October	St. Aidan's Hall, Dublin, Ireland
17th October	The Crescent Ballroom, Athlone, Ireland
23rd October	Town Hall, Newry, Northern Ireland
24th October	Dundalk, Ireland
29th October	National Stadium, Dublin, Ireland *Supporting Fleetwood Mac*
30th October	The Television Club, Dublin, Ireland *R.T.E Like Now!*
30th October	Catholic University School, Dublin, Ireland
31st October	St Paul's College, Raheny, Dublin, Ireland
1st November	Crystal Ballroom, Dublin, Ireland *Afternoon gig*
1st November	Town Hall, Newbridge, Ireland *Evening gig*
2nd November	CYMS, Tralee, Ireland
5th November	Abbey Theatre & Peacock Theatre (National Theatre of Ireland), Dublin, Ireland *(Two separate performances for Scott English and Dick Rowe. Signed for Decca)*
7th November	Club A Go Go, Dublin, Ireland
8th November	Hotel Silver Swan, Sligo, Ireland
13th November	The Television Club, Dublin, Ireland *RTE TV Like Now?*
13th November	Mayfair, Kilkenny, Ireland
14th November	Dundalk, Ireland
15th November	Crystal Ballroom, Dublin, Ireland *Afternoon gig*
15th November	Glasnevin Lawn Tennis Club, Glasnevin, Dublin, Ireland *Evening gig*

18th November	Peacock Theatre, Dublin, Ireland *Midday session*
20th November	Franciscan Hall, Limerick, Ireland
21st November	The Crescent Ballroom, Athlone, Ireland
22nd November	The Countdown Club, Dublin, Ireland
28th November	The Star Club, Dublin, Ireland
12th December	Afton Club, Dundalk, Ireland
18th December	Peacock Theatre, Dublin, Ireland
	Lunchtime rehearsal for 'Chaos with Thin Lizzy'
26th December	Hotel Silver Swan, Sligo, Ireland
??	Rugby Club, Athlone, Ireland

1971

2nd January	Afton Club, Dundalk, Ireland
??	Highfield R.F.C, Cork, Ireland
	I believe that this gig took place in 1971 between 9th January & 16th March.
	Lizzy moved to England on 17-18 March.
22nd January	The Scaffold, Ballina, Ireland
5th February	Silver Slipper Ballroom, Strandhill, Sligo, Ireland
9th February	Examination Hall, Trinity College, Dublin, Ireland
13th February	Countdown Club, Dublin, Ireland
22nd February	Mc Grath Memorial Hall, Bagenalstown, Ireland
23rd February	Peacock Theatre, Dublin, Ireland *Lunchtime session*
23rd February	University College Dublin, Great Hall, Dublin, Ireland
25th February	Peacock Theatre, Dublin, Ireland *Lunchtime session*
27th February	Peacock Theatre, Dublin, Ireland *Lunchtime session*
13th March	Mansion House, Dublin, Ireland *Lunchtime gig*
15th March	Television Club, Dublin, Ireland *(New Spotlight Supershow)*
16th March	St. Anthony's Little Theatre, Dublin, Ireland
19th March	Sisters Club, London, UK *Cancelled*
20th March	Speakeasy, London, UK *Cancelled*
23rd March	Ronnie Scott's, London, UK *First gig in Britain*
26th March	Thingamijig Club, Reading, UK
27th March	Country Club, Kirklevington, Middlesbrough, UK
31st March	Blaise's Club, London, UK
	First gig in Britain according to Brian Downey with 25 people
2nd April	Sussex Sport Centre, Brighton, UK *Cancelled*
2nd April	Blues Loft, Nags Head, High Wycombe, UK
3rd April	Hermitage Ballroom, Hitchin, UK
4th April	Fox at Greyhound, Croydon, UK
5th April	Wall City, Quaintways, Chester, UK
?? April	Clouds, Derby, UK
9th April	Marquee, London, UK
10th April	Baston Playing Field (Marquee), Baston, Peterborough, UK
11th April	Playing Fields, Bayson, Linconshire, UK
12th April	Skindles Hotel, Maidenhead, UK
13th April	Fickle Pickle Club, Alexandra Hotel, Southend, UK
14th April	Oldfield Tavern, Greenford, UK
15th April	Skindles Hotel, Maidenhead, UK
16th April	Tomorrow Club, Wallassey, UK
21st April	Heads, London, UK
24th April	The Temple, London, UK
25th April	Lyceum Strand, London, UK
26th April	Wall City, Quaintways, Chester, UK
27th April	Fickle Pickle Club, Southend, UK
28th April	Aquarius, Harlow, Essex, UK
29th April	Risley Remand Centre, Risley, Lancashire, UK
30th April	Pavilion, Cromer, Norfolk, UK
5th May	Winning Post, Twickenham, UK
7th May	College, Bristol, UK
8th May	Hermitage Ballroom, Hitchin, UK
10th May	Horseshoe Bar, London, UK *Lunchtime gig*
14th May	Horseshoe Hotel, London, UK *Lunchtime gig*
14th May	Sisters, Tottenham, UK *Evening gig*

15th May	Blaises, London, UK
17th May	Granary Club, Bristol, UK
18th May	Speakeasy, London, UK
19th May	Heads, London, UK
19th May	Keel Club, Lancashire, UK
	Two shows the same day?
20th May	Skindles Hotel, Maidenhead, UK
21st May	Market Hall, Haverfordwest, UK
22nd May	Glen Ballroom, Glen, UK
23rd May	Burlesque Club, Rose and Crown Hotel, Wisbech, UK
24th May	Speakeasy, London, UK
25th May	Heads, London, UK
27th May	John Bull, Chiswick, London, UK
28th May	Penthouse, Scaraborough, UK
29th May	Country Club, Kirklevington, Middlesbrough, UK
30th May	Apollo, Manchester, UK
31st May	Cooks Ferry Inn, Edmonton, UK
1st June	The Fickle Pickle Club, Alexandra Hotel, Southend, UK
2nd June	Town House, Wellington, UK
3rd June	John Bull, Chiswick, UK
4th June	The Hive, Westcliff, Bournemouth, UK
5th June	Madley College, Crewe, UK
7th June	Strangeways Prison, Manchester, UK
9th June	Winning Post, Twickenham, UK
12th June	Tofts Ballroom, Folkestone, UK
13th June	Wake Arms Groovesville, Epping, UK
16th June	Winning Post, Twickenham, UK
4th June	Temple, London, UK
18th June	Devizes, Devon, UK
19th June	Royal Lines Pavillion, Cromer, UK
20th June	Redcar Jazz Club, Coatham Hotel, Windsor Ballroom, Redcar, UK
21st June	Black Swan, Sheffield, UK
24th June	Hypnotique, York, UK
25th June	The Temple, London, UK
26th June	Alex Disco, Salisbury, UK
27th June	Greyhound, Croydon, UK
27th June	Lyceum Strand, London, UK
?? June	*One week in Germany for club dates and 2 TV dates.*
8th July	Hounds Green Man, East Ham, London, UK
9th July	Pavilion Theatre, Weymouth, UK
11th July	Henry's Blues House, Birmingham, UK
12th July	Skewen RFC, Skewen, Glamorgan, UK
13th July	The Place, Hanley, UK
14th July	Keele University, Keele, UK
15th July	Red Lion, Leek, UK
16th July	Krakatora Club, West Bromwich, UK
17th July	Wake Arms Groovesville, Epping, UK
18th July	Mr Smiths, Manchester, UK
20th July	Marquee, London, UK

Back Home Irish Tour

22nd July	Mayfair, Kilkenny, Ireland
?? July	Castlebar, Ireland
23rd July	Summerhill College, Sligo, Ireland
24th July	Sligo, Ireland
26th July	Donnycarney, Ireland
27th July	Adelphi, Dundalk, Ireland
28th July	Embassy Ballroom, Derry, Ireland
29th July	Limerick, Ireland
30th July	Stephanies Discotheque, Tramore, Ireland
30th July	The Silver Slipper, Tramore, Ireland
31st July	Bundoran, Ireland
1st August	Ballina, Ireland

2nd August	Holyrood Hotel, Bundoran, Co. Donegal, Ireland
4th August	Seapoint Ballroom, Galway, Ireland
5th August	Athlone, Ireland
6th August	Arklow, Ireland
7th August	National Stadium, Dublin, Ireland
8th August	Blackrock Park, Dublin, Ireland
9th August	Drogheda, Ireland
10th August	Hangar, Galway, Ireland
12th August	The Centre, Arklow, Ireland
13th August	Rainbow Theatre, London, UK
14th August	Rainbow Theatre, London, UK
15th August	The Greyhound, Fulham, London, UK
16th August	Starkers Royal Ballroom, Bournemouth, UK
17th August	Flamingo Club, Redruth, Cornwall, UK
19th August	Hornsey, UK
25th August	Cloud Nine Club, Halcyon, Peterborough, UK
27th August	The Greyhound, Fulham, UK
28th August	Rutherglen's Southcroft Park, Glasgow, UK
29th August	Picasso Club, Glasgow, UK
3rd September	Dragonbeat, Anglesea, UK
4th September	Dragonbeat, Anglesea, UK
7th September	Tricorn, Portsmouth, UK
8th September	Dolphin Hotel, Botley, UK
9th September	The Turn Of The Century, Salthill, Ireland
10th September	Imperial Hotel, Sligo, Ireland
11th September	Countdown Club (Alice's Restaurant), Dublin, Ireland
12th September	Milltown Festival, Milltown, Ireland
13th September	Wall City Club, Quaintways, Chester, UK
22nd September	Keel Club, Bathampton, UK
23rd September	Winning Post, Twickenham, UK *Cancelled*
24th September	Brodick, Isle of Arran, UK
25th September	Whiting Bay, Isle of Arran, UK
26th September	Lamlash Village Hall, Isle of Arran, UK
2nd October	Farx, Potters Bar, UK
4th October	Borough Hall, Stafford, UK
6th October	Blow Up Club, Luxembourg,
8th October	Starkers Royal Ballroom, Boscombe, UK
9th October	Padgate College, Fearnhead, Warrington, UK
11th October	Granary Club, Bristol, UK
25th October	Surrey Rooms, Oval Kennington, London, UK
29th October	Technical College, Maidstone, UK
30th October	University, Bradford, UK
4th November	The Greyhound, Fulham, London, UK
5th November	London, UK
13th November	Bath Pavilion, Bath, UK
?? ??	Rivington Barn, Horwich, UK
17th December	Dolphin Hotel, Botley, UK
20th December	Asylum, Basildon, UK
21st December	Wyndham School, Egremont, West Cumberland, UK
24th December	The Eldorado Ballroom, Oldcastle, Ireland *Date unconfirmed*
28th December	Town and Country Inn, Newtownards, Ireland
31st December	Hangar, Galway, Ireland
??	Trinity College, Dublin, Ireland
	This gig took place after the release of the New Day EP on 20th August
??	Glen Ballroom, Llanelli, Carmarthenshire, UK

1972

1st January	Stephanies Disco, Tramore, Ireland
2nd January	Hotel Silver Swan, Sligo, Ireland
5th January	Carlton, Kilkenny, Ireland
6th January	City Theatre, Limerick, Ireland
7th January	The Bear, Birmingham, UK *Cancelled*

8th January	National Stadium, Dublin, Ireland
9th January	The Eldorado Ballroom, Oldcastle, Ireland
15th January	The Country Club, Tuam, Ireland
20th January	The Greyhound, Fulham, London, UK
21st January	Temple Club, London, UK
2nd February	College of Further Education, Coventry, UK
3rd February	Technical College (Polytechnics), Teesside, UK
4th February	College of Technology & Art, High Wycombe, UK
5th February	Mardi Gras Club, Liverpool, UK
5th February	Polytechnic, Bristol, UK
	Two gigs on the same day?
6th February	Mary Ward College, Nottingham, UK
7th February	Queensway Club, Stevenage, UK
8th February	Chelsea Village, Bournemouth, UK
9th February	Mayflower, Billericay, UK
10th February	St David`s College, Lampeter, UK
11th February	North Staffs Polytechnic, Stafford, UK
12th February	University, Reading, UK
12th February	Stockwell College, Bromley, UK
	Two gigs on the same day?
14th February	St Georges Hall, Exeter, UK
15th February	Tecnical College, Bolton, UK
16th February	Padgate College, Warrington, UK
17th February	Totton College, Southampton, UK
18th February	Tecnical College, Lowestoft, UK
19th February	Union of Colleges, Loughborough, UK
20th February	Theatre Royal, Lincoln, UK
22nd February	College of Technology, Swansea, UK
23rd February	Queen Elizabeth College, Kensington, London, UK
24th February	Town Hall or (Technical College), Ealing, London, UK
25th February	College or (Town Hall), Ludlow, UK
26th February	University, Durham, UK
27th February	The Kinema Ballroom, Dunfermline, UK
27th February	University, Glasgow, UK
	Two gigs on the same day?
28th February	University, Aberdeen, UK
29th February	Solway Lido Holiday Centre, Silloth, UK
1st March	Flintshire College, Connah's Quay, Chester, UK
2nd March	Alsager College, Stoke on Trent, UK
3rd March	College of Technology, Newport, UK
4th March	Old Union University, Cardiff, UK
5th March	Civic Hall , Whitehaven, UK
10th March	College of Technology, Gloucester, UK
11th March	College, Hendon, UK
14th March	Polytechnics, Bristol, UK
15th March	Weston-Super-Mare, UK
16th March	Queens Hall, Barnstaple, UK
17th March	College of Education, Bromsgrove, UK
17th March	Training College, Hereford, UK
	Two gigs on the same day?
18th March	College of Education, Bognor Regis, Sussex, UK
20th March	Winter Gardens, Droitwich Spa, UK
21st March	Lafayette, Wolverhampton, UK
23rd March	Speakeasy, Crewe, UK
24th March	Town Hall, Lydney, UK
25th March	Town Hall, Melksham, UK
30th March	Winter Gardens, Droitwich Spa, Worcestershire, UK
?? April	Croke Park, Dublin, Ireland
9th April	Silver Slipper Ballroom, Strandhill, Sligo, Ireland
13th April	Up the Junction, Crewe, UK
14th April	College Of Further Education, Lowestoft, UK
14th April	The Mardi Gras Club, Liverpool, UK *Unconfirmed*
18th April	Bowl, Corby, UK *Richard Oliff on drums*

19th April	The Caledonian Hotel, Ayr, UK
21st April	Glasgow, UK
21st April	Glasgow, UK
	There is unconfirmed info about two gigs in Glasgow on the 21st.
22nd April	University, Glasgow, UK
27th April	Palace, Nottingham, UK
28th April	Technic, Bolton, UK
2nd May	Palace, Nottingham, UK
5th May	Tivoli Ballroom, Buckley, Flintshire, UK
13th May	College of Education, Warrington, UK
14th May	Freaks Palace, London, UK
14th May	Rings, Piccadilly, London, UK
	Two gigs on the same day?
16th May	Crown Hotel (Henry's Blueshouse), Birmingham, UK
19th May	The Mardi Gras Club, Liverpool, UK
20th May	College of Agriculture, Bishop Burton near Beverley, UK
28th May	Pied Bull, Islington, UK
?? ??	Palace, Blackpool, UK
3rd June	Drill Hall, Peterborough, UK
3rd June	The Mardi Gras Club, Liverpool, UK
	This gig was at the same day as Peterborough. They had to travel 150 miles.
17th June	Links Pavilion, Cromer, UK
22nd June	Guildhall, Plymouth, UK
23rd June	Winter Gardens, Penzance, UK
24th June	Blue Lagoon, Newquay, UK
26th June	Wall City Club, Quaintways, Chester, UK
29th June	Liberal Hall, Yeovil, UK
1st July	The Hangar, Galway, Ireland
2nd July	Imperial Hotel, Sligo, Ireland
3rd July	Ballina, Ireland
4th July	Carlton, Kilkenny, Ireland
5th July	Stardust Club, Cork, Ireland
7th July	Confraternity Theatre, Limerick, Ireland
8th July	National Stadium, Dublin, Ireland
8th July	O'Mahony's, Navan, Ireland
	Two gigs on the same day. First in Dublin then in Navan.
9th July	St Mary's Diocean School, Drogheda, Ireland
10th July	Kelly's Barn, Portrush, Northern Ireland
11th July	Flamingo Ballymena, Northern Ireland
12th July	King's Arms, Larne, Northern Ireland
13th July	Starkers Royal Ballroom, Boscombe, UK
14th July	Sirius Club, Southgate, London, UK
14th July	Friday Pop Club, Ballyhaunis, Ireland
15th July	Adelphi, Dundalk, Ireland
16th July	New Showboat, Youghal, Ireland
16th July	Argus Butterfly, Durham, UK
19th July?	Tivoli Ballroom, Buckley, Flintshire, UK
23rd July	New Windmill Hall, Upminster, UK
6th August	Silver Slipper, Tramore, Ireland
7th August	Town Hall, Cavan, Ireland
8th August	Hangar, Galway, Ireland
?? August	Red Island, Skerries, Ireland
11th August	Sgt. Pepper's, Dublin, Ireland
12th August	Horans, Tralee, Ireland
13th August	Town Hall, Killarney, Ireland
20th August	Chelsea Village Concert Hall, Bournemouth, UK
24th August	The Cavern, Liverpool, UK
27th August	Electric Village at Locarno Bristol Centre, Bristol, UK
29th August	Crown Hotel (Henry's Blueshouse), Birmingham, UK
22nd September	St. Georges Hall, Liverpool, UK
?? September	Munich Olympic Games Festival, Olympic Stadium, Munich, Germany
?? October	Zoom Club, Frankfurt, Germany
8th October	Jahrhunderthalle, Frankfurt, Germany

10th October	Hive Disco, Bournemouth, UK
12th October	College of Arts, Norfolk, UK
15th October	The Hardrock Concert Theatre, Stretford, Manchester, UK
20th October	St Andrews Hall, Norwich, UK

UK Slade Tour (plus Suzi Quatro)

3rd November	City Hall Newcastle, UK
4th November	Technical College, Havering, Hornchurch, UK
5th November	New Theatre, Oxford, UK
6th November	Civic Hall , Wolverhampton, UK
8th November	Winter Gardens, Bournemouth, UK
9th November	City Hall, Sheffield, UK
10th November	Rainbow Theatre, London, UK
11th November	Rainbow Theatre, London, UK
13th November	Town Hall, Leeds, UK
15th November	Free Trade Hall, Manchester, UK
16th November	Warrington Hall, Leek, UK
17th November	Victoria Hall, Hanley, Stoke on Trent, UK
18th November	Stadium Liverpool, UK
19th November	Town Hall, Birmingham, UK
20th November	Dome, Brighton, UK *Unconfirmed*
22nd November	Sundown, Doncaster, UK
23rd November	Greens Playhouse, Glasgow, UK
24th November	Empire Theatre, Edinburgh, UK
25th November	The Stoneground, Manchester, UK *(Not with Slade - With Help Yourself, Renia)*
26th November	Guildhall, Southampton, UK
27th November	The Hippodrome, London, UK
29th November	Top Rank, Brighton, UK
2nd December	Guild Hall, Plymouth, UK
3rd December	Cardiff Top Rank, Cardiff, UK
5th December	Colston Hall, Bristol, UK
12th December	Crown Hotel (Henry's blueshouse), Birmingham, UK

Irish Christmas Tour

15th December	Dublin, Ireland *RTE TV "Spinoff"*
22nd December	Hangar, Galway, Ireland
23rd December	Carlton, Kilkenny, Ireland
27th December	Hotel Hillgrove, Monaghan, Ireland
30th December	Town Hall, Cavan, Ireland
31st December	Fillmore West, Bray, Ireland
?? ??	The Harrow Inn, Culcheth, UK

1973

1st January	Hangar, Galway, Ireland
4th January	Savoy Cinema, Cork, Ireland
5th January	Tralee, Ireland
6th January	O'Mahony's Pavilion, Navan, Ireland
7th January	Silver Slipper Ballroom, Sligo, Ireland
8th January	Balbriggan, Ireland
9th January	National Stadium, Dublin, Ireland
12th January	Savoy Cinema, Limerick, Ireland
14th January	Harriers, Tullamore, Ireland
18th January	Kyteler's Beer Gardens, Kilkenny, Ireland
20th January	Morton Hall, Clonmel, Ireland
22nd January	TV Club, Dublin, Ireland
26th January	76 Club, Burton On Trent, UK
1st February	Pavilion, Bisley, UK
2nd February	Queen Margaret Hall, Glasgow, UK
3rd February	Strathclyde University, Glasgow, UK
9th February	Town Hall, Kettering, UK
10th February	Leas Cliff Hall, Folkestone, UK

15th February	Technical College, Blackburn, UK
16th February	Technical College, Salford, UK
17th February	Starlight Rooms, Boston, UK
22nd February	Heavy Steam Machine, Hanley, UK
23rd February	Corn Exchange, Devizes, UK
24th February	Links Pavillion, Cromer, UK
2nd March	South Bank Polytechnics, London, UK
3rd March	University, Reading, UK
4th March	Locarno, Stevenage, UK
5th March	Quaintways, Chester, UK
6th March	Zero 6, Southend, UK
7th March	Boobs, Bristol, UK
9th March	South Bank Polytechnics, London, UK
10th March	Ebbisham Hall, Epsom, UK
17th March	Village Blues Club, Roundhouse, Dagenham, UK
23rd March	Rainbow Theatre, Finsbury Park, London, UK
24th March	Technical College, The Rookery, Bromley, Kent, UK
25th March	Town Hall, Birmingham, UK
30th March	Town Hall, Cheltenham, UK
31st March	County Rock, Northampton, UK
1st April	Greyhound, Croydon, UK
2nd April	National Stadium, Dublin, Ireland *(15 minute set)*
7th April	Corn Exchange, Cambridge, UK
8th April	Queens Hotel, Southend, UK
13th April	Technical College, Maidstone, UK

Irish Tour

Supported by Deke Leonard and Mystery guest. Taken from New Spotlight Magazine 26th April 1973.
Many of the gigs in this article were changed during the tour.

21st April	Lake County Hotel, Mullingar, Ireland
22nd April	Las Vegas Ballroom, Templemore, Ireland
23rd April	National Stadium, Dublin, Ireland
24th April	Savoy Cinema, Limerick, Ireland
25th April	Hotel Hillgrove, Monaghan, Ireland
26th April	Limerick, Ireland
27th April	Talk Of The Town, Galway, Ireland
28th April	Wagon Wheel, Roscommon, Ireland
29th April	Embassy Ballroom, Castleblayney, Ireland
30th April	TV Club, Dublin, Ireland
4th May	Mount Brandon, Tralee, Ireland
5th May	O'Mahony's, Navan, Ireland
6th May	Roseland Ballroom, Moate, Ireland
?? May	College, Swindon, UK
20th May	Chancellor Hall, Chelmsford, UK
21st May	Playhouse Theatre, London, UK
9th June	Waldbühne, Berlin, Germany
10th June	Radstadion, Frankfurt, Germany
12th June	Donnybrook, Dublin, Ireland *Lizzie on the lawn" RTÉ Television*
12th June	Donal Corvin's "Gonzo Rock Palace" at Moran's Hotel, Dublin, Ireland
15th June	Carousel, Manchester, UK
22nd June	Mayfair Ballroom, Newcastle, UK *Date unconfirmed*
22nd June	Locarno, Sunderland, UK
27th June	Top Rank, Sheffield, UK
28th June	Marquee, London, UK
30th June	Village Blues Club, Roundhouse, Dagenham, UK
?? June	Braintree, UK
6th July	Racecourse, Wincanton, UK
7th July	Leas Cliff Hall, Folkestone, UK
14th July	Links Pavilion, Cromer, UK
19th July	Woods Leisure Centre, Colchester, UK
21st July	Ballroom, Waddington, UK
22nd July	The Greyhound, Fulham, London, UK *Gary Moore guests*

24th July	Bridge End, Somerset, UK
24th July	Borough Hall, Stafford, UK
	Two gigs on the same day?
25th July	Meadow Vale Country Club, Glamorgan, UK
26th July	Golders Green Hippodrome, London, UK *Recorded for In Concert. BBC Radio 1.*
27th July	Global Village, London, UK
30th July	Wall City Club, Quaintways, Chester, UK
1st August	Marquay Town Hall, Torquay, UK
2nd August	City Hall, Truro, UK
?? August	Mother's, Birmingham, UK
?? August	Wall City Club, Quaintways, Chester, UK
?? August	Boat Club, Nottingham,UK
?? August	Winning Post, Twickenham, UK
?? August	Farx Club, Southall, UK
?? August	Marquee, London, UK
5th September	Radio and Television Exhibition (Funkausstellung), Berlin, Germany
6th September	Revolution Club, Copenhagen, Denmark
14th September	Paradiso Club, Amsterdam, Netherlands
15th September	Maaslandcentrum, Elsloo, Netherlands
21st September	Winter Gardens, Penzance, UK
22nd September	Blue Lagoon, Newquay, UK
26th September	Marquee, London, UK
29th September	Leas Cliff Hall, Folkestone, UK
2nd October	Town Hall, Cheltenham, UK
3rd October	Boobs, Bristol, UK
4th October	Treforest Polytechnics, Glamorgan, UK
5th October	Racecourse, Wincanton, UK
6th October	St. Mary, University, Glasgow, UK
6th October	University, Loughborough, UK
	Two gigs on the same day?
8th October	Wall City Club, Quaintways, Chester, UK
10th October	Civic Hall, Barrow in Furness, UK
11th October	Cavern, Liverpool, UK
12th October	Mr Badger, Southgate, London, UK
13th October	Lanchester Polytechnic, Coventry, UK
14th October	The Greyhound, Fulham, UK
15th October	Winter Gardens, Cleethorpes, UK
16th October	Warren Country Club, Stockport, UK
18th October	Top of the World, Stafford, UK
19th October	Intercon, Nottingham, UK
20th October	Corn Exchange, Bourne, UK
21st October	Lord's Club Civic Hall, Gravesend, UK
24th October	Town Hall, Birmingham, UK
25th October	Civic Centre, Bedworth, UK
26th October	City Hall St Albans, UK
3rd November	Hitchin College, Hitchin, UK
9th November	Mayfair Ballroom, Newcastle, UK
12th November	Top Hat Club, Spennymoor, UK
13th November	The Marquee, London, UK

German Tour

16th November	Mic-Mac, Tönning, Germany
16th November	Zentralstudio, Friedberg, Germany
17th November	Gasthof Post, Nenndorf, Germany
18th November	Ranchbeitriebe, Kirberg, Germany
19th November	Club Big Apple, Wiesbaden, Germany
20th November	Club Las Vegas, Geilenkirchen, Germany
22nd November	Zoom Club, Frankfurt, Germany
23rd November	Rock-In, Emmendingen, Germany
23rd November	Club Black Mustang, Reutlingen, Germany
24th November	Stadthalle , Oker, Germany
24th November	To Act Club, Weissenhoe, Germany *Date unconfirmed*
25th November	Brauerie Sauer, Genzendorf, Germany

26th November	Stadthalle , Kassel, Germany
26th November	Club Village, Augsburg, Germany
27th November	Stadthalle , Wolfsburg, Germany
28th November	Atelier Disco, Lübbecke, Germany
29th November	JUVI-Klubben, Kalundborg, Denmark
1st December	Revolution Club, Copenhagen, Denmark
5th December	Caerton College, Newport, UK
7th December	University, Southampton, UK
8th December	Leas Cliff Hall, Folkestone, UK
9th December	Greyhound, Fulham, UK
14th December	Red Lion, Leytonstone, UK *Cancelled*
	Brian Downey was taken ill. Rescheduled for 15th February '74
15th December	Pier Pavilion, Hastings, UK *Cancelled*

Irish Christmas Tour

Pearce Kelly plays as additional drummer on some dates due to hand injury to Brian Downey. Downey played with his right hand and Pearce Kelly doing all the fills.

20th December	City Hall, Cork, Ireland
21st December	Mount Brandon, Tralee, Ireland
22nd December	Ritz, Carlow, Ireland
23rd December	Caroline Club, Clonmel, Ireland
26th December	Hotel Hillgrove, Monaghan, Ireland
26th December	Cavan, Ireland
27th December	Kelly's, Portrush, Ireland
28th December	Culdaff Arms, Culdaff, Ireland
30th December	Lake County Hotel, Mullingar, Ireland
31st December	Queen's University, Belfast, Northern Ireland *Eric Bell breaks down on stage*
??	Viking Club, Seahouses, UK

1974

Gary Moore joins, initially on a temporary basis until Eric Bell recovers. Gary has six hours rehearsal before his first gig. Gary becomes official member when Eric decides not to return.

1st January	Butt Hall, Ballybose, Ireland *Cancelled*
2nd January	Strathearn, Ireland *Cancelled*
4th January	Red Island, Skerries, Ireland *First gig with Gary Moore*
5th January	Ardrie, Waterford, Ireland
6th January	Killarney, Ireland
11th January	Newtownards, Northern Ireland
11th January	The Royal Arms Hotel, Omagh, Northern Ireland
12th January	Newtown Ards, Northern Ireland *Date unconfirmed*
12th January	Ulster Hall, Belfast, Northern Ireland
13th January	Athy, Ireland
15th January	Dromore, Northern Ireland
16th January	National Stadium, Dublin, Ireland
17th January	New University of Ulster, Coleraine, Northern Ireland
1st February	Polytechnic, London, UK
2nd February	University of Science, Manchester, UK
5th February	The Marquee Club, London, UK
7th February	The Cavern Club, Liverpool, UK
8th February	University, Aberdeen, UK
9th February	University, Glasgow, Scotland
	Brian Robertson went to Downey's hotel room after the gig & played Lizzy songs.
10th February	Barbarella's, Birmingham, UK *Moore joined*
11th February	Tiffany's or Boobs, Merthyr Tydfil, South Wales
13th February	Top Rank, Cardiff, UK
14th February	Memorial Hall, Northwich, Cheshire, UK
15th February	Red Lion, Leytonstone, UK
16th February	Corn Exchange, Kings Lynn, Norfolk, UK
17th February	The Roundhouse, Chalk Farm, London, UK
18th February	Top Hat, Spennymoor, County Durham, UK
22nd February	Polytechnic, Oxford, UK
23rd February	Baths Hall, Scunthorpe, UK

24th February	Woodville Hall, Gravesend, UK
28th February	The Cavern Club, Liverpool, UK
2nd March	Westminster Tech, London, UK
5th March	The Countdown Club, Dublin, Ireland
8th March	University Rag Ball, Bristol, UK
9th March	Trinity College, Dublin, Ireland
10th March	Liberty Hall, Dublin, Ireland
16th March	Village Blues Club, Roundhouse, Dagenham, UK
28th March	The Astor , Dublin, Ireland
30th March	Links Pavilion, Cromer, UK
10th April	Leas Cliff Hall, Folkestone, UK
13th April	Bracknell Sports Centre, Berkshire, UK
14th April	Locarno, Bristol, UK
24th April	The Carousel, Belfast, Northern Ireland
26th April	Polytechnic, Newcastle, UK
27th April	Corn Exchange, Cambridge, UK
3rd May	Olympen, Lund, Sweden *Cancelled*

German Tour
With Andy Gee & John Du Cann.

11th May	Beat Club, Langelsheim, Germany
12th May	Club Bonanza, Dortmund-Nette, Germany
15th May	Club Mausefalle, Stuttgart, Germany
16th May	Jahnhalle, Crailsheim, Germany
17th May	Hall Radolfzell, Bodensee-Scheffelhof, Germany
18th May	Rheinhalle, Lustenhau, Austria
19th May	Stadthalle, Lörrach, Germany
21st May	Discotheque Blow Up, Lüneburg, Germany
22nd May	Discotheque Manhattan-Bar, Peine, Germany *Unconfirmed*
23rd May	Popmeeting (Pop Festival Open-Air), Lochem, Netherlands *Cancelled*
24th May	Aula Gesamthoch-Schüle, Hoxter, Germany *Cancelled*
25th May	To Act Club, Weissenhoe, Germany *Cancelled*
26th May	Rhein-Mosel-Halle, Koblenz, Germany *Cancelled*
6th June	Village Blues Club, Roundhouse, Dagenham, UK *Cancelled*
14th June	Wirrina Stadium, Peterborough, UK *Cancelled*
21st June	Mayfair, Newcastle, UK
5th July	Lafayette, Wolverhampton, UK *Date unconfirmed*
	First gig with Robertson and Gorham in front of 6 people.
6th July	The Cavern, Liverpool, UK *Date unconfirmed*
7th July	Pandora's, Swansea, UK *Date unconfirmed*
9th July	The Marquee, London, UK
	Playing in front of Phonogram reps resulting in new record contract.

Summer Tour of Ireland
US-Tour planned between 7th August-15th September was cancelled.

14th July	St. Aidan's Hall, Dublin, Ireland
24th July	Hot Summer Day, Bochum, Germany *Cancelled*
25th July	Zero's Club, Dublin, Ireland
26th July	Golf Links Hotel (Kelly's), Portrush, Northern Ireland
27th July	Deerpark Hotel, Antrim, Northern Ireland
28th July	King's Club, Bangor, Northern Ireland
29th July	Imperial Hotel, Dundalk, Ireland
30th July	Horans Hotel, Ballybunion, Ireland
31st July	Salthill Ballroom, Galway, Ireland
1st August	Deerpark Hotel, Antrim, Northern Ireland
2nd August	The Atlantic Ballroom, Tramore, Ireland
3rd August	Zero's Club, Dublin, Ireland
4th August	Red Island, Skerries, Ireland
5th August	Horan's Hotel, Tralee, Ireland
6th August	Carlton, Kilkenny, Ireland
7th August	Leisureland Ballroom, Salthill, Galway, Ireland
8th August	Deerpark Hotel, Antrim, Northern Ireland
9th August	Ulster Hall, Belfast, Northern Ireland

11th August	Zero's Club, Dublin, Ireland *Date unconfirmed*
23rd August	The Reading Festival, London, UK
28th September	Teacher Training College, Bedford, UK
29th September	Winning Post, Twickenham, UK *Unconfirmed*
1st October	Barbarella's, Birmingham, UK *Unconfirmed*
3rd October	University, Warwick, UK *Unconfirmed*
4th October	University, Aberystwyth, UK
5th October	Stadium, Liverpool, UK
8th October	The Marquee, London, UK
9th October	Stadium, Liverpool, UK
12th October	The Corn Exchange, Cambridge, UK
13th October	Chesford Grange, Kenilworth, UK
18th October	Caledonian, Inverness, UK
19th October	University, Glasgow, UK
25th October	Locarno, Sunderland, UK
26th October	Village Blues Club, Roundhouse, Dagenham, UK
27th October	Greyhound, Croydon, UK
28th October	Boobs, Bristol, UK
31st October	Top Of The World, Stafford, UK
3rd November	Roundhouse, Chalk Farm, London, UK
5th November	The New Theatre, Oxford, UK
6th November	University, Keele, UK
7th November	Alsager College, Stoke on Trent, UK
9th November	(Boxing) Stadium, Liverpool, UK
10th November	The Rainbow Theatre, London, UK
11th November	The Rainbow Theatre, London, UK
13th November	Lafayette Club, Wolverhampton, UK
15th November	University, Salford, UK
15th November	Technical College, Ewell, UK *Date unconfirmed*
16th November	Technical College, Ewell, UK
17th November	Boobs, Bristol, UK *Date unconfirmed*
18th November	Boobs, Bristol, UK
22nd November	College (Great Hall), Derby, UK
23rd November	North East London Polytechnic, Barking, UK
26th November	Top Of The World, Stafford, UK
27th November	The Hippodrome, Golders Green, London, UK
29th November	College of Education, Swindon, UK
30th November	Town Hall, Skipton, UK
1st December	Winning Post, Twickenham, UK
2nd December	Guild Hall, Plymouth, UK
3rd December	Top Rank Cardiff, UK
4th December	Vooruit, Gent, Belgium
5th December	Ixelles, Belgium
7th December	Paradiso, Amsterdam, Holland
15th December	Sporthalle, Böblingen, Germany

Irish Christmas Tour

13th December	Tara Towers Hotel Reception, Dublin, Ireland *Date unconfirmed*
20th December	Leisureland, Salthill, Galway, Ireland
21st December	The National Stadium, Dublin, Ireland
24th December	Zero's, Dublin, Ireland *Skid Row reformation gig*
26th December	Golf Links Hotel (Kelly's), Portrush, Northern Ireland
27th December	St Johns, Limerick, Ireland
28th December	Romano's , Belfast, Northern Ireland
29th December	Derry, Ireland
31st December	Horans Hotel, Tralee, Ireland

1975

3rd January	Flamingo Ballymena, Ireland
5th January	St. Marys Hall, Portadown, UK
12th January	Greyhound, Croydon, UK
18th January	Malvern Winter Gardens, Malvern, UK

25th January	Imperial College, London, UK
26th January	Woodville Halls, Gravesend, UK
29th January	Winning Post, Twickenham, UK
12th February	Queensway Hall, Dunstable, UK
15th February	Hawthorn Hall, Leicester, UK

US Tour
Supporting Bachman Turner Overdrive, Bob Seger, Joe Walsh

15th March	Michigan Palace, Detroit, Michigan, US
16th March	Louisville, Kentucky, US
17th March	Louisville, Kentucky, US
20th March	Hulman Civic University Centre, Terre Haute, Indiana, US *Unconfirmed*
21st March	Veteran's Memorial Coliseum, Evansville, Indiana, US
?? March	War Memorial Auditorium, Syracuse, New York, US
22nd March	Illinois State University, Normal, Illinois, US
23rd March	Palace Theatre, Dayton, Ohio, US
27th March	Kenosha Arena, Kenosha, Wisconsin, US *Thin Lizzy cancelled*
30th March	The Palace Arts and Leisure Centre, Newark, New Jersey, US
31st March	Civic Auditorium, Grand Rapids, Michigan, US
3rd April	Dane County Memorial Coliseum, Madison, Wisconsin, US
4th April	Halenbeck Hall St. Cloud State College, St. Cloud, Minnesota, US
5th April	Chicago Stadium, Chicago, Illinois, US
6th April	St. Paul Arena, St. Paul, Minnesota, US
7th April	Milwaukee Arena, Milwaukee, Wisconsin, US
8th April	Veterans Memorial Auditorium, Des Moines, Iowa, US
9th April	Pershing Auditorium, Lincoln, Nebraska, US
10th April	Laramie, Wyoming, US
11th April	Henry Levitt Arena, Wichita, Kansas, US
12th April	Pavillion, Tulsa, Oklahoma, US
13th April	Oklahoma City, Oklahoma, US
16th April	Elgin, Illinois, US
19th April	Detroit, Michigan, US
23rd April	National Stadium, Dublin, Ireland

European Tour
Supporting Bachman-Turner Overdrive

29th April	Falconer Centret, Copenhagen, Denmark
30th April	Scandinavium, Gothenburg, Sweden
1st May	Apollo, Glasgow, UK
2nd May	Free Trade Hall, Manchester, UK
3rd May	Hammersmith Odeon, London, UK
4th May	Hammersmith Odeon, London, UK
5th May	Volkshaus, Zurich, Switzerland
6th May	Stadthalle Offenbach, Germany
7th May	Congress Centrum, Hamburg, Germany
8th May	De Doelen, Rotterdam, Holland
9th May	Forest-National, Brussels, Belgium
10th May	Philipshalle, Düsseldorf, Germany
11th May	Eberthalle, Ludwigshafen, Germany
12th May	Circus Krone, Munich, Germany
13th May	Messehalle, Sindelfingen, Germany
17th May	Corn Exchange, Cambridge, UK
31st May	Albert Hall, Nottingham, UK *Unconfirmed*

UK Club Tour

1st June	The Greyhound, Croydon, UK
6th June	Locarno, Sunderland, UK
7th June	The Village Blues Club, Roundhouse, Dagenham, UK
8th June	Winning Post, Twickenham, UK
10th June	St Catherines College, Cambridge, UK
12th June	Cleopatra's, Derby, UK

14th June	Links Pavilion, Cromer, UK
15th June	Mister Georges Club, Coventry, UK
17th June	Barbarellas, Birmingham, UK
20th June	Maidstone Technical College, Maidstone, UK
21st June	Pier Pavilion, Hastings, UK
22nd June	The Roundhouse, Chalk Farm, London, UK
27th June	Teacher's Training College, Hereford, UK
10th July	College, Walsall, UK
12th July	The Cardiff Castle Festival, Cardiff, UK
19th July	Spurriers in Harlow Town Park, Harlow, UK
1st August	Brunel University, Brunel Rooms, Swindon, UK
3rd August	Douglas Palace, Lido, Isle of Man
8th August	Rock Island Festival, Ginsheim, Germany
16th August	Johnson Hall, Yeovil, UK
17th August	Pavilion Theatre, Torquay, UK
22nd August	City Hall, St Albans, UK
23rd August	The Reading Festival, Reading, UK
30th August	Links Pavilion, Cromer, UK
2nd September	Village Bowl, Bournemouth, UK
4th September	Circus Krone, Munich, Germany
6th September	Radstadion, Ludwigshafen, Friesenheim, Germany
7th September	Philipshalle, Düsseldorf, Germany
8th September	Festzelt, Miltenberg, Germany
9th September	Westfalenhalle, Dortmund, Germany
10th September	Stadthalle Gutersloh, Germany *Unconfirmed*
12th September	Schwarzwaldhalle, Karlsruhe, Germany *Unconfirmed*
13th September	Weser Ems Halle, Oldenburg, Germany *Unconfirmed*
14th September	Stadthalle Wolfsburg, Germany *Unconfirmed*
16th September	Musikhalle, Hamburg, Germany *Unconfirmed*
17th September	Deutschlandhalle, Berlin, Germany *Unconfirmed*
18th September	De Doelen, Rotterdam, Netherlands *Cancelled*
19th September	Paradiso, Amsterdam, Netherlands
20th September	Tivoli, Lepelenburg, Utrecht, Netherlands
21st September	Stokvishal, Arnhem, Netherlands
27th September	Town Hall, Birmingham, UK *BRMB Radio*
29th September	Colston Hall, Bristol, UK
30th September	Top Rank, Cardiff, UK
2nd October	City Halls, Candleriggs, Glasgow, UK
4th October	Leith Theatre, Edinburgh, UK
8th October	Free Trade Hall, Manchester, UK
10th October	City Hall, Newcastle, UK
11th October	Stadium, Liverpool, UK
12th October	New Victoria Theatre, London, UK
17th October	Pireus, Malmo, Sweden
18th October	Barbarella, Vaxjo, Sweden
20th October	Concerthouse, Turku, Finland
22nd October	Jarlateatern, Stockholm, Sweden
23rd October	Hard Rock Cafe, Copenhagen, Denmark
24th October	Folkets Park, Kalmar, Sweden
25th October	Club Ron Ronneby, Sweden
26th October	Söderportskolan, Kristianstad, Sweden
7th November	Queen Mary College, London, UK
8th November	Roundhouse, Dagenham, UK
14th November	Thames Polytechnics, London, UK
15th November	Champness Hall, Rochdale, UK
16th November	The Palace, Newark, UK
17th November	University, Swansea, UK
21st November	College (Great Hall), Derby, UK
22nd November	Kursaal, Southend, UK
28th November	Winter Gardens, Malvern, UK
29th November	Technical College, Guildford, UK
30th November	Winning Post, Twickenham, UK

2nd December	Fiesta, Plymouth, UK
4th December	Crucible Theatre, Sheffield, UK
5th December	Chamber of Commerce, Hull, UK
6th December	St Georges Hall, Middleton, UK
9th December	Savoy Cinema, Limerick, Ireland
10th December	The National Stadium, Dublin, Ireland
12th December	University, Bath, UK
14th December	Greyhound, Croydon, UK
16th December	Ivanhoes, Huddersfield, UK
20th December	Sports Centre, Bracknell, UK
31st December	The Great British Music Festival, Olympia, London, UK

1976

16th January	Warwick University Coventry, UK
17th January	University, Leeds, UK
25th January	Civic Hall, Wolverhampton, UK
6th February	Tiffany's Pub, Great Yarmouth, UK
7th February	Links Pavilion, Cromer, UK
10th February	Ivanhoe's, Huddersfield, UK
5th March	University, Sheffield, UK
6th March	Essex University. Dance Hall, Colchester, UK
7th March	Greyhound, Croydon, UK
8th March	Winter Gardens, Bournemouth, UK
9th March	University, Southampton, UK
10th March	Civic Hall, Guildford, UK
11th March	Town Hall, Cheltenham, UK
12th March	Corn Exchange, Cambridge, UK
13th March	University, Exeter, UK
15th March	Town Hall, Birmingham, UK
16th March	Tiffanys, Scunthorpe, UK
17th March	St. Georges Hall, Bradford, UK
18th March	City Hall, Newcastle, UK
19th March	Free Trade Hall, Manchester, UK
20th March	Stadium, Liverpool, UK
21st March	Colston Hall, Bristol, UK
22nd March	Top of the World, Stafford, UK
23rd March	Guildhall, Portsmouth, UK
24th March	Top Rank, Cardiff, UK
25th March	University, Aberystwyth, UK
26th March	Brunel University, Uxbridge, UK
27th March	Kursaal, Southend, UK
29th March	City Halls, Candleriggs, Glasgow, UK
30th March	Albert Hall, Stirling, UK
31st March	Citidel Theatre, Leith, Edinburgh, UK
1st April	Town Hall, Middlesbrough, UK
2nd April	The Column, (Nelson), Burnley, UK
3rd April	Skindles, Maidenhead, UK
4th April	New Victoria Theatre, London, UK

US Tour April-June
Lizzy should have played 37 gigs in 38 days supporting Aerosmith, The Tubes, Be Bob Deluxe, Journey, Aerosmith, REO Speedwagon , Styx and Rush at different gigs but the tour was cancelled because Philip took ill.

US Tour June-July
Supporting Rainbow. Taken from NME 26th June 1976: We never played a single note on that tour because Phil was suffering from hepatitis weeks before we even got to "Ohio" where the tour was to begin. The day we got to "Ohio" Phil more or less nearly collapsed with exhaustion and was taken to the hospital where he was told that he had contracted hepatitis and was to immediately fly back to London. Back in London he was put in the intensive care unit for a couple of weeks. It's a shame, cause it would have been a great tour for Lizzy.

11th July	Hammersmith Odeon, London, UK

4th September	Philipshalle, Dusseldorf, Germany
15th September	Moran's Hotel, Dublin, Ireland
	Lynott, Downey & Eric Bell with Jimmy Faulkner and Ditch Cassidy
	play Lizzy numbers and blues standards.
30th September	Konserthus, Stockholm, Sweden
1st October	Konserthus, Gothenburg, Sweden
2nd October	Olympen, Lund, Sweden
7th October	Musikhalle, Hamburg, Germany
8th October	Stadthalle, Offenbach, Germany
9th October	Freidrich Ebert Halle, Ludwigshafen, Germany
10th October	Stadthalle, Erlangen, Germany
11th October	Philipshalle, Düsseldorf, Germany
16th October	Koninklijk Cirkus (Cirque Royal), Brussel, Belgium
17th October	RAI Congress Centre, Amsterdam, Holland
18th October	Pavillion De Paris, Paris, France *Lizzy cancelled*
20th October	New Theatre, Oxford, UK
21st October	Capitol, Cardiff, UK
22nd October	Colston Hall, Bristol, UK
23rd October	Sports Centre, Bracknell, UK
24th October	Pavilion, Hemel Hempstead, UK
25th October	De Montfort Hall, Leicester, UK
26th October	Odeon, Birmingham, UK
27th October	Winter Gardens, Malvern, UK
28th October	Empire, Liverpool, UK
29th October	Free Trade Hall, Manchester, UK
30th October	The Apollo, Glasgow, UK
31st October	Usher Hall, Edinburgh, UK
1st November	City Hall, Newcastle, UK
2nd November	Civic Hall, Wolverhampton, UK
4th November	City Hall, Sheffield, UK
5th November	University, Lancaster, UK
6th November	University, Leeds, UK
7th November	Victoria Hall, Hanley, UK
8th November	The Guildhall, Portsmouth, UK
9th November	New Theatre, Coventry, UK
10th November	St. Georges Hall, Bradford, UK *Cancelled*
11th November	St. Georges Hall, Bradford, UK
13th November	Kursaal Ballroom, Southend, UK
14th November	Hammersmith Odeon, London, UK
15th November	Hammersmith Odeon, London, UK
16th November	Hammersmith Odeon, London, UK
18th November	The National Stadium, Dublin, Ireland

US Tour

The night before the band were due to travel to the States, Brian Robertson had become involved in a brawl in the Speakeasy in London and injured his hand so the tour was **cancelled**.

BIBLIOGRAPHY

Although I pride myself on not having directly quoted from any of these fine books, they nonetheless proved to be useful research and corroboration tools. Good folks, all!

Bailie, Stuart. *The ballad Of The Thin Man: The Authorized Biography Of Phil Lynott & Thin Lizzy* (Boxtree, 1997)
Lynott, Philomena. *My Boy: The Philip Lynott Story* (Hot Press Books, 1995)
Putterford, Mark. *The Rocker* (Castle Communications, 1994)

Additional Citations

Some of these citations are incomplete. If informed or corrected, I would be pleased to expand or amend any and all credits in future editions.

And Now, A Drop Of The Really Hard Stuff: Thin Lizzy by Keith Altham.
Breaking Through On The Road by Tony Norman. 1973.
Disc. Vagabonds Of The Oirish World by Brian Southall. October 6, 1973.
Disc. Disc Guide To Young British Rock: Thin Lizzy by Brian Southall. March 10, 1973.
Festival of living music in Wexford by G.D.H. 1970.
First tango from Lizzy. May, 1973.
Gun. Song Writer's Column: Phillip (sic) Lynott by Steve Bolger. 1971.
Lizzy – Three's Company by Pat Prentice. 1973.
Los Angeles Times. Dennis Hunt.
Melody Maker. Review of Shades Of A Blue Orphanage by C. W. May 27, 1972.
Melody Maker. Lizzy in a tizzy by Michael Benton. February 10, 1973.
Melody Maker. Lynott Sick: Lizzy Cancel American Shows. June 26, 1976.
Melody Maker. Unlikely lads with a lead for Lizzy by Harry Doherty. July 31, 1976.
Melody Maker. Ireland's own by Harry Doherty. January 8, 1977.
Music Star. We Want Lizzy. 1973.
New Musical Express. Musicians Talk Tape: This Week Phil Lynott of Thin Lizzy. 1973.
New Musical Express. Vagabonds Of The Western World record review. 1973.
New Musical Express. How the laid-Back California met the Drunken Scot and the Heavy Black Irishman... by Chris Salewicz. December 18, 1976.
New Musical Express. The Boys Are Back In Town review by Phil McNeill. May 8, 1976.
New Record. 1970.

Philomena record review. 1974.

Record Mirror. You all know Phyllis. Well, this is her son Phil by Shelia Prophet. November 27, 1976.

The Rocker review. 1973.

Rolling Stone. Vagabonds Of The Western World record review by Gordon Fletcher. August 29, 1974.

Scene. Thin Lizzy: Challenging The Champs by Cliff Michalski. June 10 – 16, 1976.

Sounds. Drum Sounds: The Lizzy combination. July 26, 1975.

Sounds. Malady of a thin man by Pete Makowski. October 16, 1976.

Trouser Press. Phil Lynott talks… and talks… Catching up with Thin Lizzy's big bass man by Peggy Wolfe and Dave Schulps. No. 19. April/May 1977.

Vagabonds Of The Western World record review by B.S. 1973.

The World Of Thin Lizzy… Is Changing. 1973.

CREDITS

Author's interviews:

Bell, Eric. June 29, 2011.
Carroll, Ted. September 19, 2011.
D'Ardis, John. August 23, 2011.
Downey, Brian. February 26, 2009.
Downey, Brian. February 11, 2011.
Downey, Brian. March 30, 2011.
Fitzpatrick, Jim. June 21, 2011.
Gee, Andy. August 2, 2011.
Gorham, Scott. February 24, 2004.
Gorham, Scott. February 11, 2009.
Gorham, Scott. March 4, 2011.
Grainge, Nigel. July 4, 2011.
Lindberg, . September 15, 2011.
Moore, Gary. December 4, 2002.
Moore, Gary. July 2, 2007.
Murray, Frank. September 7, 2011.
Nevison, Ron. March 4, 2011.
O'Neill, Terry, July 1, 2011.
O'Neill, Terry, September 1, 2011.
Robertson, Brian, February 17, 2009.
Robertson, Brian, January, 2011.
Robertson, Brian. March, 2011.
Robertson, Brian. September 8, 2011.
Scott, Andy. February, 2011.
Shiels, Brendan "Brush." August 30, 2011.
Tauber, Nick. June 23, 2011.
Tauber, Nick. June 28, 2011.
Waybill, Fee. April 9, 2011.
White, Benny. July 27, 2011.
Wright, Raymond. September 20, 2011.

ABOUT THE AUTHOR

Martin Popoff has been described as "the world's most famous heavy metal journalist." At approximately 7900 (with over 7000 appearing in his books), he has unofficially written more record reviews than anybody in the history of music writing. Additionally, Martin has penned over 50 books on hard rock, heavy metal, classic rock and record collecting. He was Editor In Chief of the now retired *Brave Words & Bloody Knuckles*, Canada's foremost metal publication for 14 years, and has also contributed to *Revolver*, *Guitar World*, *Goldmine*, *Record Collector*, bravewords.com, lollipop.com and hardradio.com, with many record label band bios and liner notes to his credit as well.

Born April 28, 1963 in Castlegar, British Columbia, Canada and raised in nearby Trail, Martin went on to complete an MBA, work for Xerox, then co-own a graphic design and print brokering firm, before becoming a full-time rock critic in 1998. Gillan, Max Webster, Deep Purple, ZZ Top and Black Sabbath are his favourite five bands of all time. An incurable collector, Martin's music archive consists of approximately 12,000 LPs, 15,000 CDs, 3,000 45s, 1400 backstage passes, 2900 personally obtained autographed items, and the tapes, digital files and hard copies of his approximately 1500 interviews conducted since 1994 (but he really wants to paint and maybe have his work appear on a ZZ Top album cover one day).

Martin currently resides in Toronto and can be reached through martinp@inforamp.net or www.martinpopoff.com. His website includes detailed descriptions and ordering information for the books of his that are currently in print.

Martin Popoff - A Complete Bibliography

Fighting My Way Back: Thin Lizzy 69–76 (2011)

The Deep Purple Royal Family: Chain Of Events '80 – '11 (2011)

The Deep Purple Royal Family: Chain Of Events Through '79 (2011)

Black Sabbath FAQ (2011)

The Collector's Guide To Heavy Metal: Volume 4: The '00s (2011; co-authored with David Perri)

Goldmine Standard Catalog Of American Records 1948 – 1991, 7th Edition (2010)

Goldmine Record Album Price Guide, 6th Edition (2009)

Goldmine 45 RPM Price Guide, 7th Edition (2009)

A Castle Full Of Rascals: Deep Purple '83 – '09 (2009)

Worlds Away: Voivod And The Art Of Michel Langevin (2009)

Ye Olde Metal: 1978 (2009)

Gettin' Tighter: Deep Purple '68 – '76 (2008)

All Access: The Art Of The Backstage Pass (2008)

Ye Olde Metal: 1977 (2008)

Ye Olde Metal: 1976 (2008)

Judas Priest: Heavy Metal Painkillers (2007)

Ye Olde Metal: 1973 To 1975 (2007)

The Collector's Guide To Heavy Metal: Volume 3: The Nineties (2007)

Ye Olde Metal: 1968 To 1972 (2007)

Run For Cover: The Art Of Derek Riggs (2006)

Black Sabbath: Doom Let Loose (2006)

Dio: Light Beyond The Black (2006)

The Collector's Guide To Heavy Metal: Volume 2: The Eighties (2005)

Rainbow: English Castle Magic (2005)

UFO: Shoot Out The Lights (2005)

The New Wave Of British Heavy Metal Singles (2005)

Blue Oyster Cult: Secrets Revealed! (2004)

Contents Under Pressure: 30 Years Of Rush At Home & Away (2004)

The Top 500 Heavy Metal Albums Of All Time (2004)

The Collector's Guide To Heavy Metal: Volume 1: The Seventies (2003)

The Top 500 Heavy Metal Songs Of All Time (2003)

Southern Rock Review (2001)

Heavy Metal: 20th Century Rock And Roll (2000)

The Goldmine Price Guide To Heavy Metal Records (2000)

The Collector's Guide To Heavy Metal (1997)

Riff Kills Man! 25 Years Of Recorded Hard Rock & Heavy Metal (1993)